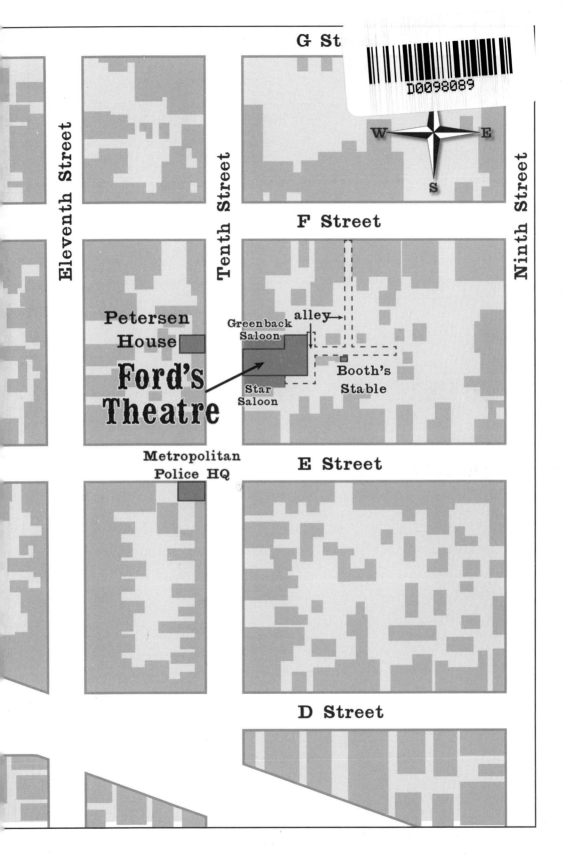

PRAISE FOR
☞ BACKSTAGE ☜
AT THE LINCOLN ASSASSINATION

"Dr. Bogar's scholarship is original and impeccable. With stunning clarity, this vivid narrative shines a light into the shadows and behind the scenes of the most resonant crime in American history. *Backstage at the Lincoln Assassination* is an indispensable resource for understanding the width, breadth, and scope of the tragedy at Ford's Theatre."

—**ERIK JENDRESEN,** writer and producer of *Killing Lincoln* and *Band of Brothers*

"Just when we thought there was nothing new to learn about the assassination of Abraham Lincoln at Ford's Theatre comes this important book by theater historian Tom Bogar. It brings the actors and actresses of Ford's Theatre finally—and fully—to life. In a masterpiece of skillful research and synthesis, Bogar immerses us in one of the most dramatic moments in American history while answering questions we thought were unanswerable. A definitive treatment."

—**TERRY ALFORD,** author of *Fortune's Fool: The Biography of John Wilkes Booth* and *John Wilkes Booth: A Sister's Memoir*

"Most Lincoln assassination books follow the well-documented trail of Booth into Maryland and Virginia, repeating often-told stories. *Backstage at the Lincoln Assassination* stays behind at Ford's Theatre, giving an old tale a new, fresh focus that other historians missed for the past 150 years."

—**CLINT JOHNSON,** author of *"A Vast and Fiendish Plot": The Confederate Attack on New York City*

"Thomas A. Bogar's innovative investigation of the traumatic event of April 14, 1865, at Ford's Theatre will quickly become an essential study among the plethora of books on Lincoln's assassination. This lively and engrossing narrative reveals the impact of the assassination on the forty-six people involved with the theatrical performance that fateful evening. Bogar follows all of them from their activities that day to their deaths, recalling controversies and questions still unanswered. Even the most ardent of Lincoln assassination addicts will find much to savor and learn in this terrific book."

—**DON B. WILMETH,** editor of *The Cambridge Guide to American Theatre*, co-editor of *The Cambridge History of American Theatre*, and editor of the series Palgrave Studies in Theatre & Performance History

"*Backstage at the Lincoln Assassination* is a must-read for anyone interested in Lincoln's assassination or history in general. Tom Bogar brings to life the many people whom other accounts mention only in passing, if at all. It's difficult to call any Lincoln assassination book unique—there are over 120 of them—but Bogar's book is indeed a unique addition to Lincoln assassination lore."

—**ROGER NORTON**, founder and moderator of the
Lincoln Discussion Symposium and the Abraham Lincoln Research Site

"Though many books have been written about the Lincoln assassination, many gaps in the story remain. One of the most obvious of these surrounds the people who worked at the scene of the crime—the actors, managers, and stage crew of Ford's Theatre in Washington. Being acquainted with, and in some cases close to, the assassin, they were potential suspects in the case. Some were arrested in the aftermath of the shooting, and one was convicted on the strength of divided testimony from his colleagues. They all survived the experience and moved on with their lives. A few continued their careers on the stage, but most faded into oblivion. Now, with the publication of this marvelous book, Professor Bogar has brought those forty-six important characters back into the spotlight. He clears away a century and a half of folklore and mythology and reminds us how even the minor figures have fascinating stories to tell. They were there, they saw it all, and now at last, their stories will be heard. This is long overdue."

—**MICHAEL KAUFFMAN**, author of *American Brutus*

"By uncovering the stories of the largely anonymous actors, managers, and stage-hands whose lives were changed forever at Ford's Theatre, Tom Bogar has found a fresh and exciting angle on the events of April 1865. This is a fascinating account, and an important piece of research."

—**DANIEL STASHOWER**, author of *The Hour of Peril:*
The Secret Plot to Murder Lincoln before the Civil War

"History tells us that the Lincoln assassination was more than the work of lone gunman John Wilkes Booth. Tom Bogar shows us in this revealing and riveting book just how much more. Bogar has fleshed out stunning details involving more than a few suspects who were inside Ford's Theatre that fateful night—along with other never-before-seen primary source material. Highly recommended."

—**MARC LEEPSON**, author of *Flag: An American Biography*,
Saving Monticello, *Desperate Engagement*, and *Lafayette*

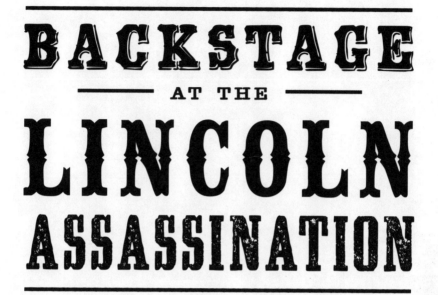

BACKSTAGE AT THE LINCOLN ASSASSINATION

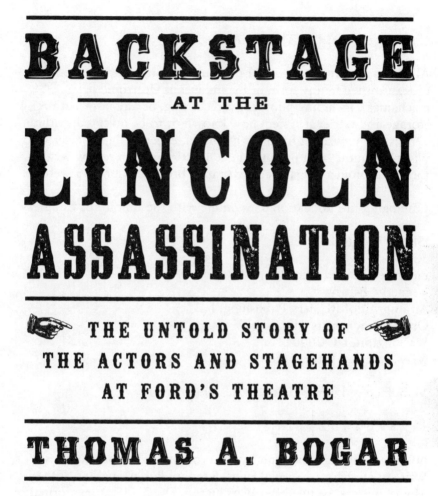

BACKSTAGE
AT THE
LINCOLN
ASSASSINATION

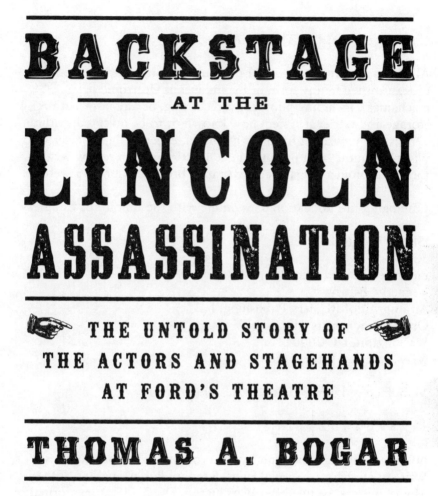THE UNTOLD STORY OF
THE ACTORS AND STAGEHANDS
AT FORD'S THEATRE

THOMAS A. BOGAR

REGNERY
HISTORY

Copyright © 2013 by Thomas A. Bogar

Cataloging-in-Publication data on file with the Library of Congress

ISBN 978-1-62157-083-7

Published in the United States by
Regnery History
An Imprint of Regnery Publishing, Inc.
One Massachusetts Avenue NW
Washington, DC 20001
www.RegneryHistory.com

Manufactured in the United States of America

10 9 8 7 6 5 4 3 2 1

Books are available in quantity for promotional or premium use.
Write to Director of Special Sales, Regnery Publishing, Inc., One
Massachusetts Avenue NW, Washington, DC 20001, for information
on discounts and terms, or call (202) 216-0600.

Distributed to the trade by
Perseus Distribution
250 West 57th Street
New York, NY 10107

*Life's but a walking shadow, a poor player
that struts and frets his hour upon the stage
and then is heard no more.*

—**MACBETH,** Act V, Scene v
(Abraham Lincoln's favorite Shakespearean play)

CONTENTS

THE FORTY-SIX ACTORS, MANAGERS, AND STAGEHANDS

Brink, Catherine "Kittie"—Edwin's (see below) new fourteen-year-old bride, helped backstage

Brink, Edwin Hunter—actor, forty-two, singing in quartet, Union Navy veteran, yet close friend of Booth

Buckingham, John E. "Buck"—doorkeeper, thirty-seven, Union veteran and Navy Yard worker

Burroughs, Joseph "Peanut John"—street urchin errand boy, about seventeen, held Booth's horse

Byrne, Charles Francis—actor, twenty, played small role of DeBoots

Carland, Louis J.—costumer and occasional actor, twenty, Secessionist but rabidly antiwar

DeBonay, John L.—prompter, seventeen, acted small role of gardener Wicks, Confederate veteran

Dyott, John—lead actor, fifty-three, traveled with Laura Keene, played Murcott

Emerson, Edwin "Ned"—actor, twenty-five, played Dundreary, relatives in Confederate Army

Evans, Johnny—actor, twenty-eight, played small role of Buddicomb, the butler

Evans, Kate—Johnny's wife, actress, twenty, played small role of Sharpe, the maid

Ferguson, William J. "Will"—callboy, nineteen, acted small role of Lt. Vernon, was staunch Unionist

Ford, Harry Clay—daily manager of Ford's Theatre, John's youngest brother, twenty-one, friend of Booth

Ford, James R. "Dick"—third Ford brother, box office treasurer, twenty-five

Ford, John T.—owner/manager, thirty-five, away in Richmond that night, ardent states-rights advocate

Gifford, James Johnson—head carpenter backstage, fifty-one, surly Secessionist but hated Booth

Gorman, Edward—gasman

Gourlay, Jeannie—promising actress, twenty, played Mary Meredith

Gourlay, Maggie—actress, seventeen, played small role of Skillet, the maid

Gourlay, Thomas J. "Tom"—their father, actor, forty-five, played Sir Edward Trenchard

Hart, May—novice actress, eighteen, played Georgina

Hawk, William Henry "Harry"—lead actor, twenty-seven, traveled with Laura Keene, played Asa Trenchard

Hazelton, Joseph H.—program boy, eleven

Hess, Courtland Van Rensalaer "C. V."—actor, twenty-five, ill but sang in quartet, Unionist, brother killed at Gettysburg

James, Henry M.—stagehand

Johnson, L.—actor, played bailiff

Keene, Laura—featured star actress, thirty-nine, played Florence Trenchard, cradled dying president's head

Lamb, James—scenic artist, forty-seven, Secessionist

Lutz, John S.—Keene's husband and business manager, forty-nine

Maddox, James L. "Jimmie"—head property man, twenty-six, Secessionist

Mathews, John—actor, thirty, played Coyle, friend of Booth

Miles, John—stagehand

Muzzy, Helen—actress, fifty-three, played Mrs. Mountchessington

Otis, William H. "Billy"—Keene's dresser and errand boy, twenty-eight

Parkhurst, George—actor, twenty-five, played bailiff

Phillips, Henry B.—acting manager, forty-five, ardent Unionist

Raybold, Thomas J. "Thomas"—box office assistant, house manager, general factotum, thirty-one, Union veteran

Rittersbach, Jacob "Jake"—stagehand for only three weeks, twenty-five, Union veteran

Selecman, John T.—property assistant, sixteen

Sessford, Joseph J.—box office assistant, thirty-two

Simms, Joe—stagehand

Spangler, Edman "Ned"—stagehand, thirty-nine, friend/eager drudge for Booth, Secessionist

Spear, George Gaines—actor, fifty-five, played butler Binny, son died from wounds incurred fighting for Union

Truman, Helen—actress, nineteen, played Augusta, devoted to Lincoln

Withers, William S. "Billy," Jr.—orchestra conductor, twenty-eight, Union veteran

Wright, John Burroughs—stage manager, fifty, Unionist

NOTE ABOUT
THEATRICAL TERMS

ALL STAGE DIRECTIONS in this account are described from the actors' viewpoint: thus, stage right is the audience's left and vice versa; going upstage (literally, because it sloped) is moving away from the audience, and downstage is toward it. "Stage business" is anything done by an actor beyond moving across the stage, especially when handling stage properties. "The house" refers either to the area of the theatre where the audience sits or to the audience itself. "The wings" are the areas immediately offstage, to the right and left, where scenery and properties are stored and the actors wait to make their entrances.

PREFACE

IMAGINE FOR A MOMENT that the president of the United States has just been murdered in your workplace by one of your most admired and charismatic colleagues, as you stood nearby. Picture the chaos that erupts around you as your mind races, fearing for your own safety and of being thought complicit, recollecting in panic any ill-chosen words you ever uttered that could be construed as hostile to the president, as well as the times you were seen socializing with the assassin—as recently, in fact, as the drink you took with him a few hours ago in the bar next door.

From that instant onward, your world would never be the same. You would be interrogated, perhaps imprisoned; you would have to provide testimony—scrupulously accurate and consistent—and endure interview after interview for weeks, months, years, constantly retelling and reliving every detail of an event that occurred in less than thirty seconds. For the rest of your life, you would move frequently, avoid reporters, and perhaps change your name. "That night" would define the rest of your life and headline your obituary.

Precisely that scenario became the terrifying new reality for forty-six all-too-human individuals employed by Ford's Theatre in Washington, D.C., on the night of April 14, 1865. The events of that night have been told and retold ever since, etched deeply into our national consciousness. But this is not the story of its two central figures, John Wilkes Booth and Abraham Lincoln, and the catastrophic four years that brought assassin and martyr together. Rather, it is that of the largely anonymous actors, managers, and stagehands of Ford's Theatre on that fateful night and what befell them afterward.

Most of the forty-six were completely innocent—unsuspecting of any plot, regardless of whether it was the original plan to abduct the president or the final one to assassinate him—yet they were nevertheless caught up in a terrifying round of arrests, interrogations, and life-altering consequences. Some unquestionably were complicit in one or the other of the plans; evidence suggests that Ford's Theatre was a hotbed of secessionist thought and sympathy. But most of those involved shrewdly managed to escape detection and punishment. A few exceptionally fortunate ones had the night off or had finished their parts early and left for the evening, and thus escaped infamy.

Previous retellings of the events of that night have followed either Booth out the back door to his fate in a burning barn at the Garrett farm, or Lincoln out the front to his, in a bedroom across the street in Petersen's boardinghouse. Those left behind, huddling in fear on the stage, listening to cries of "Burn the place down!" filtering in from the furious crowd outside as soldiers took up stations throughout, deserve to have their story told.

Some of these actors, managers, and stagehands never spoke of that night again except privately; others were considerably, almost competitively, voluble. Several divulged pieces in various interviews over many years but never provided one coherent narrative. Their reticence or insistence in telling their version of its events would vary over time and according to their audience.

Any definitive account of the details of the assassination must by necessity incorporate the most credible and objective fragments from all of these accounts, which emerged anywhere between one hour and sixty years after the fact. I have consciously given preference to the perceptions and words of those who experienced that night, and its subsequent harrowing days, from backstage, rather than to accounts by audience members, as has largely been the case to date.

Sadly for the historian, these were not public figures who left their papers to posterity. Quite the opposite: think how many letters were thrust into fireplaces in the days immediately following the terrible event, and how many correspondents held their breath waiting for the knock on the door that indicated the discovery of letters they had written to the murderer. Certainly, the loss of any normal paper trail, coupled with the silence of those involved and the questionable veracity of those who did speak out, has made it exceptionally difficult to uncover and relate their stories.

Most of these unfortunate figures have faded into obscurity. After strutting and fretting their hour upon the stage, they have become "walking shadows" from whom we have "heard no more." If anything is remembered of them, it is usually, erroneously, that they were members of "Laura Keene's Company," which in reality was only three visiting actors: Keene, Harry Hawk, and John Dyott; the rest were members of the resident stock company of Ford's Theatre. But they were all casualties, collateral damage from Booth's rash act.

They were, for the most part, "war actors" and recently hired workers, a ragtag group who had only worked together a few months, in some cases a few weeks or even days. While some were seasoned professionals with Broadway credits, others had barely set foot on a stage. A handful of the backstage staff were skilled craftsmen and shrewd businessmen; a few were simply supplementing day jobs, performing menial tasks.

The lives of those who were present backstage that night would forever be divided into Before and After. They would always feel a surreal bond with those they had worked beside that night, even a few they had met only days before. Whenever they encountered each other again, or dared to speak of it, it would always be "that night," with no further reference needed.

For some, the assassination meant the end of their careers, and for more than one, nearly the end of their lives. Others forged ahead, coping as best they could with being imprisoned and interrogated as suspected co-conspirators. A few were able to put it all behind them and go on to fulfill successful careers for forty, fifty, even sixty more years. Several of the forty-six kept in touch with each other, monitoring publicly and privately who would be "the last survivor." Most of them carried to their graves the extent of their friendship with John Wilkes Booth, that most charismatic of fellow actors. But without question, he haunted their lives from that fateful moment forward.

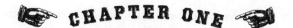

CHAPTER ONE

"IS JOHN BOOTH CRAZY?"

I N THE HALF-LIGHT BACKSTAGE, where sound meant more than sight, hardly anyone took it for a gunshot. Actor Ned Emerson, leaning against a piece of scenery in the stage left wings, studying his lines, thought it came from the apparatus of scene shifting, or from out in Tenth Street—part of the week's continuing celebration of the war's end. John Mathews, waiting behind the scenery to go on in the next scene, thought it might be a piece of new stage business introduced to frighten the character of Lord Dundreary. To one actress waiting in the wings, it sounded like the pop of a champagne cork; to someone else it resembled a lone hand clap out in the audience. Callboy Will Ferguson, standing by the downstage right prompter's desk beside the evening's star, Laura Keene, thought a stack of books he had preset for the next scene had fallen to the floor. Keene herself was sure she knew better, and was incensed; she sent her personal dresser to demand that the stagehands stop firing weapons backstage.[1]

Harry Hawk, playing Asa Trenchard, the titular *American Cousin*, was alone out on the sloping forestage, his back to the president's box, delivering a cutting retort to Mrs. Mountchessington (actress Helen Muzzy) as she exited through the curtained archway of the drawing room set. For a moment he froze, wondering what had exploded backstage in the property shop. He opened his mouth to finish his line when a male shout of "*Sic semper tyrannis*!" spun him back toward the audience.[2]

Above him to his left he saw a dark figure vault the railing of the presidential box as a puff of bluish-gray smoke drifted from its opening. Then came the sound of ripping cloth and a heavy thud, and he recognized his sometime friend John Booth only a few feet away, crouching in an odd, off-balance way. Hawk watched, stunned, as Booth, clad in a black frock coat over a blue flannel shirt, dark britches, and tall riding boots, stamped his foot to shed the shreds of a regimental flag he had pulled down with him along with shards from a picture frame, knocked askew above.

Booth straightened up, raising high an immense, gleaming, double-edged Bowie knife in his right hand. His hair disheveled, face drained of all color, ebony eyes afire, and lips drawn back over his teeth, he rushed at Hawk, who threw up his hands and backpedaled frantically toward the stage right wings, then bolted in terror up the stairs to his dressing room, certain Booth was out to harm *him*. Behind him Hawk heard Booth clearly: "The South shall be free! I have done it. Virginia is avenged!" Then only heavy panting and clumping footsteps.[3]

Shoving past Ferguson, Keene, and stage manager John Wright, and knowing the backstage area of Ford's in the dark as well as anyone, Booth lurched through the narrow wing space toward a little-used door to the back alley. In his way were actress Jeannie Gourlay and conductor Billy

Withers, their hushed conversation interrupted by the sound of the shot. Snarling "Let me pass!" Booth slashed at Withers, leaving two gashes in his coat, and shoved Gourlay back into a pile of stored scenery. Emitting an inarticulate mixture of growls and cries of pain, Booth stumbled to the door, wrenched it open with both hands, and was gone.

Just outside, Peanut John, the theatre's slow-witted teenage "basket boy," who had been holding Booth's spirited bay mare, received a blow to the head from the hilt of Booth's knife for his trouble. "Boy, give me my horse," the assassin growled and in a flash mounted it and galloped out of Baptist Alley, the sound of departing hoof beats echoing loudly across the cobblestones.[4]

In the theatre's box office, the sound of the shot sent manager Harry Ford, ticket agents Joe Sessford and Tom Raybold, and Keene's manager-husband John Lutz rushing for the tiny window that looked out into the house. Raybold and Sessford got there first, in time to see Booth land off-balance on the stage. Both men recognized him immediately. Sessford spoke for them all: "My God, then, is John Booth crazy?" Harry ran out into the house in time to see Booth lurching across the stage, knife in hand. Sessford gathered up all their remaining tickets and cash, Lutz grabbing his wife's share. Raybold ran outside to alert stage carpenter James Gifford to secure the backstage area.[5]

Inside the theatre, for the first few seconds there was total, stunned silence. Then a shriek rent the air from the president's box, along with a male voice from the front row: "Stop that man!" Others in the audience took up the cry, as Mrs. Lincoln began to shriek incoherent words, some of which sounded like "My husband is shot!" From the front row of the orchestra seats, the formidable figure of Major Joseph Stewart leapt to the stage and ran in pursuit of the assailant, but, impeded by darkness and actors in the wings, he reached the alley too late to stop him.

Then, as if at a common signal, an infernal, terrified roar engulfed them all: screams, moans, wails, and cries of "The president has been shot!" Without warning, the audience was on its feet and swarming over the orchestra's instruments left behind after intermission. They surged onto the stage, crying, "Hang him! Kill him! Shoot him! Lynch him!" not even sure whom they meant by *him*. Some rushed up the stairs to Hawk's dressing room, demanding that whoever was inside emerge, until he did so and was recognized, and the searchers turned their attention elsewhere.

By now the other dressing rooms had emptied, and panicked actors still in costume filled the stage, their greasepaint smeared and garish in the footlights' glare. They were quickly caught up in what Emerson later termed "a whirlpool, [an] inextricable chaos of mad humanity [swirling] hither and thither in hysterical aimlessness.... No one seemed to have retained a scintilla of self-possession." To nineteen-year-old actress Helen Truman, it was "the hell of hells ... an inferno of noise." For the rest of her life there would "never be anything like it on earth. The shouts, groans, curses, smashing of seats, screams of women, shuffling of feet, and cries of terror created a pandemonium terrible to hear."[6]

Gasman Ed Gorman worked feverishly in the far downstage right corner of the wings to turn down the footlights, lest the clothes of theatregoers clambering onto the stage catch fire, while simultaneously raising the house lights from half to full to quell the rising panic and signal the audience to leave the house. Stagehands Ned Spangler and Jake Rittersbach, who had futilely rushed after Booth, returned to center stage to pull the opposing halves of the scenery back into the wings, opening up the stage space.

"That was John Booth!" exclaimed Rittersbach. "Hush your mouth!" blurted Spangler. "You don't know whether it's Booth or not." That utterance would be twisted into something quite different in the coming months and prove to be Spangler's undoing. Leaving the scene did nothing to help him. Grabbing his coat, he rushed through the door Booth had taken, only to be confronted by two women—future witnesses whose house faced the back of Ford's—who accused him of being up to no good.

Loudly denying it, Spangler wrestled himself into his coat and hurried up the alley in the rain in search of Booth for an explanation.[7]

Inside the theatre, women began to faint. The first was Gourlay, but Emerson reached her in time, fanning her with his Dundreary wig as others helped her off into the wings. Turning, he caught another young woman who had ascended from the audience only to collapse onto the apron of the stage, setting her down in the box immediately below the president's. Wright rushed to rescue his wife, who had fallen when she tried to reach the stage by standing atop an abandoned bass viol.

Cautiously emerging from his dressing room, Hawk encountered acting manager H. B. Phillips, who demanded, "Who did it?" "An actor," replied Hawk. "What's his name?" Phillips asked. "I won't tell," Hawk said. "There'll be a terrible uproar, and I want to keep out of any trouble." Phillips exploded: "Don't be a fool! This man has shot the president, and you'll be hanged if you hesitate to give his name." Only then came the admission, "It was John Booth." Just as Hawk uttered the name, Mathews stepped between them. "You're a liar!" he asserted, but Hawk held his ground. "I am not a liar, and you know that I am not. I could swear to it if I was on my death bed." Phillips urged Hawk to tell what he knew to the authorities as soon as he changed out of his costume and rubbed off his greasepaint.[8]

The rest of the cast and crew huddled in small, frightened groups in the center of the stage staring up into the president's box, where he remained slumped in his chair, his head on his chest with his eyes closed and a slight smile still on his face. His frantic wife fluttered beside him. From the ledge of the box, Clara Harris called for water, and property manager Jimmie Maddox ran to fill a pitcher. Seemingly out of nowhere, two men appeared to hoist a young naval officer from the audience onto their backs, up toward the lip of the box nearly twelve feet above the stage. They could hear someone pounding on its door from the dress circle above, but no one had entered yet to assist the stricken president.

Actors Emerson and Tom Gourlay, Jeannie's father, brought a table out from the wings to boost them higher, and soon Dr. Charles Taft made it up and over, losing his cape in the process.

With an instinct born of years of her own theatrical management, Laura Keene strode to the footlights and called out repeatedly, "Order, gentlemen! Order! For God's sake have presence of mind and keep your places and all will be well." Gourlay, more familiar than Keene with the passages backstage, led her through the stage left door, then left to an outside stairway up to the Fords' apartment next door, through which they reached a reception room that connected back with the theatre's dress circle.

By now another doctor, Charles Leale, had made it through the door into the box, and Keene followed. As the doctors lowered the president to the floor, tearing at his clothing to find the wound, with Leale's permission she knelt at Lincoln's side and cradled his head in her lap. It struck her how much from that perspective he resembled Mantegna's *Dead Christ*. When Maddox's pitcher arrived, she bathed his face. Gourlay hovered in the doorway along with Ferguson, who had worked his way through the audience to the box.[9]

Below them in the house, Harry Ford knew he had to act, and quickly. He summoned doorkeeper "Buck" Buckingham, who had frozen in the act of filing away ticket stubs, and sent him in search of Washington Mayor Richard Wallach, whom he remembered seeing in the lobby. Alerted, Wallach fought his way down the center left aisle nearly to the stage and took command, ordering the theatre cleared. At first, no one moved. Then the crowd began to inch toward the exits thrown open onto Tenth Street, but a roiling crowd out there made it almost impossible to leave. Word had reached the outside world.

Then movement at the top of the stairs curving down into the lobby caught their eyes, and a funereal hush settled over the house. Four soldiers and the doctors who had been attending the wounded president carried him, nearly naked to the waist, toward the stairs, using a shutter they had grabbed from the box's narrow passageway, with Tom Gourlay assisting them around the curve of the dress circle. Turning the president to keep his head elevated, they inched their way down, a young army lieutenant clearing the way. Keene, supporting the sobbing Mary Lincoln, followed.

As they reached the bottom of the stairs and turned to enter the crowd outside, Ford stepped up to the actress, putting his arm around her waist to keep her from the crowd in the street. Her hair in disarray, her dress bloodied, she beseeched the provost guard and patrolmen rushing in to take control of the theatre, "For God's sake, try to capture the murderer!" When asked by someone in the crowd if the president still lived, she gasped, "God only knows!"[10]

Backstage, the actors frantically gathered up personal possessions, not bothering to change out of costume, as rumors flew that they would all be arrested, or that the theatre was about to be torched. On Wright's orders, the men high in the fly loft rang down the curtain, not to rise on another production for over a century.

CHAPTER TWO

"A HOTBED OF SPIES AND SEDITIOUS PLOTS"

SOMEONE SHOULD HAVE SEEN it coming. The most remarkable thing about the atmosphere backstage at Ford's was that partisan feelings managed to stay suppressed for so long. Day after day, night after night, veterans of both Union and Confederate armies, some with relatives and friends still in the field, worked side by side through tiresome rehearsals and performances. Their professed—or suppressed—political sentiments ranged from ardent Unionism tempered by years of harrowing military service to bitter secessionist ideals crushed by recent events at Appomattox. A clash was inevitable. In the fatal night's aftermath, these suppressed agendas and unsettled scores drove some to turn upon, and others to turn in, their fellow workers.

Ironically, despite all this, Ford's was just reaching its height of popularity and profitability. That success—in fact the theatre's very existence in the city of Washington in 1865—was a testimonial to the foresight and business acumen of owner-manager John T. Ford. Short, stocky, and pugnacious—friends preferred "strong in his convictions"—Ford conducted himself at all times with dignity and propriety. His strongest traits were his sharply-focused intelligence, artistic sensibility, and keen sense of fair play. Gregarious and good-humored, he made friends easily and could be charming, especially to anyone professionally helpful. Fiercely loyal to his friends and his actors, he took particular pleasure in nurturing the careers of promising young performers.

Born in Baltimore on April 16, 1829, Ford learned self-discipline at fifteen working as a clerk in his uncle's Richmond tobacco factory (which would be confiscated early in the war by the Confederate government and converted into the infamous Castle Thunder prison). At twenty he married eighteen-year-old Edith Andrews, a petite, frail, soft-spoken Quaker from Hanover County, Virginia, to whom he remained deeply devoted all his life. Leaving his uncle, he opened a newspaper stand at Seventh and Broad Streets, opposite the Richmond Theatre. Its actors congregated there, drawing him in with their talk of performances, and he was soon spending every possible minute at the theatre, where he found his true calling.[1]

1850s Richmond was a lively cultural center whose plantation society readily embraced the theatre's stars. Whether melodramas, minstrel shows, or Shakespearean tragedies held the boards, Ford was fascinated more with the conduct of the audience, and quickly developed an eye for eccentric and ostentatious behavior. He captured much of it in a local-color farce he titled *Richmond as It Is*, which he submitted to theatre managers George Kunkel and Thomas Moxley, who staged it to popular acclaim. Ford quickly accepted their offer to become advertising manager and sometime playwright at a salary of $7.50 a week, which soon was doubled as he entered into a full partnership with the managers. Traveling with their minstrel Nightingale Serenaders, he learned to craft enticing publicity notices, a skill that served him well for life.

By 1855 the three men were jointly managing theatres in Richmond, Baltimore, and Washington, sharing a common stock company (a stable of actors who could support a visiting star or carry a whole play by themselves). To provide audiences with variety and the actors with greater experience, they rotated their actors among their three theatres. Many later became major stars, including Maggie Mitchell, Joseph Jefferson, John T. Raymond, John McCullough, and young John Wilkes Booth.

Of the three cities, the managers' efforts in Washington were the least successful. The venerable National Theatre on Pennsylvania Avenue burned in 1856, and several others quickly closed for lack of business. The capital's antebellum audiences, hard to attract and fairly lowbrow, preferred circuses to legitimate theatre and lacked funds after the financial panic of 1857. By contrast the Baltimore venue, the Holliday Street Theatre, succeeded from the start. One of the oldest theatres in America at the time, from its stage "The Star-Spangled Banner" was first sung in 1819.

But for a variety of reasons, the partnership soon dissolved and Ford, brimming with confidence, branched out on his own. In 1859, with the help of Baltimore architect-builder James Gifford, he lavishly renovated the Holliday Street, enlarging its stage to accommodate opera. Success came quickly, to the point where Ford could purchase an impressive home on Gilmor Street on the northwest edge of the city. In short order he was elected to the Baltimore City Council (on the nativist American or "Know-Nothing" party ticket), then as its president, becoming acting mayor for two years.

★ ★ ★

But as the nation's secessionist crisis built to a head during the 1860–61 season, Ford and his employees found it increasingly difficult to ignore the city's rising factionalism. Many, if not most, Baltimoreans were sympathetic to the states' rights aims of the Confederacy. Rabid opposition to the draft, the war, and the president was common there, as it was in Southern Maryland and on the state's Eastern Shore, both fundamentally Southern in spirit, prejudices, and customs, including slaveholding.

In February 1861 volatile gangs of Baltimore "plug uglies" prevented President-elect Lincoln from traveling freely through the city to his inauguration. Two months later, on Pratt Street, just four blocks south of Holliday, rioting erupted that led to the deaths of four soldiers of the 6th Massachusetts Regiment as they moved through the city on their way to Washington, along with twelve citizens.[2]

For much of the war, Baltimore remained an occupied city with an army garrisoned on Federal Hill, initially commanded by the notoriously repressive Union General Benjamin Butler. A new network of forts encircled the city, one of which covered part of Ford's front yard. Even under martial law, though, Baltimore remained "seething with activity," recalled one of his actors after the war—"a hotbed of spies and seditious plots." Many in the theatrical profession "were decidedly, though not openly, on the side of the Confederacy." One reason: "Southern people had always been great patrons of the theatre, and treated actors as gentlemen and equals rather than as the vagabonds most Northerners considered them. And now the courage and gallantry of the Confederate soldiers appealed to all that was romantic in the Thespian temperament."[3]

Despite the Union fort on his property, Ford sympathized with the secessionist cause. His friendships with figures such as the city's police commissioner, George P. Kane, who was arrested and imprisoned in 1862 for aiding the Confederacy, were open secrets. (Upon hearing of Kane's arrest, John Wilkes Booth exclaimed, "I know George P. Kane well; he is my friend.") Fellow Baltimorean and actor John E. Owens, a close friend of both Ford and Kane, was a frequent star at Ford's theatres. Having lost his own New Orleans theatre to Union occupiers, Owens bitterly resented the North and remained an ardent Southern sympathizer. Captivating actress Maggie Mitchell, another frequent star at Ford's, was observed on several occasions stomping on an American flag during performances in southern cities. The *Richmond Enquirer* praised both Owens and Mitchell for their devotion to the Southern cause.[4]

Likewise, Ford's correspondence with tragedian Edwin Forrest reflected their shared antipathy to the president. At one point during the war, Forrest wrote to Ford that Robert E. Lee could easily beat Lincoln in an election in both the North and the South. It was important, he said, to "convince our Southern brethren that we are not all abolitionists in the North." If Lincoln were reelected, bemoaned Forrest, the country would be "sunk below Heaven's reaching mercy." (When that did come to pass, Forrest struggled to understand how Americans could be so blind "to their true interests.") In 1864 Ford would sign an unprecedented exclusive contract with Forrest for five months, during which he would perform only at Ford's theatres. Together, Ford and Forrest nurtured the career of John McCullough, another Southern sympathizer and close friend of Booth's who would come under scrutiny by assassination investigators.[5]

Union loyalists like Booth's brother Edwin avoided playing at Ford's theatres, preferring others more unabashedly pro-Union. As early as 1859, Edwin's wife Mary Devlin, who did act for Ford, was repulsed by his close ties to the Baltimore "plug uglies" and "riff raffs": "My pen," she informed her husband, "almost refuses to deface this sheet by the tracing of such names."[6]

Ford's partner Kunkel had exclaimed upon Lincoln's election, "The country will run rivers of blood [and our] business will now begin to fall off." Together they had staged in Richmond a production called *The Parlor and Cabin*, an anti-abolitionist rebuttal to *Uncle Tom's Cabin*.

When Joseph Jefferson appeared at the Holliday Street just after the election, Ford publicly expressed his desire to "wake up another Jefferson [Thomas] to see the land he ... strove so hard to achieve, now convulsed, almost disunited, by Northern aggression and fanaticism." A month later, Ford staged the story of a Revolutionary War rebel as a parable celebrating Southern independence from Northern oppression. He contorted the themes of another production to show the nation's being "divided into angry billows by the rude squalls of Northern Fanaticism [in which] girls can shoulder the musket [and] the irrepressible Negro will appear, homeless and disowned." He inserted a chorus singing "Dixie's Land," and within a month was billing the show as "a commentary upon the abuse of constitutional rights" by Northern forces. A March 1861 Holliday Street production lampooned Lincoln's surreptitious nighttime journey through Baltimore as "a comic view of the Flight of Abraham." Most alarming to Ford by early 1863, as he expressed in a letter to comedian James Hackett, was "the fearful work of the Negro troops ... breeding terrible events for the future. I fear worse than war will be upon us."[7]

However, by late 1863, Ford's attitude was changing. Notices for his productions no longer bore inflammatory words, and in October he donated the use of his Holliday Street Theatre for a benefit performance for the United States Sanitary Commission. By June 1864, when Confederate General Jubal Early threatened the city, Edith made a concerted effort to ensure the comfort of the soldiers stationed on their property, and John even enlisted as a First Lieutenant in the 100-Day 11th Regiment Infantry, Maryland Volunteers.[8]

Fortunately for his business, Baltimore citizens and occupying soldiers alike sought diversion. Without minimizing "the awful seriousness of the war," observed Harry Hawk, "those at home turned to the play as a means of lightening the strain of the weary weeks of silence on the part of loved ones at the front." And so Ford's Holliday Street Theatre thrived. Its 1861–62 season provided three hundred performances to good houses, the longest streak in Baltimore theatrical history to that point. By the following year, it had eliminated all competition in the city.[9]

One of Ford's strengths was recognizing and promoting young talent that he believed had the potential for true stardom. He had spotted one of the most promising of these during his days managing in Richmond: John Wilkes Booth. Ford spared no funds showcasing Booth at the Holliday Street in February 1862 in major classical roles such as Richard III, Romeo, Hamlet, and Shylock, and the engagement was a triumph. Reviewers, too, were euphoric, one exclaiming, "Mid the galaxy of stars that have illuminated our theatrical firmament, ... none have shone with greater brilliancy than [his] fervid expressions of genius." Thus was a friendship born of mutual respect strengthened, and Booth and Ford were often seen in each other's company.[10]

★ ★ ★

Despite his earlier lack of success in Washington, Ford again turned his eyes south once the war began. He was convinced there was money to be made in the capital, given the city's wartime population explosion. And so he began there in December 1861 the venture that would twice bring him heartache. He leased for five years with an option to buy a commanding building on the east side of Tenth Street, midway up the block between E and F Streets. Nestled among wooden storefronts, the building had housed the First Baptist Church, whose congregation had merged with another and moved out. Some of its parishioners, though, were unhappy about the building's being leased to Ford and predicted a dire fate for any house of worship converted to heathen theatrical purposes.

The structure suited Ford's intentions well. Its brick façade, with five arched entrances below a double row of corniced windows, suggested stability. Its interior was uncluttered, a raised platform that had housed its pulpit and choir would serve as a stage, and its pews and balcony would allow him to charge two ticket prices. Ford realized it would need improvements before he could mount full-scale theatrical productions, but the location was ideal. Prominent homes and hotels within a few blocks meant potential audiences, and major newspapers nearby would run notices of upcoming productions and eminent attendees.

His only competition would come from intermittent productions at the rundown Washington Theatre on Eleventh Street and from Leonard Grover's two venues. The first of these, the New National Theatre, was being rebuilt on the north side of Pennsylvania Avenue. It would showcase many stars but never quite shed its reputation for discomfort: it was said by some to be "an ice vault in winter and a sweatbox in summer." Grover's other theatre, on the disreputable south side of Pennsylvania Avenue at Fifth Street, was the shabby Canterbury Hall, catering to a considerably lower level of public taste, admitting only males. Dozens of popular gambling halls, too, were spread along the south side of "The Avenue."[11]

Curiously, all of these establishments flourished, patronized regularly by army officers and members of Congress alike, despite powerful forces that contrived to make the capital an unpleasant environment for entertainment. The nauseating effluvia of the city's canal, emanating from its sewage, garbage, and perennial dead animals, hovered four blocks south of Ford's, tolerable only until the wind drifted the wrong way. Yellow fever and typhoid outbreaks occurred regularly. The city's ubiquitous mud and dust—depending upon the season—were even more difficult to escape. Newspaper correspondent Noah Brooks considered Washington "probably the dirtiest and most ill-kept borough in the United States." The streets, he observed, "are seas or canals of liquid mud, varying in depth from one to three feet, and possessing ... conglomerations of garbage, refuse and trash, the odors [of which transmit] seventy separate and distinct stinks." At some sloping intersections he could watch "a torrent of thick, yellow mud flowing ... bearing on its placid surface the unconsidered trifles which have been swept out of saloons, shops and houses."[12]

Among the most notoriously ill-maintained byways was F Street between Tenth and Eleventh, a block from Ford's. Sometimes its mud trapped coaches up to their axles, and ladies and gentlemen alike donned rubber boots when venturing out. Adding to all this were large numbers of emaciated government-contract horses, near death, wandering the streets along with countless hogs, geese, and chickens. (As early as 1863, city newspapers were bemoaning the number of *dead* horses in the streets.) Cattle penned up on the grounds of the unfinished Washington Monument were slaughtered there to feed Union troops.

Any attempts at cleanliness or paving—aside from the perpetually dirt-caked cobblestones of Pennsylvania Avenue—were thwarted by the demands of a civilian and military population that exploded during the war from sixty thousand to almost a quarter of a million. Crime proved difficult to eradicate, with a police force that varied from sixteen to fifty officers on any given day, and fewer at night, to corral thousands of thugs, drunks, streetwalkers, hucksters, and pickpockets. Sizable swathes of overgrown, undeveloped property, some adjacent to government buildings, abetted by sparsely placed and poorly maintained gas streetlights, provided ample opportunity for crime to thrive. A visiting Englishman observed that even in Washington's metropolitan area "the country is wild, trackless, unbridged, uninhabited and desolate."[13]

Just below The Avenue squatted a notorious eleven-block area known as "Hooker's Division," housing the highest concentration of the city's estimated 450 brothels and five thousand prostitutes, some of whom regularly slipped into the Canterbury disguised in male attire to arrange assignations. In addition, the city's worst slum, a deplorable concentration of shanties dubbed "Murder Bay," housing thousands of "contrabands" (freed slaves who had followed the army north), lay on its southern edge. It backed against the Executive Mansion grounds and the infamous canal, which bisected it.[14]

Before the war, Washington had been a sleepy southern town with a genteel aristocracy and ample public and residential space. Now it was insufferably crowded, especially with rugged Westerners who had followed the new president to the capital, filling saloons and boardinghouses with their energy and noise. The military's presence, too, was felt everywhere. Heavily loaded quartermasters' mule trains and artillery caissons lumbered up and down city streets, and a seemingly endless stream of ambulances bore tattered, emaciated wounded to the city's twenty-one military hospitals. Companies of Union soldiers drilled on every square: it was said that officers were so thick on The Avenue that a boy who threw a stone at a dog would hit three brigadier generals instead. Yet actress Rose Eytinge found the atmosphere invigorating, "a constant state of ferment and excitement. Martial music was everywhere to be heard; aides-de-camp and bearers of despatches [sic] were galloping hither and thither; and 'contrabands' in their picturesque rags were encamped… wherever they could find an eligible spot."[15]

Curiously, this Northern wartime capital's Southern roots allowed secessionist sympathies to flourish. It had been founded by slaveholders and constructed by slave labor, and sixty years were insufficient to ameliorate deeply held beliefs. While it was primarily the older and wealthier Washington families who were Secessionists, the tremendous population increase "did not change the feelings of the natives," noted Dr. George Loring Porter, who would figure in the assassination's aftermath.[16]

Throughout the war, Southern sympathies abounded and plots simmered. The conspiratorial atmosphere fed on itself. "Every rebel victory was the signal for secret rejoicing," wrote one resident, "and every Union success became the cause of sorrow and increased hatred. In the spring of 1865 some of these people grew desperate." But by now most of them knew enough to keep their views to themselves, or, observed a loyal Unionist, "the United States Army put a check on their rebellious utterances."[17]

An increasingly circumspect John Ford wrestled his true sentiments into submission and accepted the reality that Washington was, in effect, as much an occupied city as his native Baltimore. With troop encampments everywhere, any public gathering, including his theatrical performances, was likely to include a goodly percentage of Union soldiers. (This also meant occasional raids of his theatre by Provost Marshal's men to check passes and drag out deserters.)

From the start Grover tried to paint Ford's Theatre with a broad secessionist brush, averring (then and for decades after) that *his* was the house preferred by Lincoln and most loyalists, and Ford's was a haven for Southern sympathizers. There was some truth to this, an impression held as far away as New York. In the frightening days following the assassination, the *New York Clipper*, the nation's leading source of news and information for and about actors, asserted that "there were several persons connected with this [Ford's] theatre whose secession proclivities were well known, whose violent sentiments in favor of the rebellion and the leaders have frequently been noticed by parties fulfilling engagements there."[18]

★ ★ ★

Assessing the improved tastes of his Washington audiences, Ford provided variety: ennobling Shakespearean dramas, sentimental melodramas, escapist comedies such as *Our American Cousin* and *The People's Lawyer*, old standards like *She Stoops to Conquer* and *The Rivals*, inspirational patriotic dramas such as *The Battle of Bull Run*, historical dramas like *Richelieu*, and social consciousness dramas such as *East Lynne*. His Shakespearean productions were typically edited for easier comprehension or to include a happier ending. And, he assured the public, "the most refined taste need have no apprehension of being annoyed by vulgarisms" upon his stage.[19]

In February 1862, Ford closed the theatre to undertake a $10,000 renovation designed and supervised by James Gifford, with carpenter Edman "Ned" Spangler, soon to become a pathetic figure in the assassination story, as his chief assistant. Gifford had built Tudor Hall, the Booth family's country home in Bel Air, Maryland, but they had never finished paying him for its construction, causing him to lose his own house. Out of revenge, he ripped the tin roof off Tudor Hall and for the rest of his life resented the entire Booth family.[20]

Within three weeks—just ahead of Grover's renovations of the National—Ford reopened his theatre as Ford's Atheneum [sic]. It featured lavish furnishings, the latest innovations of ventilation and lighting, and seating for 2,500 patrons. For three months, Ford gave his audiences top-rate entertainment—from Forrest to Hackett to Italian opera, and Washingtonians responded by filling the house nightly. On May 28, Ford's was graced for the first time with the presence of President and Mrs. Lincoln—likely at her urging, as the bill was opera (her preference): Donizetti's *La Figlia del Reggimento*.

After a short summer recess (the usual pattern for theatres of that era), Ford opened for a second season in late August with a strong stock company supporting visiting star John Sleeper Clarke (Booth's brother-in-law) for three weeks. This was followed for a remarkable five weeks by the exceptionally popular Mitchell, who felt so much at home at Ford's that she invested in its eventual purchase. Washingtonians were apparently so smitten with her that they ignored her political sentiments. Lincoln's secretary John Hay, under the impression that she had "throw[n] her past behind her," decreed, "Never was there a success more instant and decided." Ford reveled in the run of sold-out houses.[21]

But late on the bitterly cold afternoon of December 30, a defective gas meter under the stage sparked an inferno that within hours consumed the theatre's interior. Although no lives were lost, Ford, along with a visiting opera company, lost scenery, costumes, and theatrical furnishings worth more than $20,000. Despite this setback, from which few managers would have been able to recover, Ford's immediate decision was to rebuild.

He and Gifford gutted the building of everything but its brick façade, enlarged its cellar, and created a more elegant house on three levels that seated fewer patrons (1,720) but in greater comfort. Appended to its north face (stage right), they constructed a four-story wing containing an office, dressing rooms, and costume and scenery shops. A three-story wing to the south would house a restaurant-saloon at street level, with a narrow covered passageway separating it from the theatre. Above this, connected to the theatre's second, "dress circle" level, was an elegant reception room, or "promenade saloon," outfitted with lush carpeting, gilt mirrors, and marble-topped tables. The third floor would serve as living quarters for Ford's brothers.

Rebuilding cost $75,000, but funds appeared from willing shareholders, including Mitchell, *National Intelligencer* editor John F. Coyle, and printer Henry Polkinhorn (who would produce all playbills for the theatre), enabling Ford to pay off his lease and buy the building and land outright. Scarce lumber was made available through the intervention of none other than President Lincoln.

★ ★ ★

On August 27, 1863, in the lull between the Union's success at Gettysburg and the setback of Chickamauga, Ford's New Theatre—which would last less than two full seasons—opened to rave reviews. Audiences and critics alike praised its spacious, brightly lit interior, enhanced acoustics and ventilation—on which Gifford had consulted with the Smithsonian Institution—and its talented stock company. Its pillared white and gold interior, accented by deep rose damask wallpaper in eight private boxes, was a masterpiece of Victorian elegance "such as none of us, a year ago, would have expected to see within at least half a generation," crowed the *Washington Chronicle*.[22]

That night a plush new green curtain with a portrait of Shakespeare against a richly detailed landscape by scenic artists James Lamb and Charles Getz rose on Ford's Theatre's inaugural production, the romantic spectacle *The Naiad Queen*. It featured special effects by Gifford, new backdrops by Lamb, and a large cast that included a bevy of sprightly dancers.

One of Ford's most promising young actors, James A. Herne, delivered a dedicatory prologue, the first words spoken from the new stage: *As from the ashes Cinderella rose / Rise we—all radiant from our night of woes*. Ford had selected him for this honor as a way of nurturing his budding career, despite the trouble Herne kept getting into. He and a band of fellow performers refused to take their careers seriously, constantly playing practical jokes, drinking, and brawling. On at least one occasion, Ford had had to rescue them from police custody. "Their ringleader," remembered Herne's daughter, "was John Wilkes Booth." But that friendship ended when Booth tried to kill Herne after a particularly bitter disagreement, thought to be over a woman.[23]

Throughout that 1863–64 season at the resplendent new Ford's Theatre, a line of theatergoers appeared night after night at the box office window just inside the lobby. Orchestra seats were priced at a reasonable single dollar ($14.20 today), with reserved seats fifty cents extra; boxes that could seat four people cost six dollars (lower level) or ten dollars (upper); parquette seats (those behind the orchestra seats) and dress circle above were seventy-five cents. It was not an expensive evening: for a Washington theatregoer of 1865, despite a 75-percent annual inflation rate on many goods during the war, one dollar represented a five-pound sack of sugar, five haircuts, ten shots of liquor, or a third of the cost of a night in a good hotel.

For a half hour before curtain time each evening, patrons would drift in, have their tickets torn by the doorkeeper, then move into the theatre itself or head up the stairs to the dress circle. For anyone wanting even cheaper seats, tickets for the topmost "family circle" were available for only a quarter at a smaller box office window facing into a tiny foyer just inside the first door (approaching from the south). These ticket-holders then ascended a separate spiral staircase from the foyer to the third tier, called the gallery in other theatres.

As early as 1855, Ford had used this new name, "family circle," for the topmost gallery as a means of fighting the widespread and decades-long practice of that level being a haven for prostitutes and their clients. Furthermore, he refused to install a bar in the lobby. "I neither admit nor permit prostitutes or bar rooms," he asserted, determined to earn his money only by what he presented on the stage. He had no intention of making an "assignation place of my gallery or a rum mill of my lobby" and arranged for a regular police presence outside and part-owner Alphonso Houck to patrol the theatre to eject unruly patrons. But this morality came at a cost: men buying theatre tickets simply out of thirst or lust could have brought him an additional four to five thousand dollars a year, he figured.[24]

The theatre's wiry, jovial doorkeeper, John E. "Buck" Buckingham, was a welcome fixture in the lobby. Born in Baltimore in 1828, he worked there and in Boston as a callboy (making sure actors made it onto the stage in time for each entrance) for almost two decades, a job that meant occasionally searching nearby saloons at curtain time to ferret out the famously unpredictable, alcoholic, yet brilliant tragedian Junius Brutus

Booth Sr. In the process, Buck had witnessed the embryonic but equally inconsistent genius of that actor's son, John Wilkes.

Now Buck lived with his wife of fifteen years, Margaret Jemima, and their four children in southeast Washington near his day job as a gun carriage builder at the Navy Yard. His hours there were long, but he always reported promptly for evening duty at Ford's. He was a loyal Unionist who had served for several years in his early twenties in Washington's home guard company, the National Greys. In July 1864, he was among the Navy Yard workmen mustered in to augment the First District of Columbia Cavalry when Jubal Early threatened the city. It must have rankled Buck to hear secessionist sentiments voiced backstage.

Some of his favorite evenings were those when President Lincoln attended, tipping Buck five dollars now and then as he handed over his ticket. On some visits, the president came down from his box and stood behind Buck as he sat taking tickets, "just watching the people, sometimes for nearly an hour," occasionally returning during intermissions. It later occurred to Buck that Booth may have intended to shoot the president during one of those visits.[25]

★ ★ ★

That fall Ford branched out into neighboring towns, leasing a handsome new brick theatre in Union-occupied Alexandria, Virginia, at the corner of Royal and King Streets, and the 500-seat Belvidere Hall on Baltimore Street in Cumberland, Maryland (following its use as a hospital for the wounded of Antietam). Ford chose two highly capable protégés to manage these new ventures: former Holliday Street and Athenaeum stage manager Joseph Parker for Alexandria, and stock company actor and future star John T. Raymond for Cumberland. Soon, Ford would also lease Philadelphia's Academy of Music, the fifth theatre under his control. Again, Ford rotated his actors among these venues to save money and provide his audiences with continual novelty, meeting with tremendous success in both locations. On its opening night, October 12, the Alexandria Theatre was "crowded from pit to galleries and numbers could not obtain admittance."[26]

The first full Washington season of Ford's Theatre, which closed on Independence Day 1864, was a qualified success. The drama critic for the *Intelligencer*, "Erasmus," compared the artistry of Ford's stage technicians favorably to those in New York. He commended a few of the actors, but the majority, as well as the orchestra, was perceived as utterly inadequate. But he had to admit that the house had been full almost every night.[27]

For the 1864–65 season, which would run a typical forty-two weeks, Ford heeded Erasmus's advice as well as his own finely honed managerial instincts. He hired an almost completely new stock company at salaries ranging from five to thirty dollars a week (considerably less than the average for New York performers, who could earn forty to sixty dollars, but well above the dollar-and-a-half weekly wage of a shopgirl). Ford quickly discovered, though, that the capital offered little in the way of experienced actors and actresses, especially charming ingénues who could attract crowds in this masculine, political city. In August, he wrote to stage manager John Wright, working out of town that summer, "We want Ladies badly, can you find any in Boston?" Six of the new company members had almost no acting experience.[28]

Even so, most of these new ones were gone by April. They felt neglected as Ford poured his energy and funds into securing revenue-drawing stars, to the detriment of properly developing and paying his stock company, who by now were being shunted among five theatres. Some defected to Grover's or to the Washington Theatre under new star-managers E. L. Davenport and J. W. Wallack. Others were drafted into the Union Army or released for unreliability or incompetence. "Frequently," remembered callboy-actor Will Ferguson, "an actor from the [war] front with his discharge would walk into the theatre, doff his uniform, and take up a part." At one point Ford even hired some London actors off a British ship caught trying to run the blockade, heading for Richmond.[29]

The remaining assemblage, referred to derisively by some as "war actors," ended up being inferior even to those of the previous season. Ford shuddered at hiring them, telling Wright, "I have a horror of novices that words can't express." He watched helplessly as Erasmus stepped up the attacks: "What abominable conduct of most of the stock actors. Such a manifestation of bewildered stupidity [leads to] the amazement, ridicule, and disgust of the audience." Their acting blunders "were so excuseless as to amount to insulting carelessness"; they were apparently incapable of "uttering a single connected or intelligible sentence."[30]

In addition, Ford sorely needed someone who could improve the caliber of his musicians, and so hired Billy Withers. This tall, thin, mustachioed orchestra leader, twenty-eight, already had strong feelings about how things should operate, being used to military preparedness. Born at West Point, where his father was leader of the band, he had enrolled at nineteen as a musician in the 62nd Regiment Pennsylvania Volunteers along with his father and two brothers. Discharged two years later, he had taken on the direction of the orchestra at the old Washington Theatre (under Ford's unsuccessful management). But when the war began, he and his father and brothers re-enlisted, this time with the 12th Regiment, First Infantry, New York Militia. His father's trumpet and his brother Reuben's drumming were always in demand, but there was little call in a regimental band for Billy's primary instrument, the violin. Still, his fiddling beside the campfire was always welcome.

By cruel necessity the brothers had become more than musicians, carrying litters of wounded and assisting field surgeons throughout the summer of 1862's Seven Days' Battles on the Peninsula, notably at Malvern Hill and Gaines Mill, after which Reuben was discharged due to illness. Billy continued to perform similar duties for a few more weeks, but when regimental bands were abolished by Congress, he, too, was discharged.

Now, at Ford's, he dedicated himself to improving the quality of its music, spending a great deal of time there, boarding nearby on I Street with his father and Reuben, both of whom he added to his orchestra. He pushed Ford to hire more musicians, despite an agreement Ford had with Grover to keep the size of their orchestras equal. But Ford held firm: the money just wasn't there. He told Wright, "If Grover wants Withers, he can go. I can easily supply his place.... My honor is pledged to this." Weighing his options, Withers stayed.[31]

His orchestra became a presidential favorite and performed at Lincoln's second inaugural ball. Understandably, Withers preferred patriotic airs and often wrote new music for his orchestra, but neither he nor Reuben nor their father had any tolerance for the "Secesh" sentiments they heard all too often backstage.

★ ★ ★

By now Ford's theatrical empire was expanding almost faster than he could adequately administer it. He had committed himself to annual operating expenses totaling nearly $100,000 (about $1.4 million today). Though he would be tragically identified with his eponymous Washington theatre from the night of the assassination on, he was in fact by 1865 often absent from it. Living in Baltimore and devoting most of his time to his Holliday Street and Philadelphia ventures, he installed his brothers, Harry and Dick, as treasurer and business manager, respectively, to manage things in Washington, and only stopped in there occasionally.[32]

Both Harry and Dick were physically unassuming: dark-complected, with bushy brown hair and brown eyes. The former, stocky (just under five foot six) and moon-faced, resembled John the most; the latter was thinner and an inch taller. Harry, perpetually upbeat and outgoing, had disliked the shoemaking trade into which he had been apprenticed as a teenager under their father in Baltimore. He was grateful to John for taking him under his wing to learn the basics of theatrical management and quickly demonstrated a natural ability for it. Although he had just turned twenty-one, he played by far the greater role in management in Washington, entrusted with nearly all of the theatre's operations except the hiring and casting of the stock company, explicitly left to Wright. Dick, twenty-four, had started out as a streetcar and train conductor in Baltimore and still worked as one part-time in Washington. Reserved and tentative, he deferred to Harry despite their ages, serving as his assistant. John, more than a decade their senior, was fiercely protective of both brothers.[33]

Settling into rooms above the Star Saloon next door, Harry and Dick cut a doorway through to the theatre's dress circle to avoid traipsing through the rain and mud of Tenth Street. Nearly from the start, their effective management yielded a steady stream of box office revenue. Except for the previous summer, when the city's political and military fortunes were uncertain, the wartime economy in Washington had allowed theatres to flourish regardless of their offerings. By fall, as war news began to turn hopeful for the North, audiences seemed increasingly inclined to celebrate with an evening out. Erasmus had quipped that "the theatres are coining money." The Fords capitalized on the favorable war news by interrupting performances with updated bulletins read from the stage, such as the announcement of the fall of Atlanta in September and of election returns in November.[34]

To help contend with the increased business, the Fords had brought on Joe Sessford the previous season and Tom Raybold in December. The tall, lean Sessford, at thirty-two a lifelong Washingtonian, had briefly been a Metropolitan policeman. His stylish mustache, muttonchops, and dark, wavy hair helped disguise a thin face and generous nose. He lived with his mother, his wife, Sarah, and their young son (a three-year-old daughter had died in 1863) on C Street at Eleventh. Before coming to Ford's he had worked as a ticket seller and assistant treasurer at the National and Washington Theatres. His duties at Ford's involved selling tickets, counting the house each night (to assure accuracy of sales and detect any theft), and maintaining the "comp list" (those who were admitted free of charge—a practice that some managers, such as Grover, were trying to curtail). Sessford spent his free time at the nearby picture-frame gallery of Francis and James Lamb (who was Sessford's brother-in-law and Ford's scene painter).

Raybold, thirty-one, lived with his wife and young daughter on Saratoga Street in Baltimore, but while in Washington boarded around the corner from the theatre. He was multi-talented and eminently useful to the Fords, becoming at one time or another their upholsterer, paper hanger, doorkeeper, clerk, advertising manager, telegraph dispatch handler, and ticket agent or, as he himself put it, "general office factotum." Like Buck, he had served the Union well, having enlisted in 1861 in the 3rd Maryland Infantry Regiment, where he had been quickly promoted to second lieutenant, commanding a company at First Bull Run and up the Shenandoah Valley under General Pope, and finally to captain after Cedar Mountain, at which time he fell ill and was sent home to recover and be mustered out.[35]

★ ★ ★

During this 1864–65 season at Ford's it was again Forrest and Mitchell who drew the biggest houses and the most effusive reviews. John Sleeper Clarke, dramatic actress Mrs. D. P. Bowers, Irish comedians Mr. and Mrs. W. J. Florence, and Junius Brutus Booth Jr., had also done well. A high point of the season had come on March 18 when, for John

McCullough's benefit, his devoted friend John Wilkes Booth had joined him for a memorable performance of Richard Lalor Sheil's Moorish tragedy, *The Apostate*.

Certainly, the new members of the Ford's stock company had opportunities this season to observe and learn from some of the most skilled, experienced performers on the American stage, Booth among them. The fact that there were so few experienced performers in the company to serve as emotional anchors in case of problems backstage could prove unfortunate, but in time that, too, might be overcome. With two more months of the season still before them and the war over, the Ford's actors, finally beginning to function as a cohesive ensemble, seemed poised on the morning of April 14 to achieve a level of success and accomplishment greater than anything they had known.

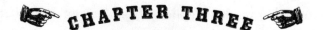

CHAPTER THREE

"IT IS A LOTTERY, THIS PROFESSION OF OURS"

T HE CAST TRICKLED IN through the stage door of Ford's Theatre that Good Friday morning a little before 11:00. They gathered around Wright and Phillips on its bare stage bathed in the morning sunlight filtering down from the building's roof hatches and high front windows. Seven blocks away, President Lincoln's cabinet was convening in the Executive Mansion to chart the course of the postwar nation. In another hour the Union flag would be ceremonially raised 550 miles away over Fort Sumter in Charleston, South Carolina, four years to the day since its lowering at the onset of war.[1]

The actors had relished their walk to work. The morning's warm, sunny weather, carrying the promise of a beautiful spring day, with dogwoods, lilacs, and Judas trees in bloom, put everyone in an expansive mood. Most felt a residual euphoria from last night's jubilant grand illumination in the city. It had been an unforgettable display of torch- and gas-lit patriotic banners and decorations splashed across storefronts and homes, still celebrating Sunday's historic signing at Appomattox. "Night was turned into day by the rejoicing residents of Washington," enthused actress May Hart. But John Ford had even bigger plans for his establishment tonight: stage carpenter Gifford was installing a Drummond "limelight," the newest and brightest of theatrical lights, atop a pole at Tenth and E Streets to illuminate the theatre's façade.[2]

Everyone wore street clothes for this morning's rehearsal, saving for the evening's performance the costumes that they themselves had to provide. Neither would the rehearsal use scenery or properties—only the most essential furniture, set out by property man Jimmie Maddox. Recording everyone present except actor Courtland V. Hess, who had reported in sick, Wright told callboy Will Ferguson to play Hess's tiny role tonight. Seventeen-year-old prompter John DeBonay, whose regular station was at a small desk just offstage left, would be needed for another minor role, so Wright himself would prompt whenever DeBonay was on stage.

Hopefully, little prompting would be required. But Phillips, as acting manager, would have his work cut out for him. This cast was younger and less experienced than he would have preferred; their average age was under thirty, and eight of them were younger than twenty.

The distinguished, Charleston-born Phillips, about to turn forty-six, carried three decades of acting, prompting, and stage managing experience. He had studied law at fourteen, but through the efforts of his playwright brother had switched to acting, playing supporting roles in New York, Boston, Montreal, and Baltimore. Throughout the 1850s, he had been especially popular at Wallack's Theatre in New York, where he had acquired modest reviews and received numerous "benefit nights"—performances, usually toward the end of the season, when the honoree(s) would take all revenue minus basic production costs.

In 1853 Phillips had married Mary Taylor, a Wallack's dancer and actress, who retired from the stage to raise their three daughters while he toured, first with actress-manageress Joey Gougenheim and then with Laura Keene (who was doubtless pleased in April 1865 to see him in charge of the Ford's company). Hired by John Ford in December 1863, he had quickly become a stalwart, valued member of the company, coaching the novice actors and taking on vital supporting roles, including First Witch to Forrest's Macbeth—a common practice at the time being the playing of that eccentric role by an older man—and Polonius to Junius Brutus Booth Jr.'s Hamlet. (He had known all of the Booths since childhood, including Edwin and John Wilkes and their famously unstable father, Junius Sr.)

As a measure of his worth, Ford had guaranteed him three benefit nights per season, an almost unprecedented privilege. But Phillips earned it, quickly becoming a popular mainstay, performing almost every night at one of Ford's theatres. His few newspaper mentions were highly favorable, except for occasional rebukes for ad libbing lines to get cheap laughs. Between seasons at Ford's Phillips spent his summers acting at Montreal's Theatre Royal, ensuring his family a stable income, a rare accomplishment in the theatrical profession.[3]

Out of necessity, Phillips had only this spring been moved up to "acting manager," a position that more and more companies at mid-century were forced by necessity to create. It really did seem, as Edwin Forrest wryly observed, "Whenever a young man is incapable of learning a trade, is incompetent to be a store porter, is too lazy to beg, and afraid to steal, he takes to the stage as a proper field for the profitable exercise of his idiocy."[4]

To Phillips, then, fell the unenviable task of training the latest raw recruits in the ways of the theatre, everything from how and when to make an entrance, to how to stand and gesture once onstage and how to deliver a line in something other than a recited monotone. Little or no time was left for developing individualized characterizations; that would only emerge later in the century when the modern theatrical director assumed responsibility for the process.

Phillips, along with Wright, began to conduct longer rehearsals to compensate for the company's inadequacies. Slowly, a few actors, like Jeannie Gourlay (whom Ford had hired away from Grover) and Ned Emerson, began to show promise. They understood beyond basic stage technique what it meant to "make a point"—that is, to strike a pose on stage and deliver a line so effectively that it elicited applause. Phillips's other responsibility was composing advertising copy for the Fords. For the past few weeks he had also been trying his hand at poetry, including a piece called "Honor to Our Soldiers," which Withers had set to music. It was to be played tomorrow night before Gourlay's benefit performance in *The Octoroon*.

Phillips would have performed tonight in *Our American Cousin* had not John Dyott, touring with visiting star Laura Keene, taken his role. A few regular members of the stock company who had supported Keene all week would spend the rest of their lives counting their blessings, for they would not be needed for tonight's cast of *Our American Cousin*. Only the luck of the draw, determined by Keene's choice of script and the actors needed for it, decided who would appear on the stage of Ford's each night. As with most tragic events, utter randomness would play a role tonight.

Audiences for the past two weeks had not been all that they had hoped for. The week's unseasonably warm weather and political excitement had kept many Washingtonians out of doors. But the patrons who had attended had been wonderfully receptive, thrilling with the melodramatic suspense of *The Workmen of Washington* and laughing generously at the predicaments of *The School for Scandal*. Good Friday ordinarily would not draw much of a crowd, but tonight was Miss Keene's farewell benefit, so a full house was possible.

★ ★ ★

In the lobby, Dick Ford had already opened the box office, assisted by ticket agents Raybold and Sessford. Raybold had been the first to arrive, well before 9:00, letting in John Lutz around 9:30 to assist with preparations for rehearsal. Raybold hoped to get his work done early so he might head home to Baltimore for the weekend. For days he had been struggling with a painful attack of facial neuralgia.

Around 10:30 the three men had received exceptional news. A messenger from the Executive Mansion appeared at the lobby window to request four box seat tickets for tonight for President and Mrs. Lincoln, along with General and Mrs. Grant, in response to two personal invitations that had gone out for tonight's performance. Earlier in the week young Billy Otis, Laura Keene's assistant, had carried one over to Mrs. Lincoln, whose approval of family social occasions was widely known to be imperative, and early this morning Dick Ford had gone to the White House with another. Unable to find her, he had sent word to her through a friendly maid. Leaving, he had run into the president and asked, "How do you feel, Mr. President?" "Like a boy," Lincoln had quipped.[5]

Dick Ford assured the messenger that the tickets would be delivered shortly by Alphonso Houck, but the assigning of that box had to be approved first by his brother Harry, who was still at breakfast at the National Hotel (where John Wilkes Booth was also taking a late breakfast). When Harry returned, he and Dick wasted no time putting together notices for the afternoon papers, the *National Republican* and the *Star*. They knew that Grant's presence would assure a full house more certainly than that of Lincoln, who by then had attended Ford's nineteen times. His most recent visit, accompanied by Generals Grant and Burnside, had occurred on February 10 to see John Sleeper Clarke in *Everybody's Friend* and a farce, *Love in Livery*.

Now, Dick sent Raybold to the *Star* and took the notice to the *Republican* himself, heading after that to the Treasury Department to see about borrowing some flags to decorate the presidential box. As much as they tried to hide it, the Fords knew, as their actors and stagehands would shortly, that a visit to their theatre by these men at this singular point in history was an occasion to be celebrated, not least because they had trumped Grover's in obtaining them.

Performing for this president, an enthusiastic theatregoer, meant a great deal to the actors. He usually made a low-key entrance, and they came to know his habits well: sitting far back in his box, hidden from the public's view by its Nottingham lace drapes. Sometimes he attended alone but usually came with Mary, their son Tad, personal secretaries John Nicolay and John Hay, or correspondent-confidant Noah Brooks. Attending with his wife, Lincoln preferred operas; with the others it was uproarious comedies that required little thought or concentration.

He relished these rare moments when he could relax in the theatre's dark anonymity, lost in his thoughts. Rarely applauding or smiling, he would from time to time burst out with a whole-souled guffaw, almost as if it caught even him by surprise. "Some people think I do wrong to go to the opera and the theatre," he said, "but it rests me. I love to be alone and yet to be with the people. I want to get this burden off; to change the current of my thoughts. A hearty laugh relieves me; and I seem better able after it to bear my cross."[6]

Among the actors Lincoln enjoyed was John Wilkes Booth. In the nearly two years since Booth's debut at Ford's Holliday Street Theatre, he had captivated audiences and reviewers across the country, and Ford always made sure to book him months in advance. He spared no expense in promoting Booth, billing him as "the youngest star actor in the world," and assembling "all-star" companies to support him. Ford marveled later that "John Booth made more money in a single season before and during the war than any other actor that lived at that time." Contributing to this was Ford's remarkable compensation to Booth of $700 a week (more than $9,600 today).[7]

The president, along with Mary, Nicolay, and Hay, had first seen him perform on November 9, 1863, at Ford's in a dual role: Phidias and Raphael in Charles Selby's *Pygmalion*-esque *The Marble Heart; or, The Sculptor's Dream*. They thought the production was "rather tame than otherwise." Lincoln admired Booth's performance, applauding it enthusiastically, and sent word through Ford that he wished to meet the actor. But Booth refused, muttering that he would "rather have the applause of a nigger." Either unaware of actors' political sympathies or unconcerned by them, Lincoln also enjoyed performances by Edwin Forrest (twice, including a performance of *Richelieu* in which Forrest changed the wording of his lines to reflect his antipathy to Lincoln's administration of the war) and by openly secessionist comedians Maggie Mitchell (three times) and John E. Owens.[8]

As for tonight's performance of *Our American Cousin*, the president knew it was to be Laura Keene's benefit. He made it a point to attend such events whenever he could, since his presence might boost box office revenue for the chosen performer. He had admired her acting in a February 1864 production of *The Sea of Ice*, in which she had played the challenging lead role of a wild Indian girl who becomes a refined French lady, and now he wanted to see her again.

Still able, despite its shopworn characters and creaky plot, to generate some surefire laughs, *Our American Cousin* was well suited to the president's taste in comedy. It conveyed the same folksy—some would say "lowbrow"—humor that he had relished since adolescence, leading him to attend any number of minstrel shows and unsophisticated comedies over the years, despite a simultaneous reverence for the profound ideas and speeches in the tragedies of Shakespeare.

British playwright Tom Taylor's inspiration for the play had come from the boorish behavior of Americans at the 1851 Crystal Palace Exhibition in London, where he had found their cluelessness, coupled with unbridled Yankee nativism, ripe material for satire. The play had languished in the United States until Keene discovered it in 1858. Her production of it at her eponymous New York theatre, with Joseph Jefferson III starring as Asa Trenchard and E. A. Sothern as the affected Lord Dundreary, was an immediate success. It had run for 150 nights; Sothern in 1861 stretched that to nearly five hundred at London's Haymarket Theatre. "Dundreary" whiskers, coats, vests, monocles, not to mention "Dundrearyisms"—bad puns and malapropos versions of familiar sayings—were seen and heard across the nation.

The play's humor derives from the fish-out-of-water plight of the American, Asa, as he increasingly imposes on his extended family "across the pond." As played by Harry Hawk, who with John Dyott had been touring with Keene all season, Asa is rustic to the core. He is mined from the vein of humorous "Yankee" characters that had prevailed on the American stage for nearly a century since the emergence of the character of Jonathan in Royall Tyler's *The Contrast*.

Asa's manner is animated and forthright. He is eager to please, and his speech is larded with folksy vernacular, such as "consarn your picture" and "concentrated essence of baboons." He has no sense of social boundaries or proprieties, constantly back-slapping and arm-pumping, yet somehow remains an endearing eccentric, most likely one who tonight would remind the president of his own early days as a backwoodsman.

Keene had been touring the nation with the play since its New York success, and it unfailingly found favor with audiences of all classes. Ironically, its tremendous success led to unauthorized productions, which Keene fought tirelessly in the courts and newspapers to thwart. The events of the next twenty-four hours would compound her anguish whenever she heard the play mentioned for the rest of her life.

Keene remains today something of an enigma, her legacy unfortunately stemming more from her association with the assassination than from her professional accomplishments or her forceful personality. In an

era of overwhelming male dominance in the field of theatrical management, she succeeded for nearly a decade (1854–1863) managing theatres
in Baltimore, Philadelphia, and New York, compiling an admirable
record of artistic and financial success. Her productions were noteworthy
for their taste and attention to detail.

Without doubt, she was demanding, a perfectionist known for her
imperious conduct of rehearsals; actors called her "The Duchess" behind
her back. She ruled with an iron hand, exercising strict discipline and
enforcing stringent rules with heavy fines for their violation. Critic William Winter observed that she "looked like an angel, but was, in fact, a
martinet. You could not help liking her, and at the same time you could
not quite escape the intuition that she was a person of impetuous and
fiery temper." Yet these traits were essential to assuring high quality
productions that could compete with (and often overshadow) those of
her male peers.[9]

Keene had acquired and refined her twin crafts of acting and manage-
ment in diligent study under the equally demanding Madame Lucia
Elizabeth Vestris in London, consistently receiving praise for her graceful
stage presence, clear, strong voice, and onstage modesty. Leading New
York theatrical manager James Wallack discovered her in 1852 and that
September brought her, along with her mother and two daughters, to
America. (Her husband at the time had been convicted of a felony and
sentenced to hard labor in the Crown's Australian penal colony.) Under
Wallack's guidance, Keene became an immediate success in witty, polite
comedies that showcased her natural elegance and refinement, later
compared favorably to that of Sarah Bernhardt.

Her strongest assets in performance were her large, dark, expressive
eyes, slender, graceful figure, lustrous auburn hair, and melodious voice.
A special talent was her protean ability to mirror the changes that her
characters underwent in the course of a play. "She had," said Jefferson,

"the rare power of varying her manner [from] the rustic walk of a milk-maid [to] the dignified grace of a queen." In *The Sea of Ice*, he said, "she displayed this versatile quality to its fullest extent, [from] bounding upon the stage with the wild grace of a startled doe [to being] sent to Paris and there educated, [displaying] the fire of the wild Indian girl through the culture of the French lady. I have never seen this transparency [sic] more perfectly acted."[10]

Keene's performance was often the intellectual, if not emotional, lynchpin of a production. She commanded the stage, along with audiences' admiration and loyalty, but did not succumb to the vocal rants and melodramatic emotionalism that typified much of the acting of that era. In this she anticipated the modulated, classical style embodied by Edwin Booth that emerged toward the end of the century. Known for diligent study of her parts, she understood her characters remarkably well.

Despite a weak constitution compounded by the exhausting effects of theatrical touring, she carried herself onstage as if she possessed boundless energy and complete self-confidence. She was, recalled Ford's Theatre actor John Mathews at the close of the century [emphasis his], "an *actress, and an experienced one.* In her day the term had meaning. Today it is a hollow misnomer."[11]

Keene's mainstay was the raffish, swarthy, forty-nine-year-old John Lutz. Variously described as "a member of the card-playing sporting fraternity" and "a gambler," he had been introduced to her during her first season in New York by an associate with a penchant for looking after struggling young actresses. Jefferson regarded Lutz as "a rough man, having no dramatic experience, but gifted with keen [theatrical] sense."[12]

Lutz encouraged Keene's impetuosity, though, which often worked against her. At his urging she had left Wallack's with less than an hour's notice before an opening curtain in 1853 to head to Baltimore, where he had arranged financing for her to manage her own theatre. From there she soon traveled to California, then embarked on a tour of Australia (including a brief shipboard dalliance with costar Edwin Booth).

While there she confronted her husband, seeking a legal separation. He refused, but upon determining that his incarceration was legally tantamount to a divorce, in 1857 in Baltimore she married Lutz, whose wife had died two years earlier. Although the Keene-Lutz marriage certificate has never surfaced, several contemporaries, including Winter and the *Baltimore Sun*, avow the nuptials took place. The couple traveled together thereafter as husband and wife and widely referred to each other as such. Lutz furnished the funds necessary to keep Keene and her mother and daughters living well until his death in 1869, and in the chaotic days following the assassination would provide her with invaluable stability and direction.[13]

She would not be present at this morning's rehearsal, as was her custom earned by right of performing her role of Florence Trenchard over a thousand times already. In her absence, her touring companions Hawk and Dyott, aided by Wright and Phillips, would instruct the cast. She would not appear until 6:30, an hour and a quarter before the scheduled opening curtain.[14]

Wright, fifty, was slightly built, bushy-haired, and considered a gentleman, almost always sharply dressed. Although he conveyed a perpetually worried air, he was an exceptionally competent stage manager. He had studied backstage operations as a callboy and prompter in Boston since age fourteen under some of the most respected stage managers in the United States. Born in Newburyport in northeast Massachusetts and brought to Boston as a child, he had never moved from the area, marrying a local girl in 1849 and buying a house in nearby Allston.

In the early 1850s, he entered a series of partnerships to manage Boston theatres, personally handling all contracts, casting, and booking of stars, quickly gaining a reputation as a skilled, conscientious manager.

In 1857 his wife died, possibly in childbirth, leaving him to support two little girls, ages seven and four, as well as his mother (his father, a sea captain, was often away), on a salary of fifteen dollars a week. When Ford sought him out in May 1858, Wright demanded and got double that, plus one-third of the box office on a benefit night. As a final inducement, Ford guaranteed him [Ford's underlining] "full power in casting all pieces to the best of judgment, the entire and sole direction of the stage," and use of a private box.[15]

Just before traveling to Baltimore, Wright remarried to Ann Frances F. Cushing, twenty-four years younger, the daughter of a venerable New England family. She and the girls remained in Allston while he rented a room in Baltimore, as he would later do in Washington, keeping the Allston house for the rest of his life. They soon had a baby girl of their own, but that child and one of Wright's older daughters died within two months of each other of scarlet fever in 1862. Within a few years he also lost his parents. Compounding their shared sorrow, Annie Wright would be seated the night of the assassination in the fourth row of Ford's Theatre and become one of the few people to stay with her husband in the building throughout the hellish night.

Observant, intelligent, and industrious, Wright was an exceptional asset to Ford, admired by audiences and critics alike for his integrity and talent. One production "would have lacked half of its present superior excellence" were it not for Wright's "unusually correct judgment and most refined taste." At the end of his first engagement at the Holliday Street, Edwin Booth presented "my gentle Wright" with an inscribed silver goblet, reciting a four-stanza dedicatory poem.[16]

From the start, Ford and Wright mounted elegant, highly successful productions at the Holliday Street and Ford's Theatres that were praised for their taste and attention to detail. Dozens of extant letters between the two men reveal a relationship of close mutual trust and respect. Ford even allowed Wright opportunities to direct plays, such as a notable production of Shakespeare's *The Tempest* at the Holliday Street in 1858. Their only times apart were summers, when Wright returned to Massachusetts, or when Wright was stage-managing a tour for Forrest, although business letters continued to fly back and forth.

As stage manager, before the arrival of any scheduled traveling stars Wright would arrange with his technicians to create the scenery and properties needed for their productions, and tell the cast what costumes would be required. During performances, he meticulously followed the script, cueing (by small hand bell or bosun's whistle) all technical effects, scene changes, and stage business, along with making sure the actors actually stuck to the script (sometimes a considerable chore). Now in his seventh season with the Fords, he was the ultimate authority backstage, often making decisions on the fly to cover mistakes, miscues, or last-minute changes, able to fine actors who failed to live up to the letter of their contracts or theatre policies.

In casting the roles of a production, Wright followed the company's "Lines of Business." These were the universal categories of stock roles a given actor would consistently play, established by precedent and tradition. New would-be actors would start as supernumeraries (or "supers") and "utility players" (or "boot-jacks"), which meant they filled any minor role not taken by someone else. Onstage, they delivered messages, served the master's table, died in battle, and filled out a crowd, or if they were lucky, got to speak a few lines (usually blurted out in a nervous rush). "The utility man was generally not a man, but a large, gloomy boy, whose mustache would not grow, and whose voice would crack over the few lines he was invited to address to the public," observed actress Clara Morris. "He sometimes led mobs, but more often made brief statements as to the whereabouts of certain carriages." This was the lowest rung on the acting hierarchy, and many a star had started on it. During this season at Ford's, callboy Ferguson, property master Maddox, and costumer Louis Carland had all been pressed into double duty as utility players; stagehand John DeBonay had just graduated into its ranks.[17]

The next rung up from utility was "Walking Gentleman/Lady." These were supporting players who provided exposition in the first scene or served as confidants to the leading characters. They were depended upon to be accurate "feeders-of-lines," so that a performance might adhere reasonably closely to the script. Above this level, the lines of business became highly specialized, and an actor was often trapped for life in his line. Conversely, he could also refuse to play any role that was not "in his line."

A standard stock company of thirty to forty actors would contain a few of each of the following:

- A Singing Walking Gentleman/Lady (like the above, but able to carry a tune and entertain an audience with an "olio act," a song or dance in front of the curtain while scenery was being changed);
- A Juvenile Man/Lady (for child and teenage roles, or as young lovers);
- A Soubrette, or Chambermaid (a pert, alluring ingénue not averse to flirtation);
- A Low Comedian (whose gags and facial "mugging," coupled with a keen sense of comic timing could be guaranteed to bring down the house);
- An Old Man/Woman (fat or thin, tall or short, to be counted on for pathos, senility, or wisdom);
- A Heavy Man/Woman (in the sense of villainy, not poundage; to these actors fell the snarls, arched eyebrows, mustache-twirling, and choice soliloquies of triumphant evil);

- A Leading Man/Lady (the most important actors; physically attractive, charismatic, and dignified; whose roles, while envied, could be taken on any given night by a visiting star).

Within each specialization was a rank, with "First" always having primary choice of meatier roles over "Second," as in First Low Comedian (who would play the Gravedigger in *Hamlet*) vs. Second Low Comedian (who would play Osric, the flamboyant courtier).

★ ★ ★

Typical of actors at mid-century, the Ford's Theatre company strove to remain conscientious about basic responsibilities. Chief among these was memorizing new parts, often assigned only a few days—or a single day—before performing. This duty usually kept them up into the wee hours of the night, hence the late morning rehearsal time. Most actors were aware, as rising star and Ford's Theatre alumnus John McCullough noted, that success required "untiring industry, ... unremitting labor, patient study, and ... unrelenting self-denial.... It is a grievous mistake to think the actor's life an easy one." As Maggie Mitchell observed, "It is a lottery, this profession of ours, in which the prizes are, after all, not very considerable." Most of her days were spent far from her children and the comforts of home, "full of exhausting labor. Rehearsals and other business occupy me from early morning to the hour of performance, with brief intervals for rest and food and a little sleep." She remained, however, "the eager, yet weary, slave of my profession."[18]

Most actors led a solitary life, isolated not only by the need to return home (or to a lonely rented room) immediately after each night's performance to learn new lines, but also by the general public's disapproval of their profession, which closed the doors of fashionable society to them.

The weight of this ostracism fell most heavily on the women of a company, as the stigma of loose morality still clung to the label of "actress." Even achieving stardom was no assurance of acceptance in polite society. Actresses "labor under a double disadvantage," rued Mitchell. "They are not only subjected to severer temptations (both positive and negative) than most other women, but in the fierce white light which beats upon them their mere weaknesses are magnified into flagrant immorality." Today's tabloids and the internet only magnify and disseminate more widely the public's eternal fascination with the misdeeds of its idols.[19]

Especially during the war, actors had to remain politically circumspect. Their careers depended on their ability to cross battle lines to perform or simply to find a job. It was tacitly understood that they would keep their opinions to themselves or risk censure or arrest. In October 1864, two of Ford's Holliday Street actors were arrested by military authorities for allegedly uttering anti-Union sentiments during a performance. One had replied to the other's line identifying him as a "Yankee Doodle" by ad libbing, "No. Thank God I am not a Yankee!" As the offender was being arrested—his third time—his fellow actor interfered with the officers, so both men were hauled away. A month later, a theatrical manager in Indiana was arrested for "utterance of disunion sentiments and expressions of sympathy for the rebel cause," overheard by "loyal citizens" in a hotel dining room.[20]

John Wilkes Booth, for one, flaunted his professional amnesty: "I have a free pass everywhere. My profession, my name, is my passport," he said as he smuggled quinine to the Confederate Army. The only other options for actors were: to leave the country, as Jefferson did, performing for the duration in Australia; to take a stand against both sides, as John Brougham did, denouncing "the madness of the projected dismemberment of the union"; or to actively aid the Union effort. Lawrence Barrett served with distinction as captain of a Massachusetts regiment, and James Murdoch gave patriotic readings in countless northern cities, soldiers' hospitals, and army camps, sometimes within the range of gunfire. His two sons enlisted in the Union Army, one dying at Chickamauga.[21]

Yet an actor's life was not all weariness and drudgery. As James Herne noted at the height of his fame two decades after leaving Ford's, "Actors are by temperament gregarious, and [so] they formed a unique social group of their own.... They considered themselves bohemians and were proud of it. They worked hard, lived frugally, and their pleasures were simple enough—a glass of beer and a pipe in some friendly tavern or boardinghouse, when the performance was over, a game of cards and talk—the endless exchange of backstage anecdotes, funny stories, and discussions of the art of acting." Most companies could count on a few old-timers, too, who "recounted their youthful triumphs or those of the stars they had played with. [They were] storing up the lore of the the-atre—acquiring the great tradition." This could mean that "the way [the elder] Booth spoke the 'To be or not to be' soliloquy in *Hamlet*, the man-ner in which Forrest delivered the 'Curse of Rome' speech in *Richelieu*, had for them the finality of Holy Writ. They would argue about the validity of a reading far into the early hours of the morning."[22]

This legacy was treasured. For a lowly stock company actor such as these at Ford's, there remained the constant need to honor and master every convention of stage movement, voice, and gesture. One had to learn, recalled Herne, "the art of timing, the value of a pause, or a gesture, the way to get a laugh, and hold an audience's attention. He learned to use his wits, and to 'fill in,' or improvise speeches when someone forgot his lines.... He learned, too, some of the age-old tricks of the actor, how to 'steal a scene' or 'play upstage.'"[23]

Stage movement at mid-century was rigidly formal and ritualized: leading characters entered the stage on a diagonal, walking dramatically to its center; minor characters entered laterally from the wings and remained at the side of the stage. An actor did not speak and move simul-taneously as most do today; rather, he strode to his place ("took the stage") and delivered his speech ("making a point"). Plays were written with vividly dramatic moments intended to highlight these "points," which were calculated to draw applause. When an actor spoke, all others remained frozen in place and expression. Anything spoken at the footlights was understood to be for the audience's ears only. Nothing of an actor's craft approached twentieth century realism representing natural human interaction and dialogue.

Furthermore, when supporting a star, there was tremendous pressure on local actors to refrain from overstepping their bounds or otherwise offending the star. The wrath of an imperious visiting star could easily get them tossed from the company. Sometimes this meant nothing more than approaching too closely, or forcing the star to turn slightly upstage (thus depriving the audience of the best view of the star's stately profile), or—worst of all—dropping a line or failing to provide the proper cue.

★ ★ ★

As that morning's rehearsal for *Our American Cousin* began, stagehands in the wings were stowing the large painted canvas flats used in last night's production of *The Story of Peggy the Actress* and pulling out those that Wright had decreed were necessary for tonight. Two of these stagehands would become important figures in the aftermath of tonight's tragedy. Both men had only just arisen, having slept in the theatre's scene shop on the third floor of the stage facilities building attached to its north side. Carpenter-stagehand Ned Spangler, nursing a hangover, slouched as he worked, partnered with recently hired Jake Rittersbach.[24]

Other than their shared central Pennsylvania childhoods, sleeping quarters, and meals taken together at Mrs. Scott's on the corner of 7th and H, the two men had little in common. In fact, they held diametrically opposed views on the war: Spangler, thirty-nine, was an avowed Secessionist, and Rittersbach, twenty-four, was a Union veteran. Although they had known each other for a year and a half at Mrs. Scott's, they spent much of their time together quarreling; Spangler, especially when drunk, reviled Rittersbach as a "nigger lover," and Rittersbach deemed Spangler "the hardest kind of Copperhead."[25]

The roughhewn Spangler, barely literate, came from an established family that had first settled in York in 1729. The fourth son of the county sheriff, he never knew his mother, who died when he was an infant. A carpenter by twenty-four, he had drifted in the early 1850s down to Maryland, where he assisted Gifford in building Tudor Hall for the Booths. As he had worked, he had tussled playfully with young John Wilkes, who briefly attended boarding school in York in the home of Spangler's mother's family. In 1853 Spangler followed Gifford to Baltimore as assistant carpenter at the Holliday Street and Front Street Theatres, settling into a house on nearby Canal Street. By most accounts he was conscientious in his work, for which he earned fifteen dollars a week.[26]

In July 1858 Spangler had married Mary Brasheare, ten years his senior, but took to drinking heavily when she died in the summer of 1864. By 1861 Gifford had brought him down to Washington to help with both renovations of Ford's Theatre, and there he had renewed his friendship with Booth. Although older by thirteen years, Spangler realized the superiority that fame had brought his actor friend and was happy to bask in his attention and reflected glory.

Ever subservient and eager to please, Spangler executed with alacrity whatever tasks Booth gave him. In January he had converted an outbuilding behind Ford's into a stable for Booth's horses and buggy, which he had sold just this past Wednesday when Booth told him they were no longer needed, as he would be leaving town. At what point and how much he told Spangler about his plans remain unknown, but it's certain that Spangler would have eagerly helped him in anything. Gifford called him a good-hearted "drudge"—someone, as Jeannie Gourlay said, simply at the mercy of a man "so magnetic and persuasive" that "he could have twisted a weak-minded menial like Spangler about his little finger."[27]

Spangler's heavy build, low forehead, unkempt red hair, querulously high-pitched voice, and a demeanor and complexion coarsened by alcohol, suggested at first he would not be a pleasant companion. Yet there was an endearing, child-like quality to him that rendered him inoffensive. Happiest when crabbing in the Potomac or in the company of young children or animals, he appreciated life's simple pleasures. Frequently the butt of backstage practical jokes, he never took offense. Last winter, after he had complained that he felt left out because his name never appeared on scenery like those of other members of the crew, grumpy scenic artist James Lamb retouched a prison-yard scene to display the name "Spangler" on its gallows.

Rittersbach, born in France, had come to the United States at age eight when his family, like Spangler's, settled into Pennsylvania's immense German community, in his case, in the town of Lebanon. He had served nine months in the Union Army, in the 127th Regiment, Pennsylvania Infantry, and had seen some of the worst fighting at Fredericksburg and Chancellorsville. When his regiment had come through Washington it had, like almost every other unit, been dogged by federal detectives looking for deserters and spies. These men reported directly to Lafayette C. Baker, head of the National Detective Police, who would in time become personally acquainted with Private Jacob Rittersbach.

After mustering out in May 1863, unable to find work, Rittersbach had returned to Washington with other veterans and found a temporary home at Ford's just three weeks ago. As much as he needed a job, though, it was difficult to be met nearly everywhere he turned backstage with sentiments that maligned the flag he had fought for. No one—Gifford, Carland, DeBonay, Maddox, nor Spangler—had any reservations about expressing their secessionist sympathies as they worked. And Rittersbach was often paired with Spangler, working closely and continuously with him on the construction and shifting of stage scenery. The tenuous relationship and occasional misunderstandings between these two men would have dire consequences by nightfall.

★ ★ ★

As rehearsal began, Maddox was still at breakfast, following an early hour of work, organizing his property closet. His assistant, sixteen-year-old John Selecman, was checking off items needed for tonight's production and calculating which ones would have to be bought this afternoon. Up on the paint frame, high against the back wall of the stage, Lamb had been at work for two hours already, roughing out a new backdrop for a planned production of *Enoch Arden*. He was assisted by two young men, John Miles and Joe Simms, both free blacks, who ground the colors for him (no pre-mixed paint in those days) and ran the fly lines. Around the corner on the third floor, in the large dressing room where he usually spent most of his days and nights, Carland was already into his third hour of mending costumes and sewing accessories for tonight's production.[28]

Superintending them all would be Gifford, who had just walked through the stage door. The oldest of the backstage crew at fifty-one, this humorless Baltimorean was an imposing, squarely built, bearded German Lutheran who was dedicated to his job, yet never seemed to enjoy it. On weekends he returned to his wife and seven children in the East Fayette Street house where he had been born and where he would die. Weeknights he spent at Ford's, sleeping in the ground-floor office stage right, below the dressing rooms, arising each morning around 5:30 to let in the cleaning ladies, then going out for breakfast when the other men arrived between 8:00 and 9:00.

Although taciturn, when he gave an order it was understood it would be obeyed promptly, without needing to be repeated. Gifford's temper, once provoked, was vile, and few of the men backstage liked working under him. He was known, reported the *Philadelphia Inquirer*, "as a rather cross-grained man, and except to intimate friends, was exceedingly unsociable." He could also be obstinate: when threatened with arrest for public obscenity for the nude sculptures in his garden, instead of removing them he walled in the yard. Nearing the close of two decades' association with Ford, having personally designed and supervised the building of both his theatres, it was clear that Gifford's authority matched that of Wright. The two men differed, though, as so many Marylanders did, about the war: Wright was a staunch Unionist and Gifford an ardent advocate of the Confederate cause.[29]

John Ford depended heavily on these men and on his brothers to capably operate the theatre here in Washington, and had come down from Baltimore only twice this spring to look in on things. In fact, he felt comfortable enough in their management that yesterday he had asked Dick to take the train up to Baltimore this afternoon so he himself could make a long-overdue visit to newly occupied Richmond. He hoped to check on family members struggling under straitened conditions there and was curious about the state of the Richmond Theatre he used to manage. Dick was to monitor Lucille Western's benefit production tonight at the Holliday Street, especially the performance between acts of "The Star-Spangled Banner" and "Dixie" by the recently captured Confederate Virginia 14th Regiment's band. Some Baltimore residents, including a city councilman, had objected to the band's being allowed to play earlier in the week, saying it was offensive to loyal Unionists.

Ford had requested a pass from the War Department to go to Richmond as soon as the Southern capital fell and received it on Wednesday. Thursday evening, knowing that matters would be well in hand at the Holliday Street under Dick and Stage Manager Tom Hall, and at Ford's Theatre under his brother Harry—including the completion of new scenery and special effects for a grand upcoming production of *A Midsummer Night's Dream*—Ford had checked on his sick wife, Edith, then rushed to Baltimore's Union Dock and boarded a night steamer south to City Point, Virginia, on the James River below Richmond.

By tonight's opening curtain, he would be a hundred miles away.

CHAPTER FOUR

"OUR AMERICAN COUSIN"

WITH THE PRESIDENT VISITING tonight, strong leadership would be needed with this young cast as the rehearsal for *Our American Cousin* got underway. As Phillips hovered in the wings, Wright took his place at one of two small wooden tables near the footlights on the slanting stage apron. Beside him sat John Dyott and Harry Hawk, who had been traveling with Laura Keene since August performing that play and a repertoire of others.

These four men would guide the cast through basic blocking and stage business, sharing the only two complete copies of the script, which had been sent ahead so the stock company actors could learn their lines. But they had been given only "sides," individual sheets with just their own lines, hand-copied by Ferguson at a penny per five handwritten lines from the master script. On these "sides," each line was preceded only by a three- or four-word cue, and actors had to be on their toes to catch the cue once on stage. Thus, having learned only their own lines, many complained that they had no idea what the play they were acting in was all about.

Dyott and Hawk had walked to Ford's early this morning from their shared room in the home of Washington actors Johnny and Kate Evans, around the corner on E Street. Tall, gray, steadfast Dyott, fifty-three, was older than almost anyone else present, his greatest years behind him. A respected Shakespearean actor in an era when the Bard was the most consistently performed playwright on the American stage, Dyott projected innate nobility that bordered on hauteur. His acting style was somber, formal, and stiff, and his voice inclined to monotone, but his interpretations of characters and their speeches were consistently insightful and intelligent. He had taken to the stage at nineteen against his Methodist parents' wishes in his native Dublin, playing romantic leads in comic operas. Three years later he took his talents to England, where he married Henrietta, the daughter of a provincial theatre manager.

In August 1844 they had sailed for New York, where they were immediately hired into the stock company of the prestigious Park Theatre. John played major supporting roles, such as Edgar to the King Lear of the great William Charles Macready, while Henrietta took on lesser parts. For ten seasons they worked steadily at the best Broadway houses, with occasional performances in Philadelphia. John acted with countless other stars of the day, including James Hackett, Edwin Forrest, Charlotte Cushman, Charles Kean, and James and Lester Wallack. He distinguished himself in the first American productions of two of Shakespeare's plays, as Octavius Caesar in *Antony and Cleopatra* and as Proteus in *Two Gentlemen of Verona*.

Along the way, two tragedies clouded his life. In 1845 their only child ever, a daughter who had just begun performing with them, died suddenly.

Then, in early May 1849, he was cast opposite Forrest in *The Gladiator* at the Broadway Theatre, while the effete, egotistical Macready was playing Macbeth—a role with which Forrest was indelibly identified—at the nearby Astor Place Opera House. For a century before Forrest, the only respected tragedians in the United States had been English like Macready, despite the results of the War of Independence. But Forrest had developed his own following, consisting largely of rowdies, street thugs known as "Bowery B'hoys," while the wealthier intelligentsia supported Macready. For a week the partisans of each of the two men had derided the other's performer in increasingly strident tones. (It was said that even Forrest himself had hissed a Macready performance.) On the night of May 10, the conflict boiled over. A riot broke out between the two factions, and by the time police and militia could quell the unrest, twenty-two people lay dead in what would become known as the Astor Place Riot. Dyott, acting with Forrest that night, never forgot its trauma. (Phillips was a member of Macready's company that night, thus gaining an equally compelling perspective on the riot.)

Three and a half years later, Dyott met Laura Keene on her first day in New York as he performed in a special celebration of the centennial of theatre in the United States. A year later he encountered her again as she began her second season under Wallack. Soon he was playing dozens of leading roles opposite her, and they quickly established a trusting professional relationship. Wallack's was a wonderful training ground for them both; standards were high and the repertory varied. The company included a number of future Ford's Theatre actors, including Phillips and Jeannie Gourlay, who honed their craft there.

But Dyott soon broke out on his own. After a season as an acting manager in Charleston, he quickly rose to the pinnacle of his career in New York. From 1859 to 1864, he earned ever-greater roles and reviews opposite Cushman, Edwin Booth, and Forrest (notably including Iago to his Othello). When Keene recruited Dyott in February 1864 for her tour, trading on their friendship and shared history, she secured one of the finest supporting performers of tragic roles in the country (even though many of her scripts were comedies).

In contrast, their other touring partner, short, shambling, redheaded William Henry "Harry" Hawk, seemed tailor-made for comedy. A product of Chicago, he was two weeks shy of his twenty-eighth birthday. He had begun his career a decade ago as a callboy at McVicker's Theatre there, quickly taking on small roles. By 1861, he had twice traveled down the Mississippi River performing under manager Ben DeBar, who openly supported the Confederacy.

For two seasons Hawk learned his comedic craft at the famed Varieties Theatre in New Orleans from one of the most popular, successful comedians of the day, actor-manager John E. Owens. Hawk admired Owens greatly, calling him "the best comedian in America." As Second Low Comedian under Owens, his line of business depended more on broad character humor than wit and all too often invited "mugging" or "gagging" (overdoing comic expressions and bits of stage business, or interjecting material not in the script, just to get a cheap laugh). Having seen Owens occasionally commit this *faux pas*, Hawk began a lifetime habit of succumbing to it.[1]

Fueled by rampant secessionist fervor among the theatrical fraternity in New Orleans, Hawk enlisted in January 1861 in a paramilitary company of actors and stagehands organized to defend the city in the embryonic cause of the Confederacy. Numbering over a hundred, they called themselves variously the Variety Volunteers or the Cocktail Guards, elected Owens captain, and drilled regularly. While many gave themselves a rank, Hawk remained a private. The political climate of New Orleans, a simmering state of fear of Northern invasion and occupation, left young men with little choice but to join such organizations; they had to declare their loyalties or be thought suspect. One recalled the pressure more than thirty years later: "The actors were daily asked, 'Do you belong to any military organization?' If we replied in the negative, the next remark would be: 'Come around with me and put your name on our company roll.'"[2]

For many years after the war, especially when it impeded their professional success, various members of the Guards tried, with dramatically different results, to distance themselves from that organization and downplay its military nature, deeming it merely a "social club." Membership in it became a liability after the war when they tried to perform in the North. They were, recalled one, "marked men for a long time." Some had to publicly disclaim sympathy with the South; others never regained their reputations or were received with hostility. Owens himself was forced to discontinue an 1862 engagement in Pittsburgh and leave the city in disguise. Another member, who later joined the Confederate Army, was hissed off the stage of Grover's Theatre in Washington in 1865 until he publicly defended himself, citing his loyalty oath and pardon. Although the Guards disbanded without ever seeing action, Hawk waited almost half a century before acknowledging his youthful membership.[3]

He stayed in New Orleans until the very eve of Union occupation, taking the last boat north in April 1862 and finding work and a growing popular following in Chicago, Baltimore, and Boston. In late 1863 in Boston he supported, and was befriended by, brilliant rising star John Wilkes Booth. But it was Keene who gave Hawk his first big break, discovering him in Boston in 1864. She saw promise in this funny young performer and promoted him to First Low Comedian. His early reviews, though, were often unfavorable; one called his Asa Trenchard "simply abominable," noting that he portrayed the character as a cross between two boorish stereotypes, a Bowery fireman and a "rollicking stage Irishman," rather than Taylor's "high-minded and honorable and intelligent, though homespun Yankee."[4]

By mid-season, though, Hawk's reviews improved as he toured with Keene and Dyott. His eccentric hangdog looks and rubbery features, coupled with what one reviewer called his "dry grasshopper-like humor," rarely failed to elicit unrestrained laughter, although some critics continued to chide him for mugging. But it was impossible not to like him, and he quickly proved immensely popular with the members of any stock company he performed with. He was exactly the sort of comedian Abraham Lincoln appreciated.[5]

★ ★ ★

Also out on the apron of the stage that morning, following along in Wright's copy of the script, sat gangly callboy Will Ferguson. Only nineteen, he had come to Ford's by a different route. Raised in Baltimore across the street from John Ford's father's shoe shop, he had started work at age ten as a printer's devil, arranging and setting type for the *Baltimore Clipper*, where Clifton Tayleure, a Ford associate and playwright, was an editor. Tayleure referred him to Ford, an elder with Ferguson's father in the city's Third Presbyterian Church, who hired the youth at five dollars a week to run errands and serve as the callboy for his Washington theatre.

Ferguson found the wartime capital an exciting place, remembering for the rest of his life the scene of panicked soldiers fleeing back into the city from First Bull Run in July 1861 and the departure of others heading for later battles. He boarded with a friend of his mother's near the Capitol, but spent most of his time at Ford's Theatre. By December 1863 he was playing supernumerary roles and soon found himself speaking his first words on any stage, to the Richard III of visiting star John Wilkes Booth, whom Ferguson idolized as "a marvelously clever and amusing demigod."[6]

In tonight's performance Ferguson would speak sixteen lines as "Lt. Vernon," but fortunately he had already played the role once before, in August. Although only a General Utility player now, with luck and perseverance he might advance to Second or Third Walking Gentleman. He realized that his workplace contained adherents of both sides in the war, but was glad that many, like himself, were strongly for the Union. Others, like Booth, however, "were devout believers in the cause of the South."[7]

★ ★ ★

As the rehearsal began, five actors took the stage for the opening scene, set in Hampshire, England, at Trenchard Manor, the estate of Sir Edward Trenchard. Two women and three men played housekeepers Sharpe and Skillet, butlers Binny and Buddicomb, and gardener Wickens. The script called for them to provide an essential element of the play's exposition: the growing pile of unpaid bills confronting Sir Edward.

Playing Sharpe was twenty-year-old Baltimore native Kate Evans, who had the arts in her blood: her father was a cellist with a New York orchestra. She had debuted on the New York stage at age ten, and this was her second season with the Fords. Despite her decade of experience, though, she was still only a "soubrette." But she had potential; Harry Ford thought she was "very clever." Her husband, Johnny, twenty-eight, played Buddicomb. Married for four years with two children, they had met while playing small roles at Niblo's Garden in New York and moved to Washington when Johnny was hired as Second Walking Gentleman at Ford's. He already knew Laura Keene, having acted in her New York theatre in the late 1850s.[8]

Skillet was enacted by sixteen-year-old Maggie Gourlay, Jeannie's younger sister. The two girls, born in Edinburgh, Scotland, and brought to the United States when quite young, had performed since ages seven and nine as members of the renowned Marsh Troupe of juvenile Shake-spearean actors touring widely in the United States and Australia. Such performances had been in vogue since the phenomenal success of child prodigy Master (William Henry West) Betty just after the turn of the century. The forty Marsh Troupe children, aged seven to twelve, were extremely popular, either performing by themselves or integrated into productions with adult stock company actors. (In Richmond in December 1859, they had appeared with John Wilkes Booth, who had just returned from witnessing the hanging of abolitionist John Brown in Harper's Ferry, Virginia.)

Both Gourlay girls were slight in build, with curly dark hair and impish, endearing countenances, but Jeannie consistently outshone Maggie. With the Marsh Troupe she had first improbably played Macduff but quickly moved up to become Lady Macbeth. Between tours, both sisters had performed with their father at Burton's Chambers Street Theatre in New York, most memorably as fairies in a richly-mounted 1854 production of *A Midsummer Night's Dream*. After finishing their last Marsh tour in November 1863, they had gone straight to New York, performing at the Park and Niblo's.

When Jeannie was hired by Leonard Grover the following spring, Maggie came to Washington with her. Most memorable in the capital for the two girls was their acting in support of Edwin Booth; during that engagement, President Lincoln had attended eight times. Now, at Ford's, Jeannie was also featured as a dancer; her tambourine dance merited its own line on posted playbills. She radiated promise.

George Gaines Spear, who portrayed Binny, was another story altogether. His best years were behind him. This tall, gaunt Bostonian, the oldest actor backstage that night, had lived far more than his fifty-five years might suggest. With a perpetually sleepy expression, bald head, and stooped posture, he had acted Low Comedian roles for thirty-five years on showboats and in stock companies up and down and across the continent. His first big break on the stage had come in Boston in 1838 when he originated the role of Colonel Damas in Bulwer-Lytton's romance *The Lady of Lyons*.

Nearly twenty years ago he had married Deborah Noble, another member of Boston's National Theatre stock company, and was now the father of three. Known to his theatrical companions as "Old Spudge," he was the source of countless anecdotes. Some were inspirational (General Lafayette's visit to his theatre in 1824 was still vivid), some side-splitting (his account of getting lost in a snowstorm while driving a carriage of fellow Boston actors never got old), and a few too ribald for polite company.

For years he had been a favored drinking partner of the elder Booth, an offstage role that involved epic levels of alcohol consumption and rowdy behavior. Leaving his family behind in Boston, Spear had accompanied Booth and his sons Edwin and Junius Jr. to California in 1852. After long runs there, he and Edwin had signed on to play mining towns across Nevada. There, in the middle of a horrific blizzard, Spear received word of the death of the elder Booth and had to break the news to Edwin, who thus endured the first of many tragedies in his personal life. The two men then continued their riotously unpredictable tour throughout the West; their drunken performance in Sacramento on New Year's Eve 1855 as Polonius and Hamlet—part of which involved beating each other over the head with a live chicken—was the stuff of legends.

From 1856 to 1860, Spear had been committed intermittently to an insane asylum at the insistence of his wife—urged on, he insisted, by her sister, "an old maid whom I heartily despise"—after lengthy legal battles. According to the commitment papers, he had acted violently toward his family and himself, and his behavior manifested "the effects produced by liquor." Despite doctors' withholding of alcohol during his confinement, he hit the bottle heavily upon his release. Nearly destitute, he fought to keep from his wife what little money the Theatrical Fund, a benevolent society, made available. The Boston Museum had held a benefit for him, and he took small roles wherever he could, but he never returned to his family and hardly ever visited Boston again.[9]

In Washington, he had roomed on G Street since 1863, when the Fords took him on, giving him minor roles. Rumors persisted, though, of his performing while intoxicated—rumors that would resurface tonight. Yet audiences and reviewers continued to love his "surpassing drollery." His sympathies lay solidly with the Union; his eldest son, Felix, had been wounded while serving three years in the 63rd Massachusetts Infantry.[10]

John DeBonay played the tiny role of gardener Wickens. With less than two years' acting experience, he could expect little more. Still, he carried a wealth of worldly experience. Born in Havana, he had drifted to New Orleans as a boy, enlisting there in the Confederate Army in spring 1862 at age fourteen. As a private in the Crescent Regiment of the Louisiana Militia, he had seen action at Shiloh—including the death of his company commander—and then at Corinth. Upon mustering out at fifteen, he had headed for Boston, where he fell into acting at the Howard Athenaeum, playing the smallest of roles. There, he was befriended by both Hawk and John Wilkes Booth. Now still only sixteen, with a slight build that made him seem even younger, he had joined the Ford's company as "responsible utility" and prompter, probably recommended to the Fords by Booth, something the star had done for other young friends.[11]

★ ★ ★

Aside from establishing the indebtedness of Trenchard Manor, two other important pieces of exposition emerge in this first scene of *Our American Cousin*. One is conveyed by Sir Edward himself: he is using what little influence he still has to procure a ship's command for Lieutenant Vernon, whom his daughter Florence loves. (Considering the twenty-year age difference between Ferguson and Keene, this would ordinarily have been a little awkward, but was typical of shorthanded stock company casting and the propensity of actresses to continue to play roles younger than their own real age.)

Sir Edward was portrayed by Jeannie and Maggie's father, bearded, august Tom Gourlay. At forty-five, he was at best an adequate actor, a twenty-one-year veteran of small roles at major New York theatres that had yielded him little recognition. To support his Brooklyn family of five—a sixth, a boy, had died in 1862 at age four—he supplemented his income by giving dancing lessons. He had great hopes for Jeannie, though, and it was her being hired at Grover's the previous spring that had brought the whole family to Washington.

The other vital piece of exposition is provided by a letter from Florence's brother Ned in Vermont, reporting the death of Edward's uncle, "old Mark Trenchard," and the impending arrival at Trenchard Manor of his sole heir, Asa. Cheated out of any inheritance was Asa's sister, Mary, because she had married into the no-account Meredith clan.

After all this background information has been conveyed, the plot creaks forward. Sir Edward goes off to meet with his financial agent, Coyle, although Florence warns him "that man is not to be trusted." (Now, in rehearsal, in Keene's absence, all of Florence's lines were spoken, and her stage business described by Hawk.) The other characters are intrigued by the imminent visit of their rustic American Cousin Asa—everyone, that is, except one long-term guest, the insufferably vain, foppish, lisping Lord Dundreary, who is jealous of the attention he and his lame witticisms will lose. Playing this pivotal role for the first time in his life was Ned Emerson, who was beginning to show promise.[12]

Emerson, twenty-five, was the company's First Walking Gentleman, having been discovered by Ford in Alexandria. Poised and handsome, with dark hair and eyes and a fashionable mustache, Ned cut a striking figure on stage, closely resembling his close friend Booth. Emerson had played major roles to adoring crowds in Union-occupied southern cities during the war, including Memphis in 1863 and Nashville in 1864, sometimes performing alongside the charismatic Booth, and their friendship had flourished. "I knew John Wilkes Booth well," he recalled later, having performed with him "in dozens of cities throughout the East and Middle West. He was a kind-hearted, genial person, and no cleverer gentleman ever lived. Everybody loved him on the stage, though he was a little excitable and eccentric."[13]

This spring Booth had stopped by Ford's and the Holliday Street several times just to see Emerson. There was no question of their shared sympathies regarding the war. Ned's revered older brother, Benjamin Franklin Emerson, had perished in 1862 fighting for the Confederacy at Frayser's Farm. Two cousins and their two brothers-in-law, all from Virginia, wore Confederate butternut as well. And Ned's younger brother, Henry Clay Emerson, had been arrested in 1863 for smuggling medicine from Washington into Richmond while retrieving his brother's body; he received a lengthy prison sentence which could have been commuted had he taken an oath of allegiance and renounced the Confederacy, which he adamantly refused to do. While there is no evidence that Booth shared any details of his plans—for an abduction or otherwise—with Emerson, they were in many ways kindred souls.[14]

During this morning's rehearsal, Emerson felt exceptional pressure. Except for Hawk, who had been performing this script for months, he had the largest part to memorize: 221 lines, almost all of which came in the first two acts and included three lengthy monologues. He knew full well what a success E. A. Sothern had made of Dundreary in the original production and realized that Laura Keene's eye would be on him tonight, as well as those of a sizable crowd of keyed-up theatregoers, not to mention the critic Erasmus. This could be the role that cemented his popularity with Washington audiences, satisfied the critics once and for all, and possibly took his career to a wider national stage.

Emerson's close resemblance to Booth would bring serious consequences over the next few days for a pretty, petite eighteen-year-old in the cast. In her third season with the Fords as a supernumerary, playing such undemanding roles as "slave girl," "first page," and "vestal virgin," May Hart had only recently been promoted to Second Juvenile Lady. Needed mainly at the Holliday Street, this was only her second week this spring in Washington. She had performed on Monday and yesterday, when she had asked Ned backstage if they might rehearse their two scenes together before the others arrived this morning. They had never performed together and she was nervous. She was to play Georgina, wealthy socialite Mrs. Mountchessington's sickly daughter, who is escorted about by Dundreary and subjected to his awful puns.

Consequently, this morning around 10:00 she and Ned had gone out into the warm sunshine of the alley behind the theatre to run through their lines and stage business, which included, as part of one of Dundreary's jokes, his pointing out to her the location of some "pigeon houses." While rehearsing, they were watched by a pair of women who lived behind the theatre, who misleadingly reported to police the next morning that a woman matching Hart's description had been standing in the alley the morning of the assassination with "Booth," who had been pointing out to her various locations outside the theatre.[15]

Dundreary's mangled attempts at wit, along with his unvarnished vanity and unsuccessful attempts to cover up his clumsiness, make him the butt of much of the play's humor. His "conundrums" quickly make their presence felt in the first scene, such as one posed to Florence: "When is a dog's tail not a dog's tail? … When it's a-waggin' [a wagon]!" Predictably, he finds these more entertaining than his listeners and always has to explain, "That wath a joke, that wath!" He and Florence also belabor various puns on the word "draft," including its meanings as a bank draft, a game of draughts [checkers], and a "draught" [an archaic word for "prescription"] given to the ailing Georgina.[16]

★ ★ ★

In this first scene, the audience also meets Georgina's overbearing mother, Mrs. Mountchessington, and materialistic sister, Augusta. Portraying the former, the stately Helen Muzzy brought nearly four decades of experience to the stage of Ford's. At fifty-three she had a wide popular following in the capital, just as she also had in New Orleans, Philadelphia, New York, and Boston. Her career began in 1829 with the Drake Company, touring up and down the Mississippi River, playing in towns that rarely sported an adequate theatre. In Louisville in 1831 she met and married poet-actor-stage manager Charles Edward Muzzy, and by 1846 they were raising five children while continuing a vigorous touring schedule. Together, they had supported almost every star of the day, her "lines of business" being Female Heavy and (later) First Old Woman. Her most noted roles were Old Fadet in Waldauer's *Fanchon, the Cricket* and Lady Melnotte in Bulwer-Lytton's *Lady of Lyons.*[17]

After her husband's death in 1852, Muzzy limited her performing to Philadelphia, Baltimore, Washington, and Richmond, but she was always in demand, appearing at almost every theatre in those cities, especially in those managed by Ford. Four years ago she had remarried, and with her oldest son, Arthur, the couple maintained a home in the capital on lower Fourteenth Street, making Helen a local favorite at Ford's. Everyone regarded her as warm-hearted, affectionate, generous, and forgiving, yet fiercely determined and utterly devoted to the stage. Her stage presence was formidable and her performance ethic highly professional; she never gave interviews, even after tonight's tragedy.

Playing Augusta was demure, plain Helen Truman, who had just turned nineteen on Saturday. She had come to Ford's out of financial necessity and bore a powerful loyalty to Abraham Lincoln. Born into an old Southern family in Norfolk, Virginia, and raised in Memphis, she had naturally supported the Confederacy despite the incumbent wartime hardships. Her mother, a devout Methodist, loathed the theatre, but Helen at age thirteen had taken to the stage of the New Memphis Theatre to help provide for the family, dropping her surname, Coleman, to avoid bringing shame to her family. Her rare mentions in reviews were favorable. Along with the rest of the New Memphis company, she had been heartened by Union General Grant's assurance when his troops occupied

Memphis, that as actors they would be protected and could continue to perform. He, after all, enjoyed an occasional theatrical performance, even during wartime.

In late 1863, Helen undertook more formal training in Richmond—including an ill-fated rehearsal of a dramatic dying scene in which she crushed the life out of a cat that had wandered too close—but before she got a chance to apply her training, the war intervened in a very personal way. Her brother, a Confederate blockade runner, was taken prisoner and sentenced to death in Norfolk, causing Helen and her mother to rush there. Exhausting their savings in a vain effort to gain him a pardon, they went in desperation in September 1864 to Washington to beseech the president personally to spare the young man's life. Ten days later Lincoln did just that, helping Helen's weeping mother to her feet after she collapsed in gratitude. When her mother returned to Norfolk, Helen remained in Washington to seek employment on the stage.

Fortuitously she encountered the Fords who, of course, needed talented actresses, and she became Third Juvenile Lady behind Jeannie Gourlay and Hart. For the next seven months, as Helen performed, her unbounded gratitude to Lincoln led her to record his every attendance and observe him closely as he watched from the darkness of his box, where sometimes only the actors were aware of his presence. He generally appeared on Fridays, she noted, and especially enjoyed escapist comedies and farces. Mrs. Lincoln, Helen recalled, preferred Grover's Theatre, but her husband enjoyed performances at Ford's by comedians like Clarke and Owens, almost always remaining for the short farce that followed the main performance.

At the most recent post-performance Christmas Eve dinner, which the Fords provided for their actors, Helen had also met the dashing John Wilkes Booth, but had not seen him much until this week. She was not impressed: "He was cold, taciturn, aloof and at times seemed almost arrogant."[18]

★ ★ ★

At this point in *Our American Cousin*, following much outlandish speculation about the titular visitor's being a "wild young hunter" with a penchant for scalping (mirroring what English playwright Taylor believed to be his countrymen's misconceptions about Americans), Cousin Asa arrives. He is escorted to his room by Binny (Spear), and Florence summarizes the dilemma the Trenchards face: "What are we to do with him?" Dundreary suggests a series of practical jokes that the audience already knows will backfire. The scene ends with Asa bounding back in to make and serve them a variety of "real drinks," genuine American concoctions all (including Mint Juleps, Brandy Smashes, and Jersey Lightnings).

Scene Two opens with accountant Coyle awaiting Sir Edward and warning his clerk, Abel Murcott (Dyott), to stay sober, as his assistance will be needed soon to witness some papers (undoubtedly for nefarious purposes). Coyle informs Sir Edward that the Manor is nearly five thousand pounds in arrears, and foreclosure is imminent. A second family home as well is already mortgaged for sixty thousand. Sir Edward is astounded, as he believed this latter estate was free and clear, and might help him retain Trenchard Manor. Clearly, something is amiss, especially when it emerges that Coyle himself holds the mortgage and is willing to release it if Sir Edward assents to Florence's marrying him. In an aside, Sir Edward laments: "Oh! Florence, why did I not listen to you when you warned me against this man? ... Still the match would save *her*, at least, from ruin."[19]

After Florence enters and escorts her father off to meet Asa, a smirking Coyle recounts to the audience how he has illicitly come to hold the mortgage. He demands Murcott's complicity in the scheme, but Murcott hesitates, recalling that Sir Edward years ago had taken him in as tutor for his children, before drink got the better of him. When Coyle exits,

Murcott vows to overcome his "poor muddled brain" and warn Florence, but veers away instead in search of brandy.[20]

Playing the slimy Coyle was John Mathews, thirty, the company's First Heavy and like Ned Emerson a close friend of Booth, whom he had known since boyhood. They had acted together in Richmond before the war, and Mathews's admiration for Booth was unbounded. The two men spent considerable time together whenever their performance schedules coincided, often including Emerson and actor John McCullough.

Others tended to refer to him as "Crazy John Mathews," and his behavior was odd at times. Slight in build (a thin five feet seven inches) and prematurely balding, with small, darting eyes and hair perpetually in disarray, he projected an image of uncertainty and insecurity. This led to a lifetime of being cast in eccentric character roles, each of which, remarked one critic, Mathews played "as if it were a feeble rubber ball in the toils of a young, strong, frisky, and amusing puppy."[21]

Orphaned soon after his birth in Ohio, Mathews had been raised in the home of Cumberland, Maryland, coroner Pierce Byrne and never formally trained for the stage. He had received a first-rate education at Saint Mary's Seminary in Baltimore, but was never ordained and had been acting now for over ten years in Baltimore, Philadelphia, and Washington. He came to Ford's only the past September, performed with Forrest in Philadelphia for a few weeks in December, and then spent the rest of the winter performing as needed here and at the Holliday Street.

In Washington, he alternately rented a room at a boardinghouse on L Street or one from William Petersen across the street from Ford's, and Booth was a frequent visitor when in town. Booth would often, said Mathews, "come over from the theatre and lie on my bed and talk to me by the hour." Earlier this spring Mathews had rented the very room in which Lincoln would die, and Booth had ironically relaxed and smoked and napped on the very bed. Recently, Booth had repeatedly pressed

Mathews to assist in a plot to abduct the president, but Mathews had refused, agreeing only to transport to Baltimore a trunk containing what may have been supplies for the abduction. Booth was irked by such cowardice.[22]

The abduction of the president, who was to be seized, bound, and carried off through the backstage door and into a wagon waiting in the alley behind the theatre, had already failed twice, in January and March, despite Booth's men being fully prepared. On both occasions—one a performance by Forrest at Ford's and the other a production for convalescing soldiers at Campbell Hospital near Soldier's Home—the president had changed his mind and did not attend. Yet, as far as Mathews or anyone else privy to the abduction plan was aware, it was still under consideration; they had no inkling of any potentially fatal change of plan.

★ ★ ★

Scene Three, the last of Act One, is short, providing comic relief. Asa tries unsuccessfully to discern what Binny means by "drawing a bawth," finally telling him just to "make tracks … vamoose … absquatulate … skedaddle." He then discovers, in a bathroom cabinet, a bottle of hair dye. Dundreary enters seeking it, but Asa hides it and denies seeing it. The two men banter a bit, misunderstanding each other mightily, until Dundreary exits and Binny sticks his head in to announce the afternoon's archery contest. The scene ends with Asa thinking he is pulling a cord to recall Binny, instead turning on the shower; his cries of "Help! … I'm drowning!" bring in all the servants, who stand laughing as the curtain falls.[23]

CHAPTER FIVE

"THE HANDSOMEST MAN IN WASHINGTON!"

BY NOW IT WAS nearly noon, and Wright called a short break. But before the cast could disperse, ever-ebullient Harry Ford, striding down through the house from the box office, had exciting news for them: this evening they would be playing before the most important theatregoers in the city. Some of the stagehands muttered about the extra work that meant, but the actors were for the most part elated. For anyone privy to Booth's plans to any degree, glances were exchanged as nervous anticipation kicked in.

Phillips decided, with Wright's approval, that the quartet Withers had hired to perform "Honor to Our Soldiers" at the first intermission tomorrow night would instead sing it tonight. A few of the company's "ballet girls," who otherwise provided intermission entertainment, now would not be needed. Clustered in the alley doorway propped open to let in the afternoon sunlight, they began packing up to leave. Hart and Emerson stepped past them to briefly rehearse again in the alley.

Once outside, Hart asked why the theatre had never expanded back into the alley, and Emerson replied that the government owned the land there and wouldn't sell it to the Fords, gesturing further as he spoke. It may have been on this occasion, rather than their earlier rehearsing, or both, that Hart was mistakenly identified as standing behind the theatre with "Booth," who was pointing out various locations. In either case, it would bring her trouble.

A few actors and stage personnel headed out to the front steps of the theatre with Harry Ford to rest, smoke, and gossip. Among them were Gifford (a trifle surly about tonight), Hawk, Evans, Ferguson, DeBonay, and Scipiano Grillo, one of Withers's musicians and co-owner with Peter Taltavul of the Star Saloon next door. They watched Booth saunter down from F Street in a dapper dark suit, light drab overcoat, and kid gloves, a shiny black walking stick in his hand, and his long black hair glistening under a jauntily-tipped black silk hat. "Here comes the handsomest man in Washington!" called out Ford. His brother John would have agreed, telling a reporter later that Booth "had Apollo's own grace about him.... Four out of five on the street would turn to look at him again."[1]

Booth epitomized Byronic Romanticism. The qualities most commonly recalled of him were his strikingly handsome features, his agile, athletic physique, his blazing dark eyes (one manager swore that "sparks of genius flashed from those orbs"), his electrifying performances, and a personal magnetism that appealed to almost everyone (with the notable exception of a handful of two-timed lovers, one of whom, an actress, had tried to kill him in Albany in 1861). Actor Edward Alfriend expressed it well: "With men, John Wilkes was most dignified in manner, bearing himself with insouciant care and grace, and was a brilliant talker. With women, he was a man of irresistible fascination by reason of his superbly handsome face, conversational brilliancy, and a peculiar halo of romance with which he invested himself and which the ardent imagination of women amplified."[2]

Starstruck young actresses idolized him. One insisted later that he "was nothing like his terrible deed suggests. He was always ready for gaiety when with the company and never struck anyone as particularly serious." Clara Morris, who had acted with him in *The Marble Heart* and would later earn stardom in New York, recalled "the ivory pallor of his skin, the inky blackness of his densely thick hair, [and] the heavy lids of his glowing eyes [that] gave a touch of mystery to his face." In restaurants and hotels, she said, waitresses rushed to serve him, "crowding round him like doves about a grain basket." Hotel maids "had been known to enter his room and tear asunder the already made-up bed, that the 'turn-over' might be broader by a thread or two, and both pillows slant at the perfectly correct angle. At the theater, good heaven! As the sunflowers turn upon their stalks to follow the beloved sun, so old or young, our faces smiling, turned to him." Yet, for his impulsive tragic deed he would be for all time remembered "in the profession," Morris later believed, as "that unhappy boy."[3]

The backstage crew was particularly fond of Booth, because he treated them as equals (and to drinks), a rare practice by stars of his caliber. Most of the stagehands, drawn into his orbit, would do anything he asked of them.

Some of the actors remembered him from his attempt at management in April 1863. He had leased the old Washington Theatre and put together a barebones stock company, some of whom, like Helen Muzzy, had supported him in his earlier Washington debut at Grover's Theatre—actors whose lives he would upend tonight. He, of course, had taken all of the leading roles, billing himself as "The Youngest Star in the World; the Pride of the American People." Other leads had been played by future Ford's Theatre performers Alice Grey and Edwin Brink. The group bonded strongly. Grey's photo was one of five found on Booth's body after he was tracked down and killed, and Brink would be one of the last people to accompany him just before the assassination. Booth's management venture had lasted less than two weeks, however, due in part to audience falloff following the receipt of harrowing news of heavy losses at the Battle of Chancellorsville, and partly as a result of his heavy drinking, loss of voice, and aftereffects of surgery to remove a fibroid tumor from his neck.[4]

★ ★ ★

Ordinarily, Booth was a delight to be around. Harry Ford considered him to be "one of the simplest, sweetest-dispositioned and most lovable men" he knew. But this whole week Booth had been in a funk, ever since the news of Appomattox had reached Washington. On Monday Phillips and some government employee friends had encountered him on Fourteenth Street and asked him to join them for a drink at a nearby saloon. Booth had accepted, saying, "Anything to drive away the blues." When Phillips had asked, "What gives you the blues?" Booth had replied, "This news is enough to give any man of right feeling the blues." One of Phillips's companions thought Booth was "a rank rebel."[5]

Since Ford's was a second home to Booth in Washington, it was never a surprise to have him stop by like this. He seemed to spend the most time with various stagehands, though, especially Spangler, usually over drinks at the Star, where bartenders could count on seeing him two or three times a day. Harry swore later that for the last two years, Booth "had drawn scarcely a sober breath for a full day." Only yesterday afternoon he had downed a full bottle of brandy. This factor may well have contributed to the rashness of his decision now to change the abduction to an assassination.[6]

Even though they were friends, Booth sometimes got under Harry's skin. This past Wednesday night, for instance, around 9:00, during the performance of *Workmen of Washington*, Booth had appeared in the box office where Harry, Sessford, and Raybold were tallying tickets. After only a perfunctory greeting, Booth had sneered, "Well, we are all slaves now. If a man were to go out and insult a nigger, now he would be knocked down by the nigger and nothing would be done to the nigger." Union veteran Raybold had no patience for such tirades. He retorted that Booth, then, should simply "not insult a nigger."[7]

But Booth forged on, expelling his bile over seeing white prisoners being brought into the capital under Negro guard. It was an affront to the feelings of good Southerners, he exclaimed. To this Harry replied that even "General Lee wanted niggers to fight down there, and if niggers were good enough to fight, they were good enough to do military duty." Ignoring this as well, Booth launched with an odd kind of admiration into a spiel about the strength of slaves he had seen on his father's Maryland farm and on plantations while touring. Booth asserted that he could work as hard as any white man, but not as hard as the slaves could, day in and day out. He continued in the same vein for almost a half hour as the ticket sellers focused on their work, saying little. Finally, Booth turned on his heel and left.[8]

But Harry and Booth enjoyed a comfortable friendship that weathered such vicissitudes, and the actor had promised to perform his acclaimed role of Richard III for Harry's benefit night at the close of the season, despite having given up the stage for the more lucrative oil business, or so he maintained. Yesterday morning Harry had greeted Booth cheerfully in front of the theatre as he chatted with Grillo, asking Booth to lend him a few thousand dollars to open a gymnasium. Booth said he would think about it. Grillo, knowing Booth's political sentiments, tried to curry favor with him by saying that Lee was "the greatest General in the world." "Well," mused Booth, "he is a very good general, but I don't like the way he surrendered." Lee, he implied, was an enemy to him now because of that. Booth recalled with his unique sense of the heroic how

Lee had ceremoniously accepted his sword in the Senate Chamber at Richmond, swearing "never to surrender, that he would die on the battle-field."[9]

At that point Emerson had approached. Booth grabbed Emerson's cane, angrily gesturing with it as he denounced "that old scoundrel, Lincoln" for having dared the week before to enter the newly occupied city of Richmond and sit in Jefferson Davis's office. Booth erroneously claimed Lincoln then "threw his long legs over the arm of a chair and squirted tobacco juice all over the place." As he held the cane across his shoulders with both hands, he blurted, "Somebody ought to kill him," and brought down his arms with such force that the cane snapped into four pieces.[10]

Now, as Booth strode up to the Friday noontime assemblage on the front steps, he seemed in a little better mood, so Harry couldn't resist another jibe: "Here is a man that don't like General Lee." He and Booth shared a long-running joke, asking each other whenever they disagreed about how something was to be done, "Who is doing this, you or me?" So Harry now asked, "Who surrendered that army—you or Lee? General Lee is a good general and I guess he knowed what he ought to do and what he wants to do." Booth snorted that he was just as brave a man as Lee, but Harry silenced him with "Well, you have not got three stars yet to show it."[11]

At that moment Raybold brought out a packet of letters for Booth that had been delivered to the theatre. One was four pages long and apparently from a female admirer. Booth moved off a little to read it, laughing aloud at some spots and shaking his head over "that damned woman." Hawk glanced at him warily, for good reason. The two men had been calling on the same lady of questionable repute since last week, and Booth had warned Hawk to stay away from her. Hawk had seemed to assent but had continued to see her behind Booth's back, as recently as last night. It was best not to trifle with a man of Booth's volatile temperament, but he hadn't been able to resist.

Just then Dick Ford returned from his errands, and Harry, with a wink at his brother, thought he'd have a little more fun with Booth: "John, the president is going to be here tonight, with General Grant. They've got General Lee here as a prisoner, and he's coming, too. We're going to put him in the opposite box." Booth flared: "Never! Lee would not let himself be used as Romans used their captives, and be paraded!" Harry assured him he had only been joking—it would be only the Lincolns and the Grants tonight. Booth jumped up and grabbed the "ticket board" (which recorded the boxes reserved) from Harry's hands and turned it toward himself. There, written across its margin in large letters for the public to see, were the words "The President and party will attend tonight's performance."[12]

Booth's face darkened. Many of the figures caught up in that night's tragedy, including all three Ford brothers, would later swear that it was at that precise moment that Booth made his decision: the abduction would be an assassination. (Yet, as early as the previous Tuesday evening, when Lincoln had spoken from the upstairs window of the Executive Mansion to the jubilant crowd assembled below, Booth had purportedly stood among them and vowed, "That's the last speech he will ever make!")[13]

Soon, the actors and stagehands hustled back into the theatre to resume rehearsal, and Harry, to change the subject, broached again the subject of the gymnasium investment. "Harry, that's too much money," countered Booth. He said he would "see about it" but would not promise anything. Then, oddly solemn, he handed Harry what he said was one of his last *cartes de visite* and strode off down Tenth Street. Harry was used to these mood swings, though. He headed over to the Greenback Saloon, just north of the theatre, to urge owner James Ferguson (no relation to callboy Will) to buy tickets for the evening's performance, knowing Grant was a particular favorite of his.

Booth, halfway down the block, called back to ask Dick Ford to join him for a drink. But Dick, knowing the ill effects of alcohol on too many in their profession, made it a point not to drink, and now demurred. He liked Booth, who he claimed later had given him the mate to the Deringer that would play a fatal role that night. But Dick had too much to do to get ready for this evening's special guests and so turned back into the theatre.

Wanting to keep on good terms with Booth, Hawk said he would join him for a quick one, and they ducked into the Star Saloon. Barely more than a minute later Hawk dashed back to the theatre and Booth strode out toward The Avenue.

★ ★ ★

Inside the theatre, Phillips and Dyott had already reconvened rehearsal, starting the second act. It opens with Mrs. Mountchessington chiding Augusta for her misplaced attention to young Captain DeBoots, played by twenty-year-old supernumerary Charles Byrne, a Baltimore native in only his third year of acting here and at the Holliday Street. He, too, knew Booth but avoided him, thinking him to be "a queer, moody fellow."[14]

Mountchessington commands her daughter to invite instead the advances of their visitor, Asa. Augusta agrees and obediently hides her distaste when Asa (Hawk) bounds into the room in full archery attire à la Robin Hood. After a bit of mutually confusing repartee with him, the ladies exit and Asa withdraws to an alcove for a quick nap. He ends up overhearing, to his glee, Dundreary harass Binny about the missing hair dye.

Asa eavesdrops as well on the next pair to happen by: Florence and Murcott. Apologizing for his "shabby, broken-down drunkard" state, the abject clerk warns Florence about her father's impending ruin and Coyle's scheme to win her hand. When she asks how they might avert it, Asa emerges from hiding and offers his assistance: "I don't know much about the ways of great folks, [but] I've got a cool head, a stout arm, and a willing heart, and I think I can help you, just as one cousin ought to help another." Murcott explains the details of Coyle's trickery, and they resolve to work together to (in Asa's words) "circumvent that old sarpint." Typical of such "Yankee" characters, he may be unschooled but possessed a good heart.[15]

The next scene opens in a park, where gardener Wickens flirts with Mary Meredith, the manor's milkmaid, whose identically named late mother had been disowned by old Mark Trenchard. Playing Mary was Jeannie Gourlay, at twenty already a seasoned actress on the verge of real recognition. With alluring lavender eyes that commanded immediate attention, Jeannie had been a favorite at Grover's and the Washington Theatre, and last August was recruited by John Ford.[16]

She had taken on increasingly larger roles as the season progressed. The Fords had featured her in advertisements, grooming her to replace the company's leading lady, Alice Grey, who had New York ambitions and was increasingly absent. Earlier this season, Wright had cast Jeannie in major roles supporting visiting stars Edwin Forrest and Junius Booth Jr., including Ophelia to the latter's Hamlet. In fact, she was scheduled to have her first benefit tomorrow night, when the entire company would support her in a sumptuous production of Dion Boucicault's *The Octoroon*.

Tonight, she would have the pleasure of acting with her sister and father for an audience that included her two teenage brothers and a cousin (whose father, Alexander Williamson, was tutor to young Tad Lincoln and would take the boy to Grover's Theatre tonight to see *Aladdin*). The Gourlay brothers, like most of the Ford's actors, were hoping for a glimpse of the president and General Grant.

Jeannie's character, Mary, remains cheerful in this scene despite her disinherited state. Wickens moons over her for a while, then exits, and she soliloquizes about the kind treatment the Trenchards have shown her. Florence enters to introduce her to Asa, who immediately (in an aside) recognizes her as Mark Trenchard's granddaughter. He openly admires her spunk: "Wal, darn me if you ain't the first raal right-down useful gal I've seen on this side of the pond ... a regular snorter."[17]

When Mary returns to her milking, Asa shows Florence the will in which Mark has left his fortune to him, expressing his regret that it did not go to Mary. They leave, and Dundreary and Georgina stroll through again, conversing. She tires of him, leaving him to Asa. Several minutes of comic business follow, designed to further illustrate Dundreary's idiocy, until Asa asks his help in securing the ship's command for Vernon, to make Florence happy. To persuade him, Asa offers to return his hair dye, over which the vain Dundreary has become increasingly agitated.

Nearly the entire Trenchard household now gathers onstage, as the winners of the unseen archery contest (which presumably has been going on offstage during the previous dialogue) are to be announced. Asa has won the match, but just as the prizes are about to be bestowed, bailiffs arrive to seize Trenchard Manor. Sir Edward intones, "Florence, I am lost," and the curtain falls to end the act.

Playing one of the two bailiffs was stocky, dapper George Parkhurst, twenty-five, known as "Gentleman George." At fourteen, he had run away from boarding school and joined the navy, traveling three times around the world in five years before joining the Metropolitan Police force. Hired by the Fords to keep women of low repute from plying their trade in the third tier of the theatre, he married a Ford's actress named Catharine (Kate) and settled into a house on E Street, Southwest. When Parkhurst was "allowed to resign" (before being fired) from the police force for gambling in the saloon next to the theatre while on duty, Harry Ford took him in as a "super," and he remained an actor for life. The other bailiff was played by "L. Johnson," about whom nothing is known except his death before the turn of the century.[18]

★ ★ ★

Wright decided to run straight into Act Three without a break, knowing that when it was over, he and Withers would still need to rehearse the quartet for "Honor to Our Soldiers." It would consist of Phillips, Evans, and two members of the company not needed in *Our American Cousin*: C. V. Hess and Edwin Brink.

Courtland Van Rensalaer Hess, twenty-six, was still mired in small roles. He had accumulated ten years of experience in Philadelphia while living with his parents and seven siblings, listing himself in the city directory first as "Gentleman" and then "Comedian." When the Fords hired him this past January, he moved to a boardinghouse on Seventh Street, Southeast, near the Navy Yard. A Unionist, he was still getting over the death at Gettysburg of his older brother, George, a sergeant in the Union Army. His eldest brother, William, a telegraph service manager who would himself become involved in a minor way in the hunt for the assassin, would be attending tonight's performance to see C. V. perform (explaining, perhaps, why C. V. would sing even though he felt too ill to act).[19]

Walking gentleman Edwin Hunter Brink (known to his friends as Ted, and who in performing sometimes dropped his surname) was a promising forty-two-year-old supporting actor who usually drew favorable reviews. He had been close friends with Booth since their days together in Richmond in the late 1850s, when Booth, he said, "was the pet of Richmond and led a very wild life there" and the two had been together "almost constantly." After a season touring in Canada, Brink had come to Washington in 1861 to join the company at the old Washington Theatre. A year later he signed up with John Ford; he and Helen Muzzy were the only two performers to go the distance with Ford in Washington.

While Ford's first theatre was being rebuilt, Brink had supported Booth, first at Grover's and then during Booth's abortive "star management" of the Washington Theatre.[20]

Given Booth's political sentiments, it's curious that their friendship flourished. In August 1863 Brink had left the profession to enlist in the Union Navy, serving as an assistant paymaster on an armed ferryboat. As soon as he returned to acting in November 1864 the two men reconnected, but their friendship was always a little unequal. Brink, although older, seemed to idolize the charismatic Booth—"To know him was to love him," he claimed—and hoped to achieve greater fame by hooking his star to Booth's. And Booth, doubtless aware of Brink's Union military service, apparently never tried to involve him in any of his schemes. But on one occasion earlier that spring when the two men had been out riding, Booth had instructed their driver to follow Lincoln's carriage, telling Brink he was doing do so "just to shoot the president," and then laughed.[21]

Within weeks of resuming his theatrical career, the dashing Brink had married Catherine ("Kittie"), a New York–born Irish lass, only days after she turned fourteen. At Ford's she helped out backstage, caring for costumes and helping dress the actresses, but aspired to an acting career, happily taking any tiny roles available. There would be nothing for her tonight, so she would make herself useful behind the scenes.

★ ★ ★

Act Three of *Our American Cousin* is unusual for its time in that it contains seven short scenes, requiring stagehands to hover without a break. It opens on the same dairy set that closed the previous act, with Asa telling Mary he needs to have a serious talk with her, although "them eyes of yourn takes my breath away." She questions him about life in Vermont, which he opines she would love, and he reveals in a lengthy monologue that Mark Trenchard, her grandfather, had gone to America to search for other branches of the family. Whenever Mary's mother wrote to Mark, Asa says, he threw away her letters without opening them, since "she had gone and got married again' his will." But taken with ague and close to death, he had called Asa to his bedside to repent his mistreatment of Mary's mother, a moment Asa now relates to her in poignant detail. She remains rapt, as Hawk hoped the audience would tonight, and begins to cry.[22]

Joseph Jefferson, the original 1858 Asa, thought playwright Taylor "never drew a finer dramatic picture" than this scene. As Asa continues, seemingly preoccupied but with careful intent, he strikes a match to light a cigar, but instead pulls out old Mark's will disinheriting Mary and naming him sole heir, and burns it. Thus, Mary inherits a fortune as the only direct living descendant. In an aside, Asa acknowledges, "There lies four hundred thousand dollars, if there's a cent." As soon as he leaves, Florence enters to comfort the weeping Mary, only to pick up an unburned scrap which conveniently contains Mark's signature and the words "Asa Trenchard.... sole heir."[23]

Mary asks, "Oh, Florence, what does this mean?"

Florence replies, "It means that he is a true hero, and he loves you, you little rogue."

They rush off to find Asa as the curtain falls.

★ ★ ★

Act Three, Scene Two opens far downstage, in a chamber setting delineated only by a backdrop barely upstage of the curtain line, containing a central red-curtained archway. Mrs. Mountchessington once again urges Augusta to forget the destitute DeBoots and focus her attention on Asa. When Asa enters, the two women proceed to flatter his archery prowess. Then, unexpectedly, he announces that he is no longer heir to a fortune.

Shocked, Mountchessington chastises him for his effrontery: "I am aware, Mr. Trenchard, you are not used to the manners of good society, and that, alone, will excuse the impertinence of which you have been guilty." Mother and daughter sweep out haughtily, with Asa's retort addressed to the archway: "Don't know the manners of good society, eh? Well, I guess I know enough to turn you inside out, old gal—you sockdolagizing old man-trap!"[24]

The line never failed to generate an enormous laugh, often the largest of the evening. Anyone who knew the play well—and John Wilkes Booth certainly did, having performed in it at least fourteen times—would have known that the laugh would cover any other sudden, foreign sound. More importantly, he would also have known that only one actor remained on the stage at that moment to possibly hinder his passage across it.

A moment later, Florence and Mary rush in and smother Asa with grateful affection. Florence leaves, and within moments Mary has pledged her hand and heart to Asa "as freely as you, this morning, gave my grandfather's property to me." They walk off arm in arm, making fervent plans to live happily together among the bears and moonlight in Vermont.[25]

Then Binny enters, drunk (which Spear would find easy to enact tonight). He invites Asa to join Coyle, Murcott, and himself in the wine cellar, a scene that was pre-set behind the current one, with furniture, props, and actors already in place to facilitate a quick scene change. (When stagehands pulled apart the two halves of the chamber's backdrop, everything would be "discovered." If done smoothly, one scene would flow easily into the next.)

In this next scene, as Asa enters, Coyle, too, is quite drunk, but Murcott is only pretending to be, as he informs Asa and the audience in an aside. The four men imbibe freely and sing until Coyle falls off his chair, senseless. Murcott and Asa lift the key to his private bureau from his person, knock Binny aside, and rush out.

The transition to Scene Four reverses the preceding change, and the same chamber setting as in Scene Two is re-created by the sliding in of the two pieces of the backdrop. There, after some silly bantering about the value of a sneeze, Lieutenant Vernon thanks Dundreary for securing him his ship's command.

Scene Five, in the Trenchard Library, is a comic interlude of Dundreary preening and practicing riddles, which serves to build suspense until Asa and Murcott reach Coyle's office. There, in Scene Six, they find nothing in the bureau, but confront a locked desk. Asa grabs a nearby fire ax and begins to break it open when Coyle appears, angry and disheveled. Realizing they are close to discovering the papers that release the mortgage, cowed by Murcott's threat to expose him for embezzling, and threatened by the ax-wielding Asa, Coyle caves. He agrees to give the release papers to Sir Edward, repay the money, resign from his duties at the Manor in favor of Murcott, and relinquish any claim to Florence, apologizing to her in the bargain.

In the final scene, back in the library, all of this occurs. Then, "two by two, as if they were pairing for Noah's ark" (Asa observes), the various lovers convene: Florence claims the newly promoted Vernon, the now-wealthy Mary announces her impending marriage to Asa, Augusta stands proudly with DeBoots, and the delicate Georgina ends up with Dundreary. Then the servants enter, and Binny and Buddicomb similarly proclaim their engagement to Sharpe and Skillet. So, with everyone on stage, a quick round of bows could be executed. This was quickly practiced and everything appeared ready for tonight's performance.

It had been a good rehearsal. As high as spirits were running, a joyous evening seemed certain.

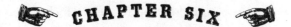

CHAPTER SIX

"HAVE YOU GOT THE KEY?"

AFEW MINUTES AFTER 2:00, the rehearsal over, the actors dispersed for dinner. Wright and Withers corralled the singers for practice that would consume another hour. As they began to work through their notes, the backstage employees began preparations for tonight's important guests.[1]

Callboy Will Ferguson remained at his desk out on the apron to write out lighting cues for stagehand Edward Gorman, twenty-six, who had only recently assumed the duties of "gasman." As was customary then, he had been trained as a plumber, but took on gas fitting responsibilities as its use spread. He lived with his wife Catherine and small son—three other children would arrive in rapid succession—on G Street near First, Northeast. Tonight his "gas plot" would be posted on the wall in the downstage right alcove, just above his four eight-inch-round valves controlling the stage and house lights.

As Ferguson worked, Tom Raybold headed up the lobby stairs toward the house right (stage left) boxes. From the dress circle he called down to Gifford to send Peanut John to the scene shop to rouse Spangler from a nap and bring him up to the box, along with Rittersbach. Peanut, perched on his usual stool beside the windowed stage left door to prevent entry by unauthorized persons, eagerly complied. Although he lived with his father a few blocks down Tenth Street, he preferred to hang out at the theatre all day long. At night he stationed himself during intermissions outside the front doors selling his namesake wares, the cracking of which could be heard throughout the audience during performances. Annie Wright felt sorry for this poor "street waif who worked all day and half the night about the stage." He did anything anyone asked of him, including posting bills all over town and carrying actors' costumes back and forth from their lodgings.[2]

Spangler and Rittersbach, rousted by Peanut, slouched their way across the stage. Harry Ford was already at work up in box number seven, one of two upper-level boxes house right. He called down to Spangler to hand him up a hammer and, reaching far over the ledge, was just able to grasp it from the stagehand's outstretched arm. He called Joe Simms down from helping Lamb with his paints to bring a stepladder, so they could drape the flags properly. When Spangler and Rittersbach appeared, Harry instructed them to remove the partition separating boxes seven and eight to create one large box to accommodate tonight's distinguished party. Peanut stayed at the ready in its doorway.

Harry had hoped for more help from Raybold, whose severe, shooting facial pains kept him from accomplishing much. Making things worse for Raybold was the fact that Dick Ford was needed tonight in Baltimore, so it was unlikely he could leave early. But when doorkeeper Buck arrived, he helped Harry, letting Raybold beg off entirely. At one point, even the clerk who had brought the flags over from the Treasury Department pitched in. Together, they placed two American flags on staffs on either side of the box's opening, hung two more over its railing along with a blue and white Treasury Guards regimental flag, and (for the first time) centered a large framed portrait of George Washington beneath them. Gifford, down on the stage, thought the whole effort was a waste of time, growling, "There is no necessity of that."[3]

As Spangler and Rittersbach wrestled with the partition, they hid their differences. Spangler seemed perpetually disheveled and morose, but even more so since Appomattox. As the men worked, his secessionist sympathies emerged. "Damn the President and General Grant," he muttered. Peanut, taken aback, asked why he would say such a thing: "He's never done any harm to you." Spangler retorted, "I don't care a damn. He ought to be cursed when he got so many men killed." To which he added—or so Rittersbach later claimed—"I wish lightning would strike that old son of a bitch." (Later, at Spangler's trial, Rittersbach would refine this to become "Well, I hope the damned son of a bitch will be killed here tonight," and conveniently omit Spangler's equal damning of Generals Grant and Lee and Confederate President Jefferson Davis.) Peanut later did not recall hearing these words.[4]

Harry directed Simms and John Miles to go around the corner into the second-floor reception lounge and bring over the velvet sofa and nine chairs—three velvet and six cane—that they would find there. When they finished, they were to go upstairs to Harry and Dick's apartment and bring down a handsome black walnut rocking chair, upholstered in red damask. Harry stored it there out of pique since noticing that its fabric was being ruined by the greasy hair of ushers lounging in it in the reception room. He made it a point to provide this special touch whenever he knew in advance that the president would attend.

The errand was a welcome respite for Simms and Miles, as Lamb could be a gruff taskmaster. Born in England, he had early become a recognized scenic artist at London's Drury Lane Theatre. Brought to America in the 1840s by a Rochester, New York, concert hall manager, he had moved to Washington in the early 1850s, advertising his artistry in "Fresco and Decorative Painting" from a studio on Pennsylvania Avenue, and by 1856 had become an American citizen. Established as the scenic artist at the Washington Theatre in the early 1860s, he caught the eye of John Ford, who recruited him with a generous contract; Lamb was the highest-paid member of the Ford's Theatre staff, including Gifford.

Disdaining to sleep at the theatre like the other stagehands, Lamb maintained a home on R Street near Fifth with his young wife, Annie. He had an address in Baltimore, too, and had pointedly told Harry Ford in completing paperwork for his pay to always list him as a resident of that city, where he remained less eligible for the draft, which he bitterly opposed. Nevertheless, he was forced to register for it in Washington (as Class 2: married and over thirty-five), but was never called up. Defiantly opposed to the war and its "butchery," he, too, was known to keep company with Booth. He had been overheard denouncing Lincoln, the draft, and the entire war.[5]

★ ★ ★

As the afternoon wore on, the stage remained a beehive of activity. Harry Hawk stopped by with a trunk that needed mending and asked the stagehands for help. Unaware of his youthful stint in the New Orleans Cocktail Guards, they taunted him for being a "damned Yankee"; he retorted that they were all "Secesh." It was good natured joshing, and they provided Hawk with the tools and hardware he needed, but a clear division remained. The only other actor still hanging around was Spear, who seemed to enjoy the company of the stagehands more than that of his younger cast mates. Plus, the theatre was a more congenial place than his solitary boardinghouse room.[6]

As soon as Spangler and Rittersbach had set the partition against the back wall of the box, they returned to the stage to repair some scenery with Gifford and Tom Hall, the Holliday Street stage manager who had come down to Washington to help out. Once Wright had determined which lightweight pine-and-muslin "flats" would be needed for tonight's performance, each had to be checked for damage and placed into the grooves in the stage floor that would allow them to slide together from the wings. Lamb's painted backdrops would be flown in from above.

As the stagehands worked, cleaning ladies bustled about among the house chairs. Since these were not fixed to the floor or able to fold up as today's seats are, cleaning around them and keeping the rows straight was a challenge. Chief Usher James O'Bryon nodded approvingly as he passed through, making sure the house looked its best for tonight. Formerly a treasurer at Grover's, O'Bryon, thirty, lived with his parents and five siblings near the theatre. Having been drafted into the Union Army in March, he served as a quartermaster's clerk, but sometimes stopped by Ford's during the day.

★ ★ ★

Just as Will Ferguson finished his copying, Jimmie Maddox strolled through the stage door, back from dinner, to make a final check of his small property room in the stage left wings. Maddox, twenty-six, was short, round, and compact, with light hair, blue eyes, and a ruddy complexion—a miniature Falstaff with a perpetual impish grin. Born in Dumfries, Virginia, but a Washingtonian for almost two decades, he had left school at fifteen to apprentice in the harness trade but left that to work backstage, first at the National and then Ford's. He ran with the rowdy firehouse "b'hoys" and was prone to bouts of drunkenness, irreverence, and practical jokes. Once when Booth had starred in *The Taming of the Shrew*, Maddox had (at Booth's suggestion) coated the underside of a prop ham with moist lampblack, so that when Petruchio used it to clout his servants (one of whom was Ferguson), they emerged from the encounter "looking like darkies."[7]

Maddox lived with his wife of two years, Maggie, a Ford's ballet girl, just around the corner on E Street. Like Lamb, he had sought to evade the draft by using a Baltimore address, but had been drafted in that city in late 1863. He had avoided service by purchasing a substitute. Like many others, he was a drinking companion of Booth's and held similar strong (some said "hard-core") "Secesh" opinions that he felt free to express with little provocation. He had on occasion been overheard denouncing the president, saying he should be shot.[8]

Around 2:45, as Maddox and Ferguson were about to leave until the evening's "call" (time to report) of 6:30, they noticed Booth seated calmly at the prompter's table, chatting quietly with Gifford, Spangler, and Spear. Booth invited everyone to join him for a drink at the Star Saloon, but only Maddox and Ferguson accepted. It was flattering to Maddox that anyone of Booth's station in life would want to associate with backstage workers. "Such men never associated with me," he said later. "They think in the profession their grade is higher than mine." Back in January, Booth had joined Maddox, Phillips, Carland, and DeBonay to celebrate Harry Ford's birthday at a fine restaurant, presenting him with a commemorative watch.[9]

Heading over to the Star with Booth was a comfortable ritual. Most of the Ford's stagehands preferred to drink there, rather than at the Greenback. Gifford, for one, had had an unpleasant exchange the week before with Greenback proprietor James Ferguson, an ardent Unionist, just after Richmond fell. Ferguson had walked over to ask if the theatre had any extra Union flags he could use to decorate his saloon. In fact, he asked, why was no flag flying above Ford's? Gifford snarled that a rope would be more appropriate, to which Ferguson prophetically retorted, "You ought to be in the Old Capitol Prison!"[10]

Like Maddox and Gifford, Carland's sympathies were staunchly with the South. Another aspiring actor, the brash costumer, in his early twenties, was born in Toronto and raised in New York, where he gained some minor experience on the stage. He, too, had fallen under Booth's spell, having known him since the late 1850s at Ford's Richmond Theatre. Carland had played tiny roles to Booth's major ones there, and the two had become friendly enough to toy with the idea of participating in a secessionist paramilitary organization. Carland considered Booth "a gentleman, who would soon get acquainted, and get familiar with people on a very short acquaintance." Now, whenever Booth or Forrest played Ford's, Carland continued to fill small roles.[11]

Carland and DeBonay, too, had had run-ins with saloonkeeper Ferguson. A few weeks ago, Carland had recounted to him a confrontation with "some damned Yankee officers" and wished they had all been killed. Ferguson called him a "damned hungry son of a bitch," ran around from behind the bar, and threw Carland out into the street. The next morning Ferguson confronted him again, in front of the theatre: "If you run across my door I'll break your neck or have you arrested and out to the Old Capitol." Carland had not attempted another visit. On the day Richmond fell, DeBonay had drowned his sorrows in the Greenback, loudly asserting that any citizen of that city who cheered the "Yanks" as they occupied the Confederate capital "ought to be hung or shot." Ferguson threw him out, too.[12]

★ ★ ★

Now, in the more accommodating Star Saloon with Booth, Maddox ordered a whiskey, and callboy Will Ferguson settled for a sarsaparilla. Booth at first declined to drink, claiming "a touch of pleurisy," but a moment later changed his mind and took a glass of ale, grousing about losing six thousand dollars in his Pennsylvania oil venture. Carland, on his way back to the theatre from buying ribbons for badges for the quartet and gloves for the actresses, joined them for a quick drink. Around 3:30, they all headed out to the street.

As they parted, Booth started down toward C Street to Pumphrey's Stable to rent a horse, but turned back to Maddox to ask, "Have you got the key?" Maddox understood this to mean the one for the stable behind the theatre that he had arranged for Booth to rent. Spangler and Gifford had made it serviceable, but earlier in the week Spangler had sold Booth's carriage, which had been stored there, bringing the money to Gifford to give to Booth.

Now, Maddox replied that no, he did not have the key on him, and headed back to the theatre for it. Carland went with him, continuing up to the wardrobe room. Looking across the empty stage, he could see Buck and Harry putting finishing touches on the presidential box. Gifford had left, Rittersbach had retreated to the scene shop, and Lamb was still painting way above them, preparing for next week's production of *A Midsummer Night's Dream*. By the stage door, Peanut John waited patiently for his next task.[13]

For a rare few hours, the theatre was almost deserted. Even Dick Ford had wrapped up his box office paperwork and was heading out to catch the 4:00 train to Baltimore. Also on that train would be General and Mrs. Grant, who, despite advance publicity, had declined the Lincolns' invitation and were heading to New Jersey to see their children.

As the Grants' carriage drove up Pennsylvania Avenue toward the train station around 3:45, they would pass Booth, astride his new bay mare, talking to John Mathews in front of Grover's. Mathews had been standing with a friend among a sizable crowd watching more than four hundred Confederate officers captured at Sayler's Creek, including General Richard Ewell, being marched under guard up the avenue to Old Capitol Prison, when Booth rode up, "pale as a ghost." At the sight of the captured Confederates, he threw a hand dramatically across his fore-head and lamented, "Great God! I have no longer a country! This is the end of constitutional liberty in America."[14]

Mathews and his friend had been headed to Shoomaker's, a nearby liquor store, but Booth reached down and detained him. The friend went on ahead, no doubt spooked by this nervous, histrionic figure on horse-back. Gripping Mathews's hand, clearly distraught, Booth asked him for a favor: "Johnny, I have a letter which I wish you to deliver to the publishers of the *National Intelligencer* tomorrow morning, unless I see you in the meantime. I may leave town tonight." *Intelligencer* editor John F. Coyle was a friend of Booth's, and the two had spoken earlier that morning.[15]

Mathews was simultaneously flattered and suspicious. True, he and Booth had been friends since boyhood, but having turned Booth down about the kidnapping, he remembered Booth's thinly veiled threat of hold-ing unspecified documents (presumably pertaining to the trunk of supplies Booth had asked him to transport to Baltimore) that would still implicate him. For whatever reason, he agreed, and Booth handed down a thick, sealed letter, which Mathews placed carefully inside his frock coat.

It was then that the Grants' barouche flew by, its top down to accom-modate a stack of luggage. Mathews remarked, "John, there goes General Grant! I thought he was coming to the theatre tonight with the Presi-dent." "Where?" Booth cried. Then he squeezed Mathews's hand tightly, uttered, "Goodbye, perhaps I will see you again," and galloped off up the avenue. Mrs. Grant would later recall a wild-eyed man on horseback who raced past them, doubled back, and then passed again, glaring at them. Mathews decided he should alert Harry Ford to Grant's obvious change in plans, and turned toward Tenth Street.[16]

About a half hour later, Booth rode the bay mare hard up Tenth Street and reined to a halt in front of the Greenback. On the front steps of Ford's were Mathews, who had just arrived, plus Carland, Spangler, Maddox, and a few others, eyed by a wary James Ferguson from his porch. "See what a nice horse I have," Booth bragged to the group. "Now watch, she can run like a cat." He spurred her down Tenth and back up, then east onto F Street, turning abruptly into the alley behind the theatre. Spangler and Maddox went inside and crossed the stage to the back door, reaching it just as Booth called in to them to bring a halter, which Spangler readily provided.

Inside the theatre, Rittersbach, who seemed to ask a lot of questions, pulled Spangler aside with another one: "Who is that?" The reply, identifying Booth, appeared to mean nothing to Rittersbach, who went back to work in the scene shop.

Peanut John, always good with horses, joined the other men in the alley. He and Spangler struggled to get the halter on, then moved to take off the saddle, but Booth told them to leave it in place, instead inserting a shawl under it. He led the high-spirited, uneasy mare into the stable, saying with some degree of pride that she was "a bad little bitch." He locked up, and the four adjourned to the Star Saloon for another round of drinks. Booth paid—as usual.[17]

★ ★ ★

Around 5:15, under a gunmetal sky and gathering clouds, the men lounging in front of Ford's watched eleven-year-old program boy Joseph Hazelton arrive, fresh from school, for his evening duties. Born in Georgia, the lad lived with his family around the corner on E Street. Harry Ford had hired him in the fall, and he had proven to be punctual and diligent, checking in every night with Buck. He was excited about Lincoln's attendance tonight, having met the president earlier in the year in the company of a relative on Grant's staff. Lincoln had taken the boy's hand warmly and enjoined him to make sure his late hours at the theatre never interfered with his schoolwork, nor gave his mother any cause for worry. The president had even inquired about his vocational plans, suggesting, "You might do worse than try the stage." It was, the president said, "a great profession." After that, whenever Lincoln came to Ford's, he greeted Joseph warmly by name.[18]

Equally fascinating to the boy was the dashing Booth, to whom he believed "a romantic aura" clung. Over sixty years later he could still envision Booth standing in front of the theatre on occasion, declaiming speeches from Shakespeare (especially those of Brutus and Cassius), "twirling his mustache and frankly exhibiting himself." The boy felt honored to be included in the fraternity of stage employees whose company Booth preferred, watching from the perimeter as the men "drank their beer and passed their leisure." He never understood why Booth was kindly towards him, but he always was, even taking Joseph to a nearby shop once to fit him out with a new cloth cap "more befitting his professional duties."[19]

Just then, Booth emerged from the Star with Spangler and Gifford and approached the group on the steps. Booth, smiling, reached down to tousle Joseph's hair, handing him a ten-cent "shinplaster" (low denomination paper currency) to buy a stick of candy. Putting it in his pocket for later, the boy went into the theatre, where he felt very grown up as he listened to Harry Ford talk about the way that "Sherman should clean up Johnston in the South." In fact, the manager surmised, the president might even receive dispatches from the general tonight during the performance and read them to the audience.[20]

Except for the box office and lobby staff, the theatre was finally quiet. Lamb, even if he knew that anything malicious was afoot, wanted no part of it; he finished up on his elevated painting platform and left, catching a streetcar out to R Street. Outside, the group on the steps dissolved as well. Spangler, Gifford, and Mathews took Booth by the arm and led him a little ways up Tenth Street in earnest conversation, but Gifford after a moment veered off to get a clean shirt from his laundress, who lived behind the theatre.

For the next hour, almost everyone connected with the coming performance was at supper. Rittersbach, though, had hung around, keeping an eye on Booth's entourage stabling the horse. At one point, he was surprised to see someone smoking a cigar up in the dress circle and pointed it out to Spangler, who was just coming in the alley door. Spangler told him to let it go, and together they headed to Mrs. Scott's boardinghouse for supper.

If the person in the dress circle was Booth, it would not have surprised the men; he had dropped by Wednesday afternoon to watch part of the rehearsal of *Peggy* from that same section of the house. And as deserted as the theatre was now, anyone sitting up there would have the perfect opportunity to bore a peephole in the door of the presidential box or carve a niche in the wall outside it for later use in wedging its outer door shut, if he were so inclined. Certainly somebody did just that.

★ ★ ★

"Call" for the cast was 6:30, just as the sun was setting. For the crew, it was 7:00. Stage manager Wright, back from supper, checked off the actors and backstage workers as they returned. No one was late, as severe penalties would have been imposed. Laura Keene and John Lutz were the first to arrive, as was her custom, having walked the four blocks from their room at the Metropolitan Hotel. She was overjoyed to hear that the president would be attending tonight and agreed that "Honor to Our Soldiers" would be a perfect addition to the evening's performance. The best spot for it would be during the first intermission. In fact, she said, the entire company should sing it, not just the quartet. She offered her own small piano to augment the orchestra, and Lutz headed for the box office to arrange for its delivery to the theatre. A perfunctory run-through of the song, less thorough than conductor Billy Withers would have preferred, would take place sometime before the 7:45 curtain.

Withers, however, was distraught. He had just suffered a deep personal setback: a striking, slender young woman with "wavy hair and big black eyes," who had promised to marry him, had that very afternoon run off and married another man. Tonight, Withers realized that his professional responsibilities took precedence, but he hoped that sometime during the evening he might find a sympathetic ear, perhaps from one of the fetching Gourlay sisters. Sometime during the half hour before the overture, he slipped next door to the Star Saloon and had a drink with, among others, Booth; if he shared his disappointment or sought any advice about the fairer sex, neither of them ever spoke of it. Withers did think that Booth appeared "more than usually fidgety and excitable" that night.[21]

★ ★ ★

By 7:15, everyone inside Ford's was in a state of nervous preparation. They had spent the afternoon running and re-running lines, double-checking costumes and props, and making sure Washington newspapers and printers had the latest advertisements touting the evening's guests. For anyone holding Southern sympathies who had been filled in by Booth on details of what was about to transpire—whether it was still to be an abduction or now an assassination—the nervousness was compounded.

In the box office, the dressing rooms, and the wings backstage, cast and crew were comforted by the warm familiar smell of the theatre's coal-oil heat and flickering gas footlights, turned up a little to "warm the curtain" (heighten audience anticipation). As Will Ferguson began his rounds, calling "half hour" (before curtain), Keene, in her first floor "star dressing room" adjacent to the stage right wings, began applying grease-paint, while her assistant, Billy Otis, laid out her dresses, hats, and gloves. On the floors above her, aided only by Carland, the rest of the cast was similarly engaged.

At the rear of the house, Harry Ford and doorkeeper Buck scanned the theatre, from the floor-level parquette seating up to the dress circle with its coveted boxes on either side, and then up again to the family circle. All of the staff were in their places: downstairs they saw program boy Hazelton and usher James St. Clair; at the top of the stairs to the dress circle was Chief Usher O'Bryon, assisted by sixteen-year-old Edmund Schreiner; up in the family circle stood Henry Sauder and Mr. Gildour.

A few minutes before 7:30, Wright ordered the act curtain lowered into place and okayed the opening of the house. Buck propped open the doors into the small lobby and then those beyond it that opened out onto Tenth Street.

Outside, an air of expectation was palpable. The temperature had dropped into the low fifties, an intermittent wind was gusting up Tenth Street, and a light drizzle had begun as the last twilight faded. Dark clouds obscured the moon, which had been full only four nights before. Patrons hustling up from Pennsylvania Avenue were guided to the theatre by torches of burning tar wedged into barrels and barkers crying, "This way to Ford's!" Clusters of men stood in the mist around bonfires that exuded thick smoke pungent with pinesap. Occasional cries of "Three cheers for the president!" or "Hurrah for Old Abe!" wafted in through the open door.

As the festive crowd poured in, Harry and Buck agreed that it might be a close-to-capacity night. Word-of-mouth and effective advertising had negated the traditional theatrical curse of "Black Friday." The dominant color of apparel seemed to be Union Blue, with more than a few gold stripes. Excited conversations bubbled up as everyone glanced toward the decorated box at house right, as yet unoccupied, as they scurried to find whichever seats might afford the best view of it.

7:45, the theatre's normal curtain time, came and went with no presidential party. Wright decided to stall and signaled via bell for Withers, back from his drink with Booth, to go ahead. Down in the orchestra pit (more of a shallow indentation, with a small door connecting it to an under-stage passageway), Withers led his musicians through a repertoire of patriotic airs to entertain the restive audience. At one point he looked up and saw Booth at the rear of the parquette section, his arms resting on the railing, watching the audience.

By 8:00, the situation had not changed. Backstage, despite reassurances from Wright, actors in the wings fretted; those already called to their places for Act One paced. Through the heavy act curtain, over the music, they could hear the excited murmur of the crowd.

Finally, at 8:15, with still no sign of the evening's most important guests (who were only now leaving the Executive Mansion), Wright decided the time was at hand. Announcing, "Clear the stage, ladies and gentlemen," he heard the actors close by in the near-darkness offer each other words of encouragement as they completed last-minute costume checks and Maddox and Selecman handed them properties. Then, Wright told gasman Gorman to dim the house lights to half and bring up the stage lights to full. He rang his little bell to signal to Mills and Simms up on the fly rail to raise the opening curtain on the drawing room of Trenchard Manor. Out on the stage Kate Evans and Maggie Gourlay, as Sharpe and Skillet, bustled about, arranging furniture, and Johnny Evans's Buddicomb lounged on a settee reading a newspaper. The curtain rose, revealing to them first the footlights, then the patrons' expectant faces in the parquette, then the dress circle, and finally the family circle above.

The orchestra faded out. *Our American Cousin* was underway.

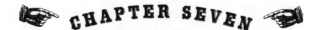

CHAPTER SEVEN

"I GUESS I KNOW ENOUGH TO TURN YOU INSIDE OUT"

ELEVEN MINUTES LATER, with the performance settling into a comfortable rhythm and the audience responding warmly, Laura Keene and Ned Emerson bantered about the various "drafts" as Helen Muzzy looked on. Keene's Florence was unable to "see the joke." Suddenly she turned full front to the audience and stood, gesturing over their heads at silhouetted figures entering the theatre behind them and ad libbed, "Well, anybody can see *that*!"

It was the presidential party: the Lincolns, accompanied by young Clara Harris and her stepbrother fiancé, Major Henry Rathbone. As they shook out the evening's mist from their bonnets and overcoats, little Joseph Hazelton nervously handed them one-sheet playbills (miniatures of the larger versions posted throughout the city), and they followed

James O'Bryon up the stairs to the dress circle, where he and Ed Schreiner led them toward their box.

Withers launched his orchestra into "Hail to the Chief" and Gorman pushed the house lights back up to full. The audience rose as one, applauding, cheering, waving hats and handkerchiefs as the onstage actors stood respectfully silent. Many of the others, along with some of the stagehands, crowded around Wright's desk in the downstage right wings (referred to as "the first entrance") to watch from across the stage.

The president paused behind the dress circle patrons, leaning against one of its white columns, his right hand over his heart, and acknowledged the hearty reception by bowing slightly, twice. His face remained a mask of ineffable weariness and sadness, his body stooped from the burden of the past four years. Catching his eye, Keene curtsied, as the musicians swung into "The Conquering Hero Comes." Mrs. Lincoln curtsied repeatedly in return, smiling uncharacteristically broadly.

Even after the presidential party had entered its specially decorated box, the applause continued. Keene, Emerson, and Muzzy, necks craned up to their left, waited for the right moment to resume their performance. After bowing solemnly once more from the front of his box and settling into his chair, the president gestured to them to continue—Emerson later avowed the president addressed him by name—and gradually the applause abated.

Keene signaled to Wright, who instructed Gorman once again to lower the house lights to half, and the scene moved forward. During the applause, Keene had whispered to Emerson that they would repeat some of their dialogue so that she could improvise a new laugh from their talk of "drafts." She knew that Secretary of War Edwin Stanton had only the day before announced an end to conscription and now, as they repeated the lines, she added knowingly, "The draft has been suspended." It drew a warm laugh, as did Emerson's lame joke about a dog's tail. This was the kind of folksy humor that Lincoln loved. Unlike Mary's polite hand-clapping, the president's appreciation of a joke was evident in a burst of hearty laughter.

From that point on, every humorous line in the play seemed to "hit," and every piece of comic business raised the level of warm, shared merriment. The cast had the audience in the palm of its hand. As Harry Hawk said later, each act "was one laugh from the time the curtain went up until it fell." Every now and then an easily identifiable guffaw would erupt from the presidential box, and the actors thrilled to see, out of the corner of their eye, that careworn, craggy face wreathed in a smile. Yet for other long stretches of time Lincoln seemed lost in a distant world. "He sat," recalled May Hart, "with his head on his hand gazing down at the stage, his eyes wide open, but not seeing.... If ever a man's face carried the expression of sadness his did that night."[1]

When the curtain came down again a shade after 9:00 amid the shared laughter over Asa's "drowning" at the end of Act One, many of the male patrons and some of the stage crew made a beeline next door for a quick intermission drink.

James Gifford, having minimal duties during performances, had spent the first act readjusting his Drummond "limelight" on a pole at Tenth and E Streets. In addition to its contributing to the city's celebratory illumination, he and the Fords knew that a well-lit theatre was a safer, well-patronized theatre. From time to time during the rest of the evening, he would return to the street to admire his handiwork, but spent intermissions checking on things backstage.

During this first break, Wright told Withers through a speaking tube down to the orchestra that the performance of "Honor to Our Soldiers" would be delayed. Miss Keene, he said, did not feel that they had rehearsed it sufficiently—she preferred it be performed later in the evening, most likely at the next intermission. For now, Withers accepted her decision but was annoyed.

Meanwhile, a train from Baltimore was approaching the District of Columbia, carrying Dick Ford back from his errand of making sure that Lucille Western's benefit at the Holliday Street Theatre had opened smoothly. The only glitch had been the cancellation of plans for the Virginia Regiment's band to play; getting the necessary sheet music, coupled with citizens' complaints about the band's Southern affiliation, had proven too difficult. Dick's only concern now was getting back to Washington to help his brother with what he knew would be a crowded house and hefty box office receipts to be counted.

Around 9:10, Will Ferguson began once again to call "places" backstage, first in the dressing rooms and then out the open door to the alley where actors were congregating, enjoying the fresh evening air despite the light rain. He noticed Spangler and Booth standing by Booth's rented mare out in the alley, but turned back inside without seeing them head over to the Star Saloon. There, the Gourlay girls' brother Robert, who had attended other performances at Ford's that spring, recognized Booth, but no one recognized the swarthy figure drinking with him: Ned Spangler. They did notice, though, how fast Booth threw back a tumbler of whiskey.

★ ★ ★

Act Two got underway around 9:15, with Muzzy in full control of the stage, urging Helen Truman's Augusta to focus her attentions on Asa during the archery contest. Waves of warm laughter flowed as freely over the footlights as they had in the first act. Near the end of the scene, out behind the theatre, Booth, back from the Star, walked his horse around to the stage door where DeBonay stood, and called in for Spangler to hold the horse for him during the rest of the act. DeBonay told him Spangler was needed for the upcoming scene shift.

The scene moved swiftly to its conclusion. As the stage lights faded, Spangler, Rittersbach, Selecman, and Maddox moved to set up the bucolic milkmaid-in-the-park scene, known to them as "the dairy scene," which took up nearly the entire stage. As soon as the scene shift was completed, around 9:40, Spangler, Selecman, and DeBonay slipped out the stage door and around into the alley to confer with Booth. Spangler agreed to hold the horse for a few minutes.

The others started back in through the alley door, but the scene was already running, with full stage lights up, leaving them no room to cross the stage, even behind the scenery. So Selecman remained stage right and helped Booth and DeBonay lift the trap door in the extreme upstage right corner, so they could duck down the stairs beneath it and cross under the stage via the musicians' T-shaped passageway. When they emerged upstage left, Spangler had already brought the horse around to the stage door and was calling in for DeBonay to get Peanut to come hold it. At first the boy objected, but Spangler ordered him to do it, saying he would take the blame if anything happened, and besides, Booth would pay him fifty cents when he returned.

So Peanut relented and walked the horse back around into the alley. There, he alternated pacing and lying on a carpenter's bench, holding the reins. Spangler slipped back behind the wings, passing DeBonay and Booth on their way out the stage door toward the Star Saloon, where they quaffed a quick whiskey and a water chaser.

Within minutes DeBonay returned to the stage, and Booth emerged from the Star puffing on a fine cigar. He passed Gifford, on his way back from taking a glass of ale up at another watering hole at Tenth and F, heading backstage.

Booth sauntered into the theatre lobby and leaned into the ticket window where Harry Ford was tallying receipts. Laying the half-smoked cigar on the window's ledge, he intoned in mock-heroic style, "Whoe'r this cigar dares displace must meet Wilkes Booth face to face." It was a parody of a sign the title character hangs on a tree along with his boots in the satirical drama *Bombastes Furioso*. Harry recognized the allusion and laughed. Booth will be Booth, he thought.[2]

Standing in the doorway behind the orchestra seats, with young Hazelton beside him, Buck reached out automatically for Booth's ticket. Taking hold of the outstretched fingers, the actor joked, "Buck, you don't want a ticket from me," then asked what time it was. The time was clearly visible on the large lobby clock, Buck retorted. Booth just grinned and slipped into the house, humming a tune. Sessford drifted over from the box office. "Wonder what he's up to. He was in here this afternoon, too." Buck just shrugged. He, Hazelton, and Sessford watched Booth stroll over to the far left side of the lobby, gaze up at the presidential box for a good five minutes, oblivious to the action on the stage, and then return to the street. It was almost 9:50, and Act Two was drawing to a close, with the bailiffs arriving onstage to arrest Sir Edward and the curtain about to descend.[3]

As soon as it did, Parkhurst and Johnson, their minuscule parts done, left for the night, thus eluding the fate of their peers. Parkhurst had only that evening come across a windfall: he had arranged with Booth earlier in the day to pick up a two-part trunk filled with costumes and properties the tragedian said he no longer needed. It was a nice gesture to a young actor just beginning his career. The trunk alone was beyond Parkhurst's means, not to mention the lavish Elizabethan and Roman period shirts, collars, tights, and sandals it contained. He had picked it up at the National Hotel on his way to the theatre and brought it backstage.

Heading out the stage door, Parkhurst stepped aside to make way for Gifford, who came inside and motioned Spangler and Carland over. The three conferred closely for several minutes, ostensibly about upcoming scene and costume changes. Nearby, Maddox and Selecman discussed stage properties needed for act three. Realizing they lacked some of the ingredients for the potion representing "wine" in the third scene, Maddox sent his young assistant off to the druggist.

The second intermission saw a repeat of the earlier enthusiastic bar patronage, including this time a backstage contingent. John Dyott, anticipating Method Acting by several decades, decided to prepare in a realistic way for the wine cellar drinking scene. He gathered up a visibly irritated Withers, who was remonstrating with Wright about the postponement *again* of his special song. Crossing the stage, they approached Carland and Gifford (Spangler having drifted away) to join them for a drink next door, and they all headed over to the Star.

Just as they arrived, Booth was leaving by its front door, strolling out into Tenth Street and over to Ford's, where he hit up Buck for a plug of tobacco and poked his head into the house again for a few minutes. After one quick drink, Withers and Dyott returned to the stage, where Withers was again told to be patient, which he did not like hearing.

Carland and Gifford left the saloon by the same door Booth had used, emerging into the street, Gifford explaining improvements he was planning to the theatre's façade. In the emerging moonlight struggling through the clouds and mist, their gesturing and pointing upward did not go unnoticed, much like Emerson's that morning in the alley behind the theatre with May Hart. Booth re-emerged from the lobby, but they studiously ignored him as he returned to the Star.

Inside the theatre, it had grown a little chilly; Annie Wright noticed from her seat in the fourth row on the opposite side of the parquette that the president had put his overcoat back on, and his wife still wore her bonnet. The stage manager's wife found it comforting that Lincoln spent the interim leaning forward in his box, his elbows on its ledge and his head in his hands, watching the audience, as if "to ascertain how many persons there he recognized." He barely moved through the entire intermission. A young woman near her had similar feelings as she regarded "Father Abraham ... there like a Father watching what interests his children, for their pleasure rather than his own." It seemed so sociable, "like one family sitting around their parlor fire."[4]

Doubtless the least sociable gathering of the theatre so far that night was the orchestra's. Withers instructed them now to disperse until after the show, when they might finally be allowed to play his composition. Leaving their instruments in place, they complied, the swiftest being Scipiano Grillo, who rushed next door to help out in the Star. Withers made up his mind to confront Wright once and for all as soon as the act was underway.

★ ★ ★

At 10:05, Gorman dimmed the house lights to half and patrons drifted back into their seats, shooed along by the ushers, who left for home after this final task. Buck, asked yet again by the hovering Booth what time it was, curtly informed him, "Look at the lobby clock and you will see." Strangely, Booth turned on his heel and went back out to the street. When Buck, his duties done, slipped next door for a nip, there, too, was Booth. They nodded, but did not speak. Whether Buck also noticed Edwin Brink, who had joined Booth, he never said.

Inside Ford's Theatre the curtain rose for the final act, displaying for a second time the "dairy scene," the background for Hawk's finest moment as Asa. Carefully spooling out his lengthy monologue to Jeannie Gourlay's sweetly attentive Mary Meredith, he carried out the seemingly nonchalant stage business of lighting his cigar with the will, all with exquisite timing. It worked to perfection. The audience remained rapt, their full attention drawn to the bench at stage center where the two actors sat while Asa related the circumstances of the death of old Mark Trenchard.

Near the end of the speech, however, just as Hawk struck the match, Gourlay's own attention wandered. Distracted by movement at the rear of the house, her eyes were drawn over the footlights and the heads of the audience to the figure of a man in dark clothes standing there. Booth had returned, but it was the first time that evening she had seen him. He paused in the dim light, his head characteristically inclined forward, then glanced upward to the presidential box. Although she was as taken by the dashing tragedian as any other girl of the day, Gourlay quickly remembered her professional responsibilities and turned back to Hawk. At the time, she thought nothing of it; Booth was often seen around Ford's. Only later did she realize the critical significance of his standing there at the very moment when the audience's full attention was drawn to the stage.

Leaving the bar, Booth had turned to Brink: "Go in and make up. Ted, old fellow, I'm going to have my name hung in a place where my father's never was." Brink thought the remark odd and inappropriate and remonstrated with his friend, telling him it would be unworthy of him "to bring shame upon the great line of Booths." His father, Junius Brutus Booth, he reminded John, was a highly distinguished actor in both England and America. Booth gave no reply, and the two friends separated in the lobby of Ford's. Now, Brink loitered downstairs in the far left aisle as Booth ascended to the dress circle. Brink would later marvel at how nonchalantly Booth picked his teeth with a penknife as he waited for access to the presidential box.[5]

On stage, Laura Keene's Florence happily explained to Mary what Asa had done for her. As they exited, the lights, but not the curtain, lowered for a quick scene change. All that was required for scene two was the stagehands' shoving together, just upstage of the curtain line, the two halves of the interior wall representing Mrs. Mountchessington's chamber. Where these met, their red-draped archway would hide the preparations for scene three (the "wine cellar") behind it. In the dim light backstage, Keene headed for the stage right wings.

A moment later the lights were back up and Helen Muzzy as Mountchessington swept onto the stage, admonishing her daughter Augusta (Helen Truman) to keep her eyes and her charms focused on Asa. But Truman's attention was distracted by the sight of Booth just outside the presidential box. Their eyes met and they subtly exchanged nods of recognition. Knowing that actors sometimes visited the president in his box during performances, she thought little of it.

At the same time, Ferguson and Maddox swooped in behind the backdrop from the wings with furniture and properties to set in place. Stage right, Withers emerged from the trap door to confront Wright over the omission of his song. By now he was livid. *When* would it be performed? At the curtain call, he was told. Miss Keene had sent word to the presidential party requesting they remain for it. Withers turned to go, but spied Gourlay back in the corner. She had always been friendly, and tonight a sympathetic ear would be most welcome. He stepped toward her.

Out in front of the theatre, Gifford and Carland were struck by the quiet of Tenth Street. Barely a soul was in sight in the mist. The temperature had dropped into the forties, and the provost guard who had checked soldiers' passes as they entered the theatre had dispersed. What few Metropolitan police there were remained near the station house a block away across the street.

Maddox darted out, impatient for Selecman's return from the druggist. He and Carland paced, fretting. But at that moment the boy arrived, nearly out of breath, and rushed with Maddox through the passageway between the theatre and saloon, toward the stage door.

C. V. Hess, dark-complected and sporting a dapper mustache, apparently recovered from his illness, approached from F Street. Asking Gifford and Carland for the time, he was told it was ten minutes after ten, so he veered off toward the same passageway back to the stage door, announcing over his shoulder that it was "pretty near time to go and get ready," presumably for singing "Honor to Our Soldiers." A minute later Johnny Evans, unneeded on stage until the quartet sang, emerged and spoke similar words to Gifford and Carland. Soon after that, DeBonay came out, exchanged looks with Gifford and Carland, then scurried back to the stage left wings.

There, preparing for his entrance as Asa triumphant (having won the archery contest), Hawk was startled to see John Mathews come in through the stage door wearing street clothes instead of his costume. Hawk, knowing Mathews was needed in the next scene, challenged him about his clothes, but Mathews told him not to worry—he would make his entrance in time, in the proper costume. It later struck Hawk as odd and troubling. Where had Mathews been during intermission and the previous scene?

But Hawk's cue came and he joined Muzzy and Truman on stage, modestly deflecting their praise of his archery prowess with words that would carry a darkly ironic significance that night. Aiming and shooting, he said, was easy; all you had to do was "look straight ... calculate the distance, and you're sure to hit the mark."[6]

Then, as Asa, he proceeded to confess his newfound indigence, causing Muzzy to exercise her forceful dramatic ability. Rising to her full height, she ordered her daughter from the room and proclaimed, "I am aware, Mr. Trenchard, you are not used to the manners of good society, and that, alone, will excuse you the impertinence of which you have been guilty."

She swept magisterially through the curtained archway, heading for the darkened stage right wings.

There she passed Billy Otis, helping Laura Keene don gloves for her entrance on the next line.

George Spear stood there, too, poised to enter the scene after Keene.

Will Ferguson, just back from getting Spear, was reassuring Keene that he knew his few remaining lines.

In the downstage right corner, Wright hunched over the stage manager's table, watching the script under a small gaslight.

Gorman stood impassively behind him, ready at his valves.

In the upstage corner, Withers leaned close in conversation with Jeannie Gourlay.

May Hart walked from Wright's table toward the greenroom, offstage right.

Inside the greenroom Kate Evans sat tatting drowsily, telling Maggie Gourlay, "Wake me up when Kirby dies" (a theatre catchphrase for the emotional end of a production, from the melodramatic death scenes of actor J. Hudson Kirby).

Tom Gourlay relaxed there with them.

Just outside the greenroom door, Charles Byrne paced, long before his cue.

One floor above them, Helen Truman dashed into the dressing room, and Kittie Brink turned to assist her.

Across the hall, H. B. Phillips was washing his hands, half-dressed for the upcoming performance of his and Withers's song.

Perched a floor above them all on the fly rail, John Miles and Joe Simms peered idly down across the stage.

Peanut John lay on the bench in the alley, the reins loose in his hand.

Dyott and Mathews (remarkably, back in costume) readied themselves behind the scenery to be "discovered" in the wine cellar.

Spangler waited just behind Rittersbach by the stage left side of the archway, to pull the scenery off.

Two stagehands named Henry James and "Skeggy" stood across from them, ready to pull away the corresponding stage right side.

DeBonay followed the prompt script at his station downstage left, just below the president's box.

Ned Emerson, beside him, leaned against some unused scenery, using the light of a gas jet to study his lines.

Maddox waited with Selecman a few feet away.

Hess stepped through the stage door.

Buck crouched in the box office, stashing ticket stubs in his little closet.

Tom Raybold and Joe Sessford stood beside him, tallying receipts.

Harry Ford and John Lutz counted heads in the house through the lobby door.

Little Joseph Hazelton, near Brink halfway down the far left aisle, eagerly awaited Hawk's retort.

Gifford and Carland lingered out in Tenth Street, ten feet from Lincoln's waiting carriage.

Dick Ford's train crossed into Washington, slowing as it approached the New Jersey Avenue depot.

John Ford sat conversing in his sister-in-law's parlor a few miles outside Richmond.

On the stage of Ford's Theatre, Harry Hawk, facing upstage and bent over in mock civility, rotated his comic face to the audience and started his retort: "Don't know the manners of good society, eh? Well, I guess I know enough to turn you inside out, old gal—"

Before he could finish, John Wilkes Booth with outstretched arm squeezed the trigger and their world turned upside down.

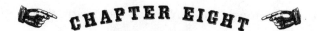

CHAPTER EIGHT

"BURN THE DAMNED PLACE DOWN!"

B Y 10:20, AS BAYONET-WIELDING soldiers cleared a path across Tenth Street, their comrades carried the unconscious president across to the Petersen house. The rain had picked up, and a frightened mob swirled in and out of the garish shadows created by Gifford's new lamp, mingling with frantic citizens rushing up from The Avenue. Directionless, ready to seize upon any rumor, follow any cry, a vigilante mentality rising among them, they threw off a terrible, unfocused energy that ricocheted back and forth across the street, the rain failing to quell their agitation.

Dick Ford, striding up Tenth Street, stopped short, stunned. "What drunken loafer is that?" he asked a bystander, thinking the supine form being carried out was just another soused theatregoer being ejected. When told the truth, he fought his way inside the theatre through horrified patrons still spilling out of its front doors.[1]

Inside, with the stage lights extinguished and only a few oil lamps lit, casting eerie shadows of their own, the terrified actors could hear the rising sounds of the mob in the street. Among the worst were strident cries of "Burn it down! Burn the damned place down!" Fleeing to their dressing rooms to frantically gather possessions, few could even think coherently enough to change out of their costumes.

At the bottom of the stairs to the dressing rooms, Harry Hawk confronted John Mathews about the street clothes he had been wearing after the last intermission. Flustered and turning red, Mathews blurted out an excuse about having forgotten part of his costume and needing to go back for it—an excuse that rang hollow to Hawk, who knew the script called for one basic outfit for Mathews throughout.

In the dim light, other actors, bundles in their arms, elbowed their way past Hawk onto the stage, having no idea where to go or what to do once they got there. They had no idea whether to be relieved or frightened further when they saw soldiers rushing in. Within minutes the 24th Regiment, Veterans Reserve Corps, had taken up stations in the dress circle, the orchestra and the lobby, with the backs of other soldiers visible out front, guarding every entrance, confronting the crowd. Ordered to remain inside, the actors huddled on the stage, sobbing, terrified. H. B. Phillips stationed himself out on the apron, trying ineffectually to keep order, his voice lost in the bedlam.

Rumors flew that they would all be arrested. The soldiers aggressively clearing stragglers from the house were hardly reassuring as they shouted, "Get out of here! We're going to burn this damned building down." Even at that, some patrons lingered, dazed. "All seemed to be groping for a way to lend a helping hand," remembered Helen Truman, "but no one had any definite idea as to the actual situation." Finally, as the last ones left, Buck locked the theatre doors and scurried home, forgetting his overcoat. (When he returned for it months later, he found it ruined by rats.)[2]

The box office staff and backstage crew, too, stayed rooted where they were. Gifford ordered Carland to stand by the alley door to prevent anyone from leaving that way. Maddox inexplicably—perhaps to "get out in front of" the night's events—bolted for the stage door and forced his way through the crowd, dashing diagonally across Tenth Street to police headquarters, arriving simultaneously with saloonkeeper James Ferguson, who had been in the audience. Bursting through the doorway, they were the first to gasp out a report and were aggressively questioned by Superintendent A. C. Richards.

A few minutes later, Hawk was brought in to the station house. He too had made a run for the stage door but was seized by soldiers, who arrested him. Hawk tentatively identified Booth as the shooter and was placed under $1,000 bond to reappear as a witness when the assassin was apprehended. Undertaker Dr. Charles Brown stepped forward to post bail for Hawk, who spent the next two hours, like countless Washingtonians, wandering the streets in a daze. For the past two weeks, he and Booth had been almost inseparable. He worried, too, about implicating the Evanses and knew he could not return to their house. Well after midnight, he reported to Dr. Brown's house to try without success to sleep.

Ferguson, Maddox, and Hawk were luckier than those who followed them to police headquarters. For the next few hours, the mob attacked anyone brought in, even witnesses to be questioned, and police had to protect them from being killed. As the tumult neared a combustion point, a police detective faced down the crowd, assuring them that the assassins would be found and that the persons being brought in now were important witnesses, not suspects. They must be allowed to provide whatever information they had!

Among the crowd in the street, mouth agape, stood little Joseph Hazelton, watching Lincoln's son Robert and various cabinet members rush into the Petersen house and countless uniformed messengers dart out from it. Suddenly, he wheeled and tore for home to cry himself to sleep. Yet with a child's curiosity he would return in the early morning hours to the same spot.

★ ★ ★

Backstage, an exhausted Laura Keene collapsed in her dressing room, steered there from the lobby by her husband. He was stunned to see her jewelry, some containing diamonds, spread out on her makeup table. Gathering the items up, he upbraided her for her carelessness. Nodding numbly, she washed the blood from her face and hands and threw a cape over her bloodstained Act Three costume, a pale gray moiré silk dress, and drew her bonnet close around her face. Somehow, they slipped out of the theatre by the alley door and made their way east on F Street to their room at the Metropolitan Hotel. No one hindered or detained them.

One floor above them John Mathews stood frozen in the dressing room, his mind racing, terrified in the certainty that he had been observed in Booth's company in recent weeks. That very afternoon he had accepted a letter from Booth in broad daylight on Pennsylvania Avenue! Worse, he might be linked to the aborted abduction of the president through the trunk he had transported to Baltimore. It hit Mathews, too, that only moments ago he had failed to silence Hawk in his backstage identification of Booth.

Donning his recently discarded street clothes, he returned to the stage in time to hear of a rumor that a mob had formed over at Willard's Hotel to come and torch the theatre. He swore later that, "but for the presence of Mr. Lincoln across the street, the house would have been burned." Enlisting one of the frightened "basket boys" to carry his costumes, he miraculously managed to slip out into the street with the last of the departing audience. With affected nonchalance he hurried to his L Street lodging, where he dismissed the boy, locked the door, and withdrew from his inner coat pocket the letter from Booth, unsealing it with dread.[3]

The contents of the three-page letter chilled him. A defiant justification for assassination, it made abundantly clear that Booth's previous plans for abduction had become untenable: "The moment has now arrived when I must change my plans." Expecting public acclaim for his deed, Booth couched his act in heroic terms, comparing himself to Shakespeare's Brutus, rescuing "a country that groaned beneath this tyranny." Reading it through twice, Mathews recognized its treasonous implications and tore the pages into tiny pieces, burning them in his fireplace grate. Years later, when the letter's existence became known, he would claim that it simply fell out of his pocket as he undressed, having "almost forgotten it in my excitement," but it certainly would have been burning a hole in his pocket all the way back to his room.[4]

★ ★ ★

Callboy Will Ferguson claimed for years to have likewise slipped out of the theatre unnoticed, to dash across the street and meet up with the Petersen's son, a boyhood chum. They then snuck into the Petersen home through the tailor shop in the basement, he said, emerging at the top of the servants' stairs to peer into the bedroom where Lincoln lay dying. He recognized the room, he insisted, as the one Mathews had rented previously, to which he had carried written-out parts for the actor to study. But no one ever mentioned seeing the boys there that night, and decades later Ferguson admitted, "That night I got myself home as quickly as possible and remained there for two days."[5]

From that room at Petersen's just before midnight, Army Major-General C. C. Augur, Commandant of the Department of Washington, emerged onto the front stoop to ask if there was anyone in the crowd who could write shorthand. Someone called down from a neighboring balcony that Corporal James Tanner, who lived above, could. Tanner, a Union veteran who had lost both legs at Second Bull Run, made his way with help down and into the Petersen house. There, in a small parlor across the hall from the room where the president lay dying, he would sit for seven hours recording interview notes across from Edwin Stanton and a hastily assembled court of inquiry consisting of District of Columbia Chief Justice David Cartter, Justice Abram B. Olin, and attorney Britten Hill. Tanner tried his best to block out the shrieks and moans of the distraught Mary Lincoln penetrating the closed doors to the front parlor.

★ ★ ★

At one o'clock in the morning, the actors were finally allowed to leave the theatre. No one was permitted to carry out any personal items, however, including their own costumes or properties. Everyone's wardrobe trunk was impounded, as were the orchestra's instruments, all scenery, all scripts, and all paperwork in the manager's office and box office. They were told, on Stanton's orders, that under no circumstances were they to leave the city, and that all of their mail would be delivered until further notice to the War Department, where they could call for it after it had been opened and read. They were to report daily to the Metropolitan Police.

Tentatively, they began to disperse. Jeannie and Maggie Gourlay, inching past the sentries through the darkened house with their father Tom and conductor Withers, were met at the front door by their anxious brothers. The four men formed a cordon around the young women, and the group cautiously made their way downhill to the Gourlay home on C Street, keeping close to the shadows. It was not until they were safely in the front parlor with the door locked that they discovered that the cuts on Withers's coat went through his shirt as well. Fortunately, these had not punctured his skin (despite his increasingly vivid assertions in later years that his arm and neck had been deeply slashed).

Supernumerary Charles Byrne wasted no time. He left immediately with the rest of the cast, defying the order to stay in Washington and returning to Baltimore. Despite an ambition since earliest childhood to become an actor, and having acquired three years' experience at it, he never set foot on a stage again. "I took one look and then fled," he said. "All of us did. We didn't want to be implicated in the terrible affair. From that night I never wanted to see a stage or act a part again."[6]

Harry Ford rushed backstage to check on the terrified actors as they left. The younger ones, such as May Hart and Helen Truman, were near hysteria, so he tried his best to calm them, personally escorting them out of the theatre. In the excitement he forgot to give them their end-of-week pay envelopes that were already in his pockets. Amid the frenzy of arrests in the ensuing weeks, it would be two years before Hart got her twenty dollars.

Those arrests began immediately. Superintendent Richards sought the apprehension of anyone who may have associated with Booth. Something about Edwin Brink, leaving the theatre with his child-bride Kittie, attracted the attention of a lieutenant, or someone had fingered him in advance for having been seen with Booth earlier that evening. He was arrested on the spot, the second actor (after Hawk) to be taken, and would be held for over a month. Richards's reach extended to Baltimore as well. He telegraphed that city's provost marshal early Friday morning, while witnesses were still giving statements to Tanner at the Petersen house, to round up two of Ford's actors who had the night off, Charles Bishop and Alice Grey. (They were not found; both were likely in New York.)[7]

The stage crew elected to remain in the theatre, except for the already-absent Spangler and for Gifford, who imperiously turned over his keys to the police and headed up the alley toward F Street. Carland retreated to the dressing room, where he and Maddox, back from police headquarters, were startled to find Kate Evans, her makeup removed, cowering among racks of costumes. Fearful that she would be questioned by detectives milling about the stage, she had run upstairs to hide. She had heard enough to know they were specifically looking for her husband, for Spangler, and for Peanut John. The men escorted her downstairs to the nearly empty theatre, but they ran into soldiers who insisted she come with them; they intended to search her house. Phillips stepped between them and insisted on accompanying Kate there.

When they reached the house, Johnny Evans was nowhere to be found. Kate considered that fortunate; someone had doubtless seen him with Booth that afternoon, putting him in danger. The soldiers swarmed through the house "from garret to cellar, upon the remote possibility that Booth was concealed somewhere under the roof. Walls were sounded, the bedding pierced through and through with swords and bayonets, the trunks and wardrobes broken open and searched, and every possible place of concealment pried into." Twice more that night they would return and plunge anew into ransacking the house, giving particular attention to the room Hawk and Dyott had shared. Within days Johnny would be found and taken in for questioning about his recent socializing with Booth, but was only held overnight.[8]

Having seen the Gourlays safely home, Withers determined to do his proper duty. Fighting his way through the mob in front of police headquarters, he provided a sworn statement to police justice Nehemiah Miller, which was both an identification of Booth and a complaint about the slashing, but contributed little new or useful information. Yes, he knew Booth and had seen and conversed with him frequently (omitting their drink together only hours ago); he was familiar with Booth's appearance and voice, he said, and thus could readily identify him. He spoke not a word about events that later became centerpieces of his version of the tragedy: that he had caught Spangler trying to turn off the gas lights and plunge the theatre into darkness but had valiantly fought the stage-hand off and prevented this from happening. Satisfied now that he had materially helped the investigation, he strode up Tenth Street toward home.[9]

★ ★ ★

Sometime after 2:00 a.m., four soldiers roused Hawk from his troubled sleep at Dr. Brown's and marched him in the slow rain to the Petersen house to provide testimony. He was one of the first to do so, but waffled in his identification: "To the best of my belief, it was Mr. John Wilkes Booth, but I will not be positive. I only had one glance at him." Then he grew more certain: "I do not have any doubt that it was <u>Booth</u> [underlined in Tanner's transcript]." He admitted knowing Booth, but only casually, never having socialized with him (despite having taken that quick drink with him around noon). Tanner later stated that Laura Keene was there as well, and that both Hawk and Keene were certain that the attacker was Booth, but no notes or other account has ever surfaced to corroborate this.[10]

Shortly after Hawk, Phillips was brought by soldiers from the Evanses to be interviewed by Stanton and Cartter. He had no trouble reporting that he heard Booth "repeatedly speak in favor of the South [and] regret the announcement of any Union victory," relating the incident on Monday in which Booth sought to "drive away the blues." Phillips freely acknowledged being "a very dear friend of the Booths almost from infancy" and confirmed Hawk's identification of Booth.[11]

Throughout these early morning hours, the sound of galloping soldiers and messengers jangled through the Washington streets, where a confused, frantic Ned Spangler wandered in the rain as Hawk had, afraid to return to either place where he normally slept—the theatre or Mrs. Scott's—yet having no idea where else to go. In the middle of the night, the Gourlays answered a knock at their door to find him huddled there, incongruously cradling a small puppy. Jeannie felt a rush of sympathy for him, regarding the child-like carpenter as "a kind-hearted, jovial ... good-natured sort of fellow without much sense." But her father turned Spangler away. Their home would not be open to suspicion or search. Spangler eventually found refuge for what remained of the night at the Evanses, despite the destruction wrought by the soldiers' search.[12]

★ ★ ★

Backstage at Ford's, Rittersbach had gone to sleep in the manager's office across from the greenroom. He was awakened in the early morning hours by Carland, who demanded to know Spangler's whereabouts. Rittersbach's disoriented first thought was that Carland was Booth, but upon collecting his senses, he told the costumer he had not seen Spangler since the night before; he had no idea where he was now. He told Carland he had recognized Booth running toward the alley door—despite his having earlier in the day asked Spangler who Booth was—but that Spangler had slapped him in the mouth and said "You don't know who it is; it may be Mr. Booth, or it may be somebody else." Carland went back out in search of Spangler, fearful what information the slow-witted stagehand might spill if caught, and whom he might unwittingly implicate.[13]

Shortly before dawn, it began to rain heavily. Stage manager Wright had remained in the theater, lit only by a garish watchman's lamp, the entire night with his wife and that of Dr. Taft (who had climbed up into the president's box and then accompanied Lincoln's unconscious form across the street). Now, at first light, just before 5:30, the Wrights yearned to go home to their room in Herndon House a block away on Ninth Street. With Mrs. Taft, who lived across from them, they slipped into the alley using the door through which Booth had escaped, following the same route he had taken up F Street, their teeth chattering from the cold and from understandable unease. "Scared about half out of our senses, for fear Booth might be laying in wait for us," Mrs. Wright forced a joke that her husband would be safe with two women to protect him.[14]

★ ★ ★

Harry Hawk, fearing for his safety in a city he felt closing in around him as he left Petersen's, decided not to return to Dr. Brown's. Instead he would break his bond and return home to Philadelphia. He headed for the railway station on New Jersey Avenue to catch the 6:00 a.m. train to Baltimore, where he could switch to the Philadelphia line. But when he got to the station, he found that all trains had been halted. Meandering in the rain up and down Pennsylvania Avenue, he heard bells tolling the death of the president. At 7:22 a.m., Abraham Lincoln had breathed his last.

As word flew through the city of the awful finality of Booth's mad act, more bells rang out, flags were lowered to half-mast, and lines formed in front of stores to purchase black crepe. Within hours none was left, some families reduced to tearing up old dark clothing to display their mourning. Nearly every home and place of business, conspicuously including Ford's Theatre at Harry's direction, was quickly draped. Soldiers warned the owners of any places lacking displays of mourning that they might be attacked for their perceived antipathy toward the martyred president.

Cavalry patrols blocked Tenth Street at both E and F, preventing anyone not authorized from nearing the theatre or the Petersen house. Yet at those intersections, thick clumps of people still stood rooted in the rain, staring dumbly at the two buildings. "Nature seemed to sympathize in the general lamentation, and tears of rain fell from the moist and somber sky," observed correspondent Noah Brooks. "The wind sighed mournfully through the streets crowded with sad-faced people, and broad folds of funeral drapery flapped heavily in the wind over the decorations of the day before."[15]

At the F Street intersection, Brooks met "a tragical procession. It was headed by a group of army officers walking bareheaded, and behind them, carried tenderly by a company of soldiers, was the bier of the dead President, covered with the flag of the Union.... As the little cortège passed down the street to the White House, every head was uncovered, and the profound silence which prevailed was broken only by sobs and by the sound of the measured tread of those who bore the martyred President back to the home which he had so lately quitted full of life, hope and cheer."[16]

★ ★ ★

At the Metropolitan Hotel, Keene and Lutz had spent a sleepless night discussing the effect this terrible deed would have on the nation and on her career. Their next engagement was at Wood's Theatre in Cincinnati, and neither her reputation nor her budget would tolerate its loss. Hearing bells early that morning, Lutz stepped outside to learn that the president had expired, just as Keene's daughters, Emma and Clara, rushed in from their residence hall at the Ladies' Academy of the Visitation Convent in Georgetown. Seeing them, Laura broke down. Emma remembered the scene for the rest of her life: "As I extended my arms to embrace her, she shook all over like a leaf. I tried to give her courage by saying 'Where is your old-time courage?' but the frightful calamity of the night before was too much, and it seemed as if grief was breaking her heart."[17]

★ ★ ★

At Ford's Theatre Gifford returned early that morning to inspect its condition, knowing well the custom of the day of relic collectors, some of whom had already slipped past the cavalry guard to whittle off pieces of the front stoop of the Petersen house. Despite the soldiers inside the theatre, or perhaps including some of them, similar vultures managed to extract about a yard square section of the green baize carpeting marking the spot where Booth's feet had struck the stage, and carved away sizable chunks from the bench out back where Peanut John had lain holding the reins of Booth's mare. Gifford asserted his authority as far as he could to prevent damage to the interior of Ford's, but that clearly did not extend to the provost guard already encamped in the theatre's boxes and waiting parlor, their muddy footprints evident throughout, their cooking smells hanging in the air.

James Lamb, unfazed by the events of the previous evening and knowing he had a job to do, reappeared around 9:00 to resume work on his *Midsummer Night's Dream* backdrops. Barely had he arrived when Rittersbach cornered him to relate the same tale of Spangler's actions the night before that he had imparted to Carland. Rittersbach appeared intent on making sure everyone knew what he had experienced, but was too new to Ford's to perceive how each would receive the information. Uttering no reply, Lamb turned back to his work, and Rittersbach headed to Mrs. Scott's for breakfast.

There he encountered Spangler, who had naïvely returned from the Evanses. Within minutes, two Metropolitan policemen were at the door to take both men in for questioning. The officers were also looking for Peanut John and soon found the boy wandering in Tenth Street. He had been trying to report to police headquarters as told, but was frightened of the crowd that still seemed intent on harming anyone who came in or out of the station house, chanting at each, "Hang him! Hang him!" Officers escorted the terrified boy inside.[18]

Rittersbach was released within minutes, but Peanut and Spangler were held for nearly four hours, compelled to provide sworn statements to Justice Olin. Peanut described the length of time he had known Booth (two months), his duties around the theatre, and his Friday afternoon and evening encounters with Booth and his horse, signing his statement with an "X." Spangler's account covered the same territory, but he acknowledged knowing Booth for nearly twelve years. So far, this was only preliminary fact-gathering, they were told, and neither was considered a suspect, but Olin reminded Spangler, "We know where to find you when we want you." Released, the frightened stagehand bolted back to Ford's.[19]

★ ★ ★

Harry Ford had retreated Friday night to the brothers' quarters above the Star Saloon, but Dick had wandered the streets for hours as Harry Hawk had. Both brothers knew they had to get word to John in Richmond. If they did send word, it never reached him. The only extant telegram from them that night was inexplicably sent to Booth's Pennsylvania oil investment partner, reporting the assassination.[20]

And so John Ford remained unaware of the tragic events unfolding a hundred miles to the north that would forever tarnish his name. His overnight trip to City Point had been pleasant, with part of it spent chatting with Colonel John W. Forney, publisher of the *Washington Chronicle* and secretary of the United States Senate. Early Friday morning he had taken the passenger steamer *Josephine* to Richmond, disembarking at the charred Rockett's Landing. His timing was fortunate, since immediately after the assassination all civilian traffic to Richmond was halted.[21]

Arriving in the devastated Confederate capital, he was prepared for the worst; a friend there had written him earlier in the week, describing the city as "a perfect Hell." Engaging a hack, he rode three miles along the James River, up through Shockoe Bottom, seeing only ashes and ruins for blocks. At Nineteenth Street he passed the infamous Castle Thunder, his uncle's former tobacco factory where he had worked as a boy, confiscated by the Confederate government but now filled with rebel prisoners of war. As he rode up Shockoe Hill, wreckage obstructed the street everywhere, and the brick shells of homes and businesses seemed about to topple at any moment.[22]

Two blocks past the capitol, on the southwest corner of Seventh and Broad Streets, he arrived at his old Richmond Theatre, which was largely intact. Rebuilt after burning in 1861, it had been damaged again last month by a fire that had inflicted thousands of dollars of damage but was contained. Within days of the Union occupation, despite the city's destitution and famine, the theatre's opportunistic manager, Richard D'Orsey Ogden, had reopened for business, hoping to attract entertainment-starved Union soldiers; the previous Monday he had staged a "Grand Entertainment" performance of *Macbeth*. (In October Ogden had attempted to flee to Fredericksburg by hiding in a ladies' train car to escape being drafted into the Confederate Army. Within days he had been caught and imprisoned—ironically, Ford must have thought—in Castle Thunder.)

Finding Ogden inside the theatre, Ford bargained for a few scenic backdrops that had been painted by his Holliday Street artist, Charles Getz, and some costumes that had been smuggled from Europe through the Union blockade during the war. Remarkably, he was able to arrange for their shipment by steamer to Baltimore.[23]

On Saturday, as Robert E. Lee returned in a driving rain to Richmond and his Franklin Street home and invalid wife, Ford tried unsuccessfully to hire transportation for the seven miles to Hanover County to comfort his wife's parents. Instead, he sent them a brief note updating them on Edith's health and the activities of their six children. No news of the assassination would reach him until Sunday afternoon—his thirty-sixth birthday—when he boarded a train to City Point to return to Baltimore.

Occupying Union forces had learned of the assassination, but had tried to keep the news from citizens until Richmond was fully secured. By Sunday, though, incoming steamboat passengers had brought word, which quickly spread. The first version that reached Ford on the train was that it was *Edwin* Booth who had killed the president. "I said it was impossible," he later recalled, "as I knew he was not in Washington." Then, it dawned on him: "I recollected Wilkes Booth was in Washington; that he was boyish and foolish enough for it. He had pluck." Now that Ford thought about it, he *had* found it odd about a week ago that Booth was still in Washington, since the actor had told him much earlier that he intended to quit the stage for the oil business.[24]

★ ★ ★

In Washington on Saturday morning, John Mathews burst into a gloomy saloon near the theatre looking for Booth. Among the patrons there, hunched over drinks, was Hawk, chaperoned by Brown, who had tracked him down and canceled his bond. (Brown, whose firm's embalming services would soon be needed for the slain president, would within the hour take Hawk to the police, who held him in D.C. jail for two days until releasing him on two new bonds posted by others.) Buttonholing Hawk, Mathews drew an angry reaction from the crowded bar's patrons, who rose en masse and threatened to hang him if he did not explain who he was and what he wanted with Booth. Mathews, terrified, rushed back into the street, where a rope was produced and only the intervention of nearby soldiers saved his life.

Clearly, it was not a good time to utter the name Booth or voice any sentiments in support of his deed. Mathews quickly adopted a motto: from that day forward, he decided, "those who were the wisest knew the least." Others, in Washington and elsewhere, learned that lesson the hard way. In the capital alone, "there were many instances of mob rule prevailing," reported a wounded veteran who ventured from his hospital bed that morning for a walk.[25]

No one was exempt. The offices and presses of a Democratic newspaper in Westminster, Maryland, were destroyed for having printed, just before the murder, an article "vituperative of Mr. Lincoln." A similar retribution befell a Southern-leaning newspaper in San Francisco, its editor barely escaping being lynched. An Ohio architect who expressed his glee was kicked down a flight of stairs by a crowd who then tried to kill him, until he was rescued by police. A Maine man who said it was the best news he had heard in four years was tarred and feathered and dragged through town with an American flag in his hands. Several men in other cities were killed for similar expressions. A young seaman who blurted, "I'm damned glad Lincoln is dead" was sentenced to two years in the brig, and another received ten years for adding, "I wish he had been killed long ago." Even one of the Veterans Reserve Corps guarding Ford's Theatre toasted the deed, saying, "Here's to Abe Lincoln, may he go to hell and be found damned; may the assassin who murdered him sit on the right hand of God forever"; he was sentenced to three years in prison.[26]

The entire theatrical profession suffered, not just from revenue lost during the mourning period, but from loss of reputation for the murder having been committed by one of their own. "Everything has been deranged by the atrocious crime," rued the *Clipper*, "engagements broken, time curtailed, entertainments postponed, speculations ruined, hopes deferred, and aspirations nipped in the bud." In Columbus, Ohio, police averted an outbreak of mob violence against a theatre where Clara Morris was performing. Its manager, John Ellsler (who had known Booth since childhood), urged his company to stay away from any public gatherings. Morris's own feelings were torn: "That the homely, tender-hearted 'Father Abraham,' rare combination of courage, justice and humanity, died at an actor's hand will be a grief, a horror and a shame to the profession forever ... Poor, guilty, unhappy John Booth! We venture to pray for His mercy upon [his] guilty soul."[27]

★ ★ ★

All day Saturday the heavy rain continued. Sometime mid-afternoon word reached Police Superintendent Richards that despite the weather an attack on Ford's Theatre was planned for that evening by an unnamed number of outraged citizens. Deciding that his force was "entirely inadequate to protect the building and property in the neighborhood," Richards urgently requested a military guard from Provost Marshal Timothy Ingraham, who readily granted it. By 7:00 seventy men of the 9th Regiment, V.R.C. under the command of Captain William McKelvey were in position on Tenth Street and throughout the theatre, setting up makeshift headquarters in the greenroom. Either their presence was effective or the threat was spurious to start with, for no assault on the theatre materialized.[28]

But that night an assault of a different kind would begin on the employees of Ford's Theatre.

CHAPTER NINE

"ONE OF THE LAST PLACES TO WHICH A GOOD MAN SHOULD GO"

SATURDAY EVENING THE HUNT for conspirators commenced in earnest, spearheaded by National Detective Police head Lafayette C. Baker. A man of feral intensity whose ego was matched only by his ambition, Baker had been recalled from New York by Secretary Stanton, to whom he now directly reported as a "War Department Special Agent" with the self-appointed rank of colonel. He immediately set out to arrest and interrogate anyone who may have been involved, even peripherally, in the assassination.

Some of his first steps were as misguided as they were zealous. Neophyte actress May Hart, although ordered like the others to remain in Washington, had returned to her hotel room in Baltimore. She had done so out of fear: "everybody who even knew Booth was suspected and to admit being a member of the cast at that performance was to court arrest."[1]

And arrested she was, that night, on Baker's orders, based solely on the word of one Mary Jane Anderson, who lived behind the theatre. On Friday, Anderson had witnessed an actress wearing an outfit like Hart's rehearsing in the alley with the mustachioed Ned Emerson, whom she misidentified as Booth—a logical misunderstanding given their similarity. The next morning she reported this to Baker, and he converted her description into an identification of Hart, who had compounded her appearance of guilt by fleeing to Baltimore, and issued the order for her arrest.[2]

Sitting on the veranda of her hotel late that night, Hart was approached by a boyish underling of Baker's who addressed her by name. She was offended by his impudence: he seemed to think that just "because I was an actress I could be addressed by strangers with impunity." When he identified himself as a detective, she ran to her room and locked herself in. But, urged by a friend in the hotel to cooperate and reassured by the detective that he only needed to get a deposition from her, she accompanied him to the street, whereupon he and his men seized her and conveyed her directly to the train station and thence to Washington, to Old Capitol Prison.[3]

Hart was understandably terrified: "I saw the gallows looming up ahead of me." Asked if she knew Booth, she denied any acquaintance with him. She had never spoken a word to him, she insisted; she had only seen him for the first time on Thursday, backstage. What she did not acknowledge to the detectives, but had admitted earlier to Helen Truman, was that she had been "greatly impressed with his handsome face and polished manner. He was the most magnetic actor and man I had ever seen." When Truman had told Hart who he was and asked if she wanted to be introduced, Hart had primly refused, but "really wished to meet him." Now, she was infinitely glad she had not. Asked about being out in the alley behind the theatre with "Booth," she insisted it was Emerson with whom she had been rehearsing. She was nevertheless held overnight in a solitary prison cell with no explanation or charges.[4]

On Sunday morning, Baker accosted Emerson in front of the theatre, asking where he had been at 10:00 Friday morning. When he replied that he had been rehearsing with Hart, Baker took him to Old Capitol, where Emerson explained the situation, and she was released. However, she was told, this time it was imperative that she stay in Washington and remain available to provide a statement. She and Emerson were to report to police headquarters daily.

Throughout that singular Easter weekend, the rest of the actors of Ford's Theatre withdrew from public view as much as possible, likely sunk in despair or pacing in confusion. In later testimony and interviews, they remained remarkably silent about their whereabouts and activities. One place they justifiably avoided was the theatre itself.

The stagehands, while undoubtedly as fearful as the actors, put on a brave front and kept about their business. None of them seemed to be aware of the intense investigation ramping up around them. By Saturday evening Louis Carland had brought Spangler back to Ford's to sleep. They too had heard the rumors that the theatre would be burned. Gifford asked them, along with Maddox, to remain with him in the theatre all night and throughout the day on Sunday; they would all be needed if a fire had to be extinguished.

Spangler was scared to sleep alone. He slept heavily, he explained (omitting the contributing factor of alcohol) and might not awaken in time if fire broke out. That could really happen, he insisted, since the street was filled with soldiers under tremendous stress. Carland took him to the carpentry room on the third floor, where they could escape down a set of outside stairs in case of fire. Rittersbach, also back in the theatre, his eyes and ears open, asserted his willingness to stay as well. At one o'clock in the morning, Captain McKelvey posted a guard outside each room where the stagehands slept, placing them under virtual house arrest. His soldiers remained on duty until 9:00 Sunday morning, when they returned the theatre keys to Gifford and left, judging that any danger had passed.[5]

★ ★ ★

There is no evidence that anyone connected with Ford's Theatre ventured out in public to attend church that clear, chilly Easter Sunday except for Carland, whose prayers were likely fervent. If they had, they would have heard their profession roundly denounced. "It will always be a matter of deep regret to thousands that our lamented President fell in the theatre," intoned the Reverend Phineas D. Gurley, Lincoln's own pastor. He was merely echoing a long-held belief that one's soul was endangered if death came while one was inside such a debauched place: "The theatre is one of the last places to which a good man should go and among the very last in which his friends would wish him to die." "Would that Mr. Lincoln had fallen elsewhere than at the very gates of Hell," cried another man of God. Yet another asked any young man who was "justly proud of your sister, would you not rather follow her to the grave tonight, than to know that tomorrow she shall stand at the altar and pledge her faith, and trust her precious future to an actor?"[6]

That afternoon, Carland led the perpetually frightened Spangler to the Gourlay home for a meager Easter dinner that doubtless no one felt like eating. There, Carland shared with Withers Rittersbach's story about Spangler slapping him, asking the conductor if he had overheard anything of the sort. Withers had not, nor had Jeannie Gourlay, despite their close proximity to both stagehands Friday night. No sooner had the meal concluded than a man came to the door to warn Spangler that he was about to be arrested as a suspect. Scared and penniless, the stagehand said he needed to find Gifford to ask for money and advice. Carland advised him instead to go immediately to the police and not wait around

to be dragged out of bed some night. But Spangler fled to Ford's, and Carland went alone to police headquarters to ask if any such warrant existed. He was told it did not.

On his way back to the theatre, Carland encountered still another detective, who curiously announced that he had orders for his and Spangler's arrest, but told him, "go home and sleep tonight." An exasperated Carland pulled Spangler from Ford's, where he had failed to find Gifford, and hauled him back to headquarters. There, Carland demanded to know: yes or no: Were they wanted? The officer on duty reiterated "no," so the two returned to the theatre for the night. This runaround typified the agonizing uncertainty under which everyone connected with Ford's lived each day for weeks, and which ultimately yielded a crueler fate for Spangler.[7]

★ ★ ★

By late Sunday afternoon, Laura Keene had determined it was imperative that she continue her tour, regardless of any travel restrictions placed on the actors. She felt she had a right to earn a living, after all, and had certainly demonstrated her devotion to the slain president on Friday night when she had cradled his head in her lap. Claiming later that she applied to military authorities in Washington for a pass to leave the city only to be told it was not necessary, she and Lutz gathered John Dyott and the newly released Harry Hawk and headed for the nearby B&O railroad station on Louisiana (now Indiana) Avenue. Lutz arranged for their wardrobe trunks to be carried over from the Metropolitan Hotel and the Evanses, but left behind his wife's little piano, still in the theatre. Inexplicably, Lutz remained in the capital; Keene's dresser, Billy Otis, may have also, for his whereabouts that weekend remain unknown.[8]

Keene, Dyott, and Hawk boarded the 5:45, one of the first trains allowed to leave the city, transferring in Baltimore to the Northern Central line to Harrisburg (the same route the president's funeral train would

take on Friday), arriving around 1:30 a.m. on Monday. Upon disembarking in Harrisburg they were arrested by Pennsylvania Cavalry Lieutenant
Charles Gresh, who notified Colonel Louis H. Pelouze in the adjutant
general's office in Washington. Pelouze asked Baker and Provost Marshal
Augur whether Keene and her party had received permission from either
of them to leave the city. The answer, of course, was negative. So for two
days the actors were held under military guard in Harrisburg's City Hotel.

A flurry of telegrams commenced. Keene and Hawk fired off separate
messages to Lutz informing him of their arrest, with Hawk adding,
"Hurry it up." Lutz set to work contacting everyone he could in the
already overworked provost marshal's office. Keene telegraphed Augur,
lamenting her detention "for want of passes which we were told yesterday
were not needed. Please expedite an answer." Lutz sought the help of
Pelouze and others at the War Department. In the meantime, Hawk
telegraphed the manager of Wood's Theatre in Cincinnati, the site of their
next engagement, to postpone their opening there.[9]

Finally, after further legwork by Lutz, the actors were released early
Wednesday afternoon and were allowed—this time with a pass—to
continue on to Cincinnati. Opening there on Thursday, April 20 (after
theatres were allowed to reopen) they performed *She Stoops to Conquer*
and *Workmen of Cincinnati* to overflowing houses and resounding ova-
tions. But public sensibilities and her own lack of a clean Act Three dress
led Keene to drop *Our American Cousin* from their repertoire—for now.

Dyott, though, had had enough. The trauma of the assassination, the
furtive travel and Harrisburg arrest, the ordering about by Keene—whose
London pedigree fell short of his own—and a pressing need to get on
with his career in New York, brought him to a boiling point. Without a
word he abruptly left Keene for good just before the opening curtain on
Saturday the twenty-second (much as she had done to Wallack twelve
years before). To Keene, this was an unforgiveable breach of professional
ethics. She lashed out at him in an angry letter, reminding him of her

Ford's Theatre: exterior (1865)
Courtesy of the Library of Congress

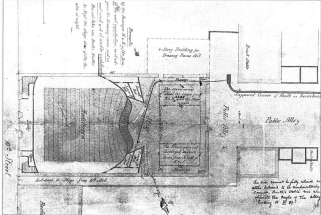

Floor plan of Ford's
Theatre created by
John T. Ford, 1865
*Courtesy of the
Library of Congress*

Left: Abraham Lincoln
Courtesy of the Library of Congress

Right: John Wilkes Booth
Courtesy of the Library of Congress

Decorated presidential box, Ford's Theatre, April 14, 1865
Courtesy of the Library of Congress

Stage setting, Act III, scene ii, *Our American Cousin*
Courtesy National Archives and Records Administration

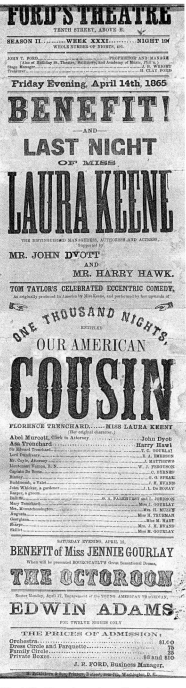

Playbill, *Our American Cousin*,
April 14, 1865
Courtesy Harvard Theatre Collection

Harry Clay Ford
Courtesy National Park Service,
Ford's Theatre National Historic Site

John T. Ford
Courtesy Harvard Theatre Collection

James R. "Dick" Ford
Courtesy Harvard Theatre Collection

William S. "Billy" Withers Jr.
Courtesy Harvard Theatre Collection

John Burroughs Wright
Author's collection

Laura Keene
Courtesy Harvard Theatre Collection

John Dyott
Courtesy Harvard Theatre Collection

William Henry "Harry" Hawk
Courtesy Harvard Theatre Collection

Edwin "Ned" Emerson
Courtesy Emerson family

Henry B. Phillips
Courtesy Harvard Theatre Collection

William J. "Will" Ferguson
Courtesy Gratz Historical Society,
Gratz, PA

Jeannie Gourlay
Courtesy Georgetown University Library

Maggie Gourlay
Courtesy Harvard Theatre Collection

Thomas J. "Tom" Gourlay
Courtesy Harvard Theatre Collection

May Hart
Courtesy Harvard Theatre Collection

John Mathews
Courtesy Harvard Theatre Collection

Helen Muzzy
Courtesy Harvard Theatre Collection

George Parkhurst
Courtesy Harvard Theatre Collection

George Gaines Spear
Courtesy Harvard Theatre Collection

Helen Truman
Courtesy Harvard Theatre Collection

James Johnson Gifford
Courtesy National Park Service,
Ford's Theatre National Historic Site

James Lamb
Courtesy National Park Service,
Ford's Theatre National Historic Site

John E. "Buck" Buckingham
Courtesy Historical Society
of Washington, D.C.

John L. DeBonay
Courtesy Harvard Theatre Collection

Joseph J. Sessford
Courtesy Arthur Loux

Old Capitol Prison
Courtesy Georgetown University Library

Edman "Ned" Spangler
Courtesy of the Library of Congress

First cell at Fort Jefferson, Dry Tortugas
Author's collection

stated policy that every actor must keep her informed of his whereabouts at all times, as if he were a novice. The faithful Hawk stayed with her tour until the summer of 1866, but fearing (needlessly) that he bore a vague resemblance to Booth, he traveled under an assumed name "to avoid further unpleasantness."[10]

★ ★ ★

Easter Monday, April 17, dawned clear and cold in the capital; the temperature all day never left the forties. That morning John Selecman, Jimmie Maddox's young property assistant, decided to spill to saloon-keeper James Ferguson what he had overheard on Friday evening.

Previously, Selecman's loyalties had been divided. Brought up on a farm in Fairfax Station, Virginia, one of five children of a single mother—his father had died before John was a year old—he had come to Washington only last fall and secured employment at Ford's. There he had found a backstage ethos sympathetic to the Southern cause. He tried to stay neutral, but soon fell under the sway of Maddox, his immediate boss. Now, though, he made a crucial choice: to distance himself from Maddox and ally himself with Rittersbach.

Furtively approaching Ferguson behind the bar, Selecman indicated he had vital information to share about the assassination, making it clear he did not want word to get back to Gifford (no problem for Ferguson, who detested the openly secessionist carpenter). Ferguson took the boy to his living quarters and locked the door. "Jim, I want to tell you something," Selecman began. "I was standing in that alley that night when Mr. Booth rode up and called Ned Spangler the carpenter and said to him, 'Now Ned, you will give me all the assistance you can,' and Ned says, 'Yes, I will, you can depend on that.'" Ferguson was intrigued and promised to respect the young man's confidence.[11]

Over at police headquarters, Judge Olin spent half that day taking sworn statements. Doorkeeper Buck appeared before him that morning as requested, to relate Booth's comings and goings on Friday evening, having easily recognized him from his frequent visits to Ford's. Appearing shortly after Buck was Carland, who had clearly come to realize over the past few days how important it was to stay on the right side of the growing investigation.

Carland's statement was obsequiously detailed: he cited occasions of Booth's socializing with the Fords and with numerous stagehands. Yes, he admitted, he, too, had attended one such event, but "that is the only occasion I have been out in company with Booth." He described the responsibilities of everyone who worked at Ford's (including the cleaning ladies), the theatre's daily routine, and (most importantly) his own hour-by-hour whereabouts on Friday. (His penchant for detail included an ingratiating but irrelevant anecdote about seeing a lady on her stoop holding a baby, and telling her that Lincoln and Grant would be at the theatre that night, so she should attend.) And oh, yes, he now remembered: he *had* had a quick drink with Booth Friday afternoon, but had merely "passed the time of day, and did not converse extensively with him [for] more than a few seconds" before "some of our people took him by the arm and walked up the street with him." He was "fairly positive one of the men was Mathews." And at the moment of the shot? He avowed he had been out on Tenth Street with Gifford.[12]

Later that morning the serving of arrest warrants on theatre employees began in earnest. Harry Ford, Maddox, and Spangler were the first to be picked up, having generated the most suspicion by their repeated associations with Booth and their overheard secessionist sentiments. Harry was taken from his room next to the theatre at 11:00 in what would be his first of three arrests and releases, and Maddox a short time later. Both were conveyed to Old Capitol in heavily curtained army ambulances.

The scene of their incarceration was formidable. Old Capitol Prison, so named for its construction as the temporary seat of Congress after the British burned the United States Capitol in 1814, was a formerly handsome but now dingy three-story red brick rectangle that squatted squarely atop Capitol Hill at First and A Streets, Northeast, where the United States Supreme Court stands today. After 1819 its two large interior chambers—one on the first floor for the Senate (45' x 15') and a larger one on the second for the House of Representatives (75' x 45')—had been subdivided into rooms. It became in turn a boarding house, a school, and a fashionable hotel (where southern firebrand John C. Calhoun had died in 1850). But falling into disrepair, it had sat vacant until confiscated by the federal government in 1861 for use as a prison.

The disrepair had not been remedied; its moldy, whitewashed walls flaked profusely, its doors and stairs creaked eerily, and grime and graffiti covered nearly every surface. Vermin owned the place. Straw beds infested with spiders, mice, and bedbugs, threadbare cotton blankets and filthy, ragged pillows, along with a smattering of crude pine chairs and tables, were the rooms' only furnishings. Crumbling, unusable fireplaces had been supplanted with meager coal stoves set out on uneven, splintered floorboards. The constant clump of sentries' boots, clanking of weapons, and guttural, shouted orders reverberated through the corridors day and night. Permeating every corner of every floor was the stench from open latrines that surrounded a muddy, fenced-in exercise yard and troop barracks out back. Looming prominently within that yard was a heavy black wooden gallows whose use prisoners were periodically required to observe.

Disease spread quickly in the prison compound: during the four years of the war, close to 12 percent of the nearly 215,000 prisoners housed there perished. Visibility and ventilation in the cells were wretched, yet prisoners were ordered to keep away from all windows—most of which were haphazardly boarded up or filled with bars loosely inserted into soft wooden frames. An incarcerated friend of Booth's had been shot and killed by a sentry three years before for precisely that infraction. In retaliation, the most unruly inmates, twenty of Confederate cavalryman John Mosby's guerillas, threw bricks dislodged from their room's fireplace down onto the sentries. All told, Old Capitol was, as Provost Marshal William Doster observed, "too lenient a punishment for the guilty, and too harsh for the innocent."[13]

Its inmates were almost exclusively prisoners of state; among its current internees were three southern governors. Less savory offenders— Union deserters, Confederate prisoners of war, bounty jumpers, smugglers, blockade runners, muggers, kidnappers, counterfeiters, and negro contrabands—were housed across the yard in a five-floor wooden overflow prison known as Carroll Annex, at the corner of First Street and Maryland Avenue, where the Jefferson building of the Library of Congress now stands. It consisted of five sizable row houses, the center one of which ironically had served as home to Abraham Lincoln during his sole term in Congress (1847–49). Although these were two distinct complexes, separated by the one-hundred-foot-square yard, the entire compound was commonly referred to collectively as "Old Capitol."[14]

During the war its population had grown steadily from eighty to an average of well over three hundred. By now, it had swollen far beyond capacity. On the night of the assassination, more than eight hundred Confederate prisoners of war awaiting transportation south for exchange, including those marched past Booth and Mathews on Friday, were "housed" in crude tents and hastily constructed wooden barracks in the yard, above the latrine trenches. (Later that night only the resolute efforts of a reinforced guard regiment had prevented these prisoners from being killed en masse and the complex burned to the ground by a violent mob of two thousand bent on misguided revenge.)

Harry and Maddox were led in through the prison's slapdash wooden First Street portico by an armed corporal, and then through a long, broad, dim entry hall lined like the sidewalk outside with sentinels gripping bayoneted rifles. Beyond this awaited room No. 19, the large office of prison superintendent William P. Wood.

A compact, muscular veteran of the Mexican War with graying brown hair and beard and twinkling blue-gray eyes—soldiers and prisoners alike avowed he resembled Santa Claus—the Virginia-born Wood, forty-five, was devoted to the Union cause. In compensation for his efforts here, he would be named in July as the first Director of the United States Secret Service by his close friend Stanton. Wood conducted his own interrogations, lately in tandem with Baker, whom he held in low regard (asserting that Baker's detective associates were "a band of thieves ... of the vilest character"). The two men tended to play "good cop, bad cop," with Wood consistently advocating for better food and decent clothing for his inmates, while Baker glowered and threatened as he grilled each detainee. Wood, though, was simultaneously capable of candor and guile, solicitous concern and vicious reprisal, never to be fully trusted.[15]

Each new prisoner brought into his office was searched for concealed weapons (if the soldiers bringing him in had forgotten to check). Wood's clerk recorded the prisoner's name, status and reason for arrest (often simply "Committed by Secretary of War"). Harry Ford was no exception. His first questioning covered general information: his duties at the theatre, how tickets for the boxes were sold, which usher stood nearest the presidential box (James O'Bryon), and the extent of his relationship with Booth.

Harry admitted a two-year acquaintance, which had warmed to a friendship within the past eight months. During that time he had "often heard J. Wilkes Booth express himself as a secessionist." Yes, he had shared drinks with the actor "about ten or twelve times, but never had any confidential relations with him." He knew none of the other suspected accomplices, and insisted that he himself was "a loyal man, having never uttered a disloyal sentence at any time since or before the rebellion."[16]

On orders from Judge Advocate Colonel John A. Foster (who had been appointed on Saturday by Stanton to head the investigation along with Colonel Henry H. Wells and Colonel Henry Steel Olcott), Wood placed Harry in "close confinement" in a "solitary" room near the top of Carroll Annex. Orders for Maddox's arrest by Provost Marshal Ingraham had been even more specific: he was "to be placed in close confinement in irons and no one allowed to see or correspond with him under any circumstances whatever."[17]

Taking his cue from those orders, Wood took a harsher tone with Maddox. He led the no-longer-jovial property man through his entire day on Friday, making him identify everyone he had seen and repeat all he had heard. Wood's primary focus was the time between 3:00 and 5:00 when Maddox had helped Booth with the mare and then joined him for a drink. Maddox was fully forthcoming, but as he was being taken to his cell, he began to tremble, a trait that would become more pronounced over the next two weeks.

★ ★ ★

Late Sunday night, soldiers of the 24th Regiment, V.R.C., under the command of Captain George R. Bell had taken permanent possession of the theatre. From that point on, no one except soldiers was allowed inside without permission, nor would anyone else retain keys.

Monday afternoon around 3:00, Gifford and O'Bryon hosted a peculiar assemblage of visitors to Ford's: Judges Olin and Cartter, Clara Harris, and her father, New York Senator Ira Harris, along with the seemingly omnipresent saloonkeeper James Ferguson. None of the brothers Ford was present. O'Bryon, unaware that Harry had been arrested, telegraphed him in Baltimore: "It is absolutely necessary that yourself or Dick should be here in the theatre."[18]

The visitors headed directly for the presidential box. They spent considerable time closely examining it by candlelight, especially a small hole in its door and a mortised niche in the wall outside it, which Friday night had held one end of a sawed-off piece of pine music stand. Once wedged in place, it had prevented anyone entering behind Booth until Major Rathbone had removed it. The party also discovered that the screws of the latch on the double box's outer door were stripped loose. Questioned about these anomalies, Gifford insisted that the niche had not existed before Friday, and that he had never seen the piece of wood before. Furthermore, he said, the blood visible on both box doors had not been there before, and he had never noticed the loose screws. The group debated about the small hole: had the shot produced it or was it a peephole bored in advance?

Perhaps put off by his tone, Olin pulled Gifford aside to formally question him about rehearsal procedures, about who had been in the theatre when throughout the day on Friday, and about the scope of each person's backstage responsibilities, including his own. Oddly, Gifford professed ignorance about who had removed the box's partition, despite having heard Harry order Spangler and Rittersbach to do it. He stressed that for much of the afternoon and evening on Friday he had not been inside the theatre.

Also present Monday afternoon was a photographer from Mathew Brady's studio. Gifford was instructed to reset the scenery for *Our American Cousin* as it had stood Friday night, so the photographer could record a series of exposures. The presidential box was similarly returned to its Friday night appearance using replacement bunting, and photographed. Artist Alfred Waud, staff artist for *Harper's Weekly*, also arrived to sketch the scenery and the interior of the theatre. Soon Stanton himself appeared and decided that a more detailed examination of the stage and scenery, including its placement during a performance, was necessary. He ordered a reenactment of the play to take place next Saturday afternoon, during which measurements would be taken of all areas backstage, at various points during the performance.

Also scurrying around inside the theatre on Monday was Provost Marshal's detective Charles Rosch, making his own "careful examination of the premises." This investigation led him to become "fully convinced that some person or persons belonging to the theater were accomplices." This particularly meant Spangler, who according to Rosch "was on very intimate acquaintances with Booth." In fact, "they were seen together on the afternoon of the murder." Rosch never reported specifically who had imparted this information to him, or what factors led to this conclusion, but he went directly from the theatre to Olcott and Wells, who ordered the stagehand's arrest.[19]

Spangler had ventured out for supper that evening at Mrs. Scott's. Leaving, he found Rittersbach waiting in the doorway, suggesting they share a friendly walk. It lasted a half hour, the main topic of conversation being Rittersbach's desire to get some of the reward money being offered. Did Spangler know of any information they could use? Rittersbach said that he, too, had given a statement at police headquarters on Saturday (although no evidence exists that he did). Spangler, as trusting as the animals he befriended, seemed completely unaware that Rittersbach had already implicated him to others.

Back at their boardinghouse around sunset, the two men parted ways (for good, as it turned out), and Spangler went upstairs to rest, asking to be awakened if anyone asked for him. He slept for nearly two hours until a serving girl knocked to say that men were downstairs looking for him. Groggily descending, he encountered the provost marshal's detective William Eaton, who arrested him, shoved him into a hack, and took him to Carroll Annex. There, Spangler, too, was placed in solitary confinement, with the additional restriction of being placed in irons.

Close behind Eaton at Mrs. Scott's was detective Rosch, who with two colleagues searched Spangler's room, confiscating a carpetbag that Rittersbach later said was all that Spangler kept there. It contained a coil of coarse rope eighty-one feet long, some blank stationery, and a dirty shirt collar.

★ ★ ★

Even more than his brother Harry or Maddox or Gifford or Spangler, manager John Ford had quickly become a major focus of the investigation. At 6:00 Monday morning at City Point, he had boarded a government tug to Fortress Monroe, changing there to a Bay Line steamboat to Baltimore. Coincidentally, it was also transporting assassination conspirator and Baltimore actor Samuel Arnold, arrested the night before, north to be arraigned. Ford kept his distance, but learned from Arnold that Booth had not acted alone. Arnold insisted, though, that the plan had been only "to kidnap the President without any violence." No one besides Booth, himself, and five others were involved, none of whom were theatre employees. That came as a relief to Ford, who from that moment on never believed Spangler was involved in the assassination.[20]

General Grant, thinking Ford was still in Richmond, telegraphed Major General E. O. C. Ord, commander of the Army of the James River, to quietly arrest Ford there. When Ord informed him that Ford had left City Point that morning, Grant then directed that he be arrested as he disembarked in Baltimore and taken immediately to Washington. However, no one detained Ford that evening, allowing him to reach his home and wife.

Aware that his reputation, if not his safety, was threatened—and on some level aware that he had tacitly encouraged the free expression of secessionist thought at his theatres—Ford worked late into the night on a statement, widely published the following day, to clear his name. Expressing first "the highest respect and reverence for President Lincoln," he went on to explain why he had been in Richmond. He made it clear that Booth was not a member of his company and had not performed for him in over a year (which was technically correct, as the March 18 benefit had been for John McCullough, and Booth had not been under contract to Ford). As with any respected actor, Ford wrote, Booth had had free access to the theatre, a privilege he abused by committing such an "infamous crime, which no one less suspected, which no one would have done more to prevent, which no one more deeply deplores, than I."[21]

Ford defended himself against charges that he had shown sympathy for the South by engaging for his Holliday Street Theatre "a Rebel Band" who were, after all, "prisoners who had taken the oath of allegiance." They had, he argued, performed patriotic songs—nothing "which could be construed as expression of Southern sentiment or sympathy, except 'Dixie,' which our now lamented President has just proclaimed a 'captured tune.'" These same musicians, he said, had also performed at the War Department and at Grover's Theatre. Ford hoped that this statement "to loyal citizens ... can partially express (I pray they may never fully know) the painful embarrassment in which this foul crime has placed me."[22]

At 8:00 on Tuesday morning, soldiers arrived at Ford's front door to arrest him. Escorted respectfully to the office of Maryland Provost Marshal James McPhail and held there most of the day, he learned more about the assassination conspiracy, which he found "intensely interesting," realizing that "it explained Booth's purpose in Washington." Brought south on the 6:00 train, Ford was ensconced in Old Capitol, facing Superintendent Wood, by 10:00. Although told he was being charged with "disloyalty," no specific charges were ever brought against him.[23]

Questioning Ford, Wood took a solicitous tone; he had, after all, enjoyed several performances at Ford's Theatre and took the manager for a gentleman. The session was more of a conversation than an interrogation, and Wood's report to Stanton conveys no suspicion of complicity. Ford acknowledged knowing Booth for more than fifteen years, adding that the actor was the only Southern sympathizer in his family, yet one who always spoke "moderately and quietly on that subject." He had last performed for Ford about fifteen months ago.[24]

Echoing his public statement, Ford clarified for Wood that Booth had had free access to his theatres and his mail sent there, "a courtesy always extended to actors in good standing." Booth had more than once offered to perform without payment for others' benefits and was popular with fellow actors as well as the management. Ford explained why he had been in Richmond, showing his official pass. Hearing of the murder of the president, he said, he had returned home at once. Summarized Wood to Stanton: "He denies having any knowledge of anything from which he might infer that Booth contemplated the murder."[25]

Within the hour Ford was installed in Room 47, another small, solitary, barred, locked garret room in Carroll Annex, to which the heat and stench of the entire building arose. He immediately began making notes, which in his thirty-nine days of imprisonment would grow to many pages, documenting his own plight as well as that of other prisoners.

His first complaint was the absence of any furnishings except for a pallet of straw, a few threadbare blankets, "a slop bucket and a stone pitcher. When I wrote, I did so on the floor and when I wished to sit down the straw was the only accommodation." If he approached the cell's small dormer window, sentries below threatened to shoot him. By the end of the week, though, Wood would provide him with a crude stool, chair and table, and allow him to purchase a washbasin.[26]

Edith Ford soon came down from Baltimore and applied to Stanton for a pass to see her husband, but was curtly refused. Ford, accustomed to living comfortably among his family, channeled his frustration into his note-taking: "The horror of that [first] week is indescribable," he wrote. "I endured my confinement with all the philosophy I could bring to bear."[27]

★ ★ ★

At police headquarters, the indefatigable Judge Olin spent Tuesday morning taking more sworn statements and issuing more arrest warrants. One of his first visitors was saloonkeeper James Ferguson with young Selecman in tow. The boy had returned first thing in the morning claiming new information imparted to him by Rittersbach: while working together on the partition in the presidential box Friday afternoon, Spangler had growled, "I hope the damned ol' son of a bitch will be killed here tonight." "Or," Rittersbach had tossed off, "words to that effect." Although no one else corroborated Rittersbach's version of these words, Olin immediately ordered Spangler's arrest, unaware that he had already been picked up the night before.[28]

But Ferguson wasn't through—he had much more to relate. He began with the incident in his restaurant the day after Richmond fell when Carland and DeBonay had openly sympathized with the South and wished for the death of all Yankees. They needed to be checked out, he declared. And Gifford, too: the man "was quite intimate with Booth and considered to be disloyal in his sentiments." Furthermore, Ferguson had proof of this: he had been in the audience Friday evening and the next day had stood in front of his saloon describing witnessing the flash of Booth's pistol. Gifford, from the front steps of Ford's, had scoffed: the assassin, Gifford said, had fired through the door (which meant he knew about the hole before Monday's inspection), and thus Ferguson "could not possibly see him or recognize it." Worst of all, asserted Ferguson now to Olin, Gifford "on various occasions attempted to prevent [me] giving testimony" (but provided no specifics).[29]

Close behind Ferguson that morning was stagehand John Miles. He and Joe Simms had observed, from their unique vantage point up in the fly gallery, Booth's Friday afternoon interaction with Spangler and Peanut about the horse, as well as his leap from the box and crossing of the stage that night. Miles, who lived at 18th and L Streets, had worked for the

Fords since May of 1863—long enough to gauge the tenor of feelings backstage. John Ford himself hardly ever came by, Miles reported, but manager Harry Ford he liked, considering him "a loyal Union man" who never uttered a word against the government. The actors, too, all seemed loyal. But Maddox, Spangler, and Gifford, the three men Miles had the most contact with except for Lamb? These without question were "hard-core Secesh."[30]

Miles had a keen eye for suspicious goings-on and memory for dialogue. He related clearly Spangler's building the stable behind the theatre and selling Booth's horse and buggy. He knew Booth well and thought it odd that Booth had come to the alley door during Friday evening's performance asking for Spangler. When he and Simms heard the shot, they had run down to the stage, where the first person they encountered was Spangler. They asked him why Booth had run outside and ridden away, but Spangler directed them to "hush and to say nothing at all about it."[31]

Miles had quickly sought out a "very much frightened" Harry Ford to report what he had seen. Harry had told him to come by the backstage office the next morning and tell him everything, which Miles dutifully did after ostentatiously kissing a Bible. Now, Olin asked him if he knew anything about the peephole that had been discovered yesterday in the door of the presidential box. Miles insisted it had not been there before. After all he had observed, he told Olin, neither he nor Simms had any intention of ever returning to Ford's. The next day, Simms corroborated Miles's testimony, emphasizing Spangler's close ties to Booth.

Olin had heard enough. Gifford, too, was arrested that afternoon and taken directly to Old Capitol. Interrogated by Wood, he shrewdly got to work distancing himself from the assassination. Proclaiming his dislike of the entire Booth family, he said it had been difficult to even be cordial when Booth had performed at Ford's. He described everyone's responsibilities backstage then inexplicably reversed his statement to Olin yesterday: it was he who had directed Spangler to take out the partition to form the presidential box. And no matter what anyone had reported, he was still a "loyal man."[32]

Apparently, Gifford had influential friends. Within days his bail, surprisingly proffered at all, was posted by *Intelligencer* editor John Coyle, and he was able to return to the theatre. It also helped that actor Sam Chester, who upon his arrest had implicated John Mathews in the abduction plot, believed that Gifford had never been part of it. Ultimately, Gifford was never charged with a crime. Yet his detention rankled; during his brief incarceration, he muttered to John Ford one morning as they passed in the prison yard, "I have lost my prosperity to the old man, and my liberty by the young one."[33]

Rittersbach, too, was brought to Old Capitol on Tuesday. His interview with Wood disclosed his Union Army service, the brevity of his tenure at Ford's Theatre, and his observations about Spangler, against whom he would become the primary witness at trial. On Wood's ledger of arrests, the line for "Remarks/Reason" is blank after Rittersbach's name and no record exists of his being interrogated despite his remaining there a month.

He was placed in a communal room in Old Capitol, perhaps as a spy, a common practice there, where an atmosphere of duplicity prevailed. "Persons are often put in the rooms with prisoners who, while posing as prisoners themselves, are really spies, [and] are looked upon with suspicion," reported one of Mosby's men. Another inmate observed that "one of the prison officials was going around the yard last night, dressed in Confederate uniform, endeavoring, by offering bribes, to test the fidelity of the guards." As legendary Old Capitol inmate Confederate spy Belle Boyd observed of Wood, "There wasn't anything going on in that prison that he didn't know of."[34]

A short time later Spangler was brought down to Wood's office to be grilled by Lafayette Baker about the sale of Booth's horse and buggy. Incapable of guile, Spangler was fully forthcoming; he had, after all, only done what he had been asked by his friend. Escorted back to his cell, he remained oblivious to the cruel circumstances closing in around him.

CHAPTER TEN

"DREADFUL UNCERTAINTY"

O N WEDNESDAY, APRIL 19, all places of business closed and tens of thousands of somber, black-gloved Washingtonians gathered along Pennsylvania Avenue under an unseemly cloudless sky for the funeral of Abraham Lincoln.

A few blocks away, twenty-two men employed by Ford's and Grover's Theatres assembled to draft a statement expressing their deepest regret over the commission of the assassination by one of their own, a "fiend ... who has used our profession as an instrument to the accomplishment of his terrible and inhuman design." Fearing guilt by association, they sought to distance themselves from Booth's irrational act, pledging themselves to abjure any contact with anyone "who has or shall give utterance to the least sympathy with secession," and to wear mourning badges for ninety days. It was particularly shameful to their profession, they agreed, that the martyred president had been an ardent theatregoer. Signing for Ford's were actors Evans, Ferguson, Gourlay, Hess, Parkhurst, Phillips, Spear, and Wright, along with conductor Withers and scenic artist Lamb.[1]

Their motivation was not hard to understand. The *New York Clipper* avowed that "there has been, and still is exhibited, a good deal of feeling touching the secession proclivities of certain members of the dramatic profession." In recent weeks it was "a common occurrence to hear these secession actors declaim loudly against the North, at the same time that they expressed themselves in favor of Jeff Davis and the Confederacy...and their unholy cause."[2]

★ ★ ★

Even during the Lincoln obsequies, the investigation to identify Booth's accomplices continued. A good deal of it, however, produced nothing but false leads and dead ends when it came to the theatre employees. Perhaps the greatest waste of time, yielding almost nothing that was prosecutable, was the lengthy interrogation of the Ford brothers.

Dick Ford, arrested in Baltimore Tuesday night, was placed early Wednesday afternoon in yet another isolated room in Carroll Annex. Harry saw him brought in and felt a keen sense of responsibility for his unassuming sibling, whose weak constitution left him perpetually susceptible to illness. But any contact among the brothers, or even permission to leave their rooms, was strictly prohibited. "It was rather rough," Harry recalled. "There we were, left alone in our dungeons in dreadful uncertainty."[3]

The most fearful dimension of that day for the Fords, as for all inmates of Old Capitol, was hearing the sounds of the funeral procession approaching the United States Capitol across the street. "I could see nothing," said Harry, "but could hear the solemn booming of guns, the dismal beating of muffled drums, playing dead marches, and the steady tramp of feet. That was not very cheering music for our ears. We did not know but the people in their excitement would mob the prison and lynch us, for some of the men arrested had been stoned in the street."[4]

The next morning soldiers escorted Harry downstairs to Wood's office for an exhaustive interrogation by Olcott. The session's transcript, the most thorough by far of anyone connected to the assassination investigation, filled thirty pages.

Olcott began slowly, and Harry did his best to cooperate. What interaction had he had with Booth recently? He narrated the incident a week ago when Booth had complained bitterly about the potential new rights of freed slaves. Who else had been present? Harry identified, and explained the duties of, Sessford and Raybold, emphasizing that all three of them had tried to reason with Booth but had failed. Next, he summarized his conversation with Booth about money for the gymnasium, as well as Booth's diatribe about the manner in which Lee had surrendered, stressing, "I contradicted him about it." He described, too, his unsuccessful attempts on Friday to joke with Booth about Lee. After that, he said, "I never saw Booth again till I saw him that night on the stage."[5]

Looking for any lead, anything that could be used later by a prosecutor, Olcott took Harry back over the same ground: was there anything he had omitted about the afternoon of the assassination? Harry described the rehearsal of *Our American Cousin* and Booth's reading his mail on the steps outside the theatre. Were these visits to Ford's typical, asked Olcott? Yes, agreed Harry, "He used to come frequently to the office and stop there." Actors and crew alike would greet Booth "and ask him to take a drink, and then he would go out. Sometimes he would come into the office, and sometimes he would stay outside. He was as intimate with me as any one, I should think."

That admission apparently triggered some internal alarm for Harry, because he then began to backpedal, distancing himself from Booth just as Gifford had done, shifting culpability to others: "Lately I have not been taking many drinks with him, though I was doing so about two or three weeks ago." Booth drank with "nearly everyone," especially Ned Spangler, "four or five times." Booth was also "very well acquainted with Mr. Gifford."

Olcott wanted details of theatre operations. How were the boxes rented out? Harry explained the process, noting that only he and Dick had the authority to reserve them. Olcott probed again for particulars about Friday night. Harry complied, describing his reaction in the box office to hearing the shot as well as that of Raybold, Sessford, and Lutz. They had all heard it "distinctly," and Harry recalled thinking that something "had accidentally gone off on the stage." He heard "a buzz all over the theatre and went in myself" in time to see Booth run across the stage. "I fully identified him. I know it was Booth." Sessford, a man of honor whom Harry trusted completely, could verify all of this, he said (Sessford, though, was never questioned).

Olcott seemed to think there was something about Ford's Theatre that was particularly attractive to Booth, a theme that would emerge in the prosecution of Spangler. Why not Grover's? Harry hedged: "I have not been in the habit of going behind the scenes at Grover's." Olcott tried another tack, equally applied later to Spangler: Who might have helped Booth backstage? Would that person have had time between scene changes? Might someone have aided Booth by clearing an exit route for him? Harry professed ignorance about scene changing—he was not familiar with backstage operations. He *was* able to list the scenic locations, in approximately the right order, for *Our American Cousin* and clarified the process of scene shifting. But, he insisted, "We always have the passageway clear."

Olcott forged ahead. How had they prepared the presidential box? Here Harry was on more familiar ground, explaining who had obtained and installed each item of decoration. No, he had not noticed a fresh hole in the door, nor had he at any time Friday afternoon seen Booth inside the theatre. He reviewed the procedures that typically took place when the president visited, recalling instances of Lincoln's attendance. Harry did think it odd that Booth had "asked me repeatedly if the President was not coming some night with some such language as this, 'Why don't the old bugger come there sometimes?'" But, he said, Booth had never expressly asked him to invite Lincoln.

What did Harry know about the stable out back? Not a thing. Then just how close were he and Booth? Well, said Harry, further distancing himself, "I used to associate with Booth a great deal, until I had a controversy with him in Mrs. Petersen's house in the room that Mr. Mathews [rented], where the President died, while talking politics. I had been drinking and expressed myself rather freely—Union sentiments—and I never associated with him so much after that." It suddenly came to him, too, that Booth had announced one day last February in a saloon on Pennsylvania Avenue that "something would happen in two weeks that would astonish the world [but] he did not say what he was going to do."

Olcott returned to the theory of backstage complicity. Think: who might have assisted Booth? "Many people," responded Harry, flustered and starting to ramble, "but no one in particular stands out.... Mr. Wright or Mr. Gifford could facilitate the escape behind the scenes. The carpenters and the property man could be the most useful in keeping the sceneries [sic] in the proper place away from the wall.... Spangler is under the control of Gifford.... When I asked for two flags to put around the picture [Gifford] said, 'There is no necessity of that,' [but] he did not make any remark about the President being there or being shot that night."

Hours had passed, and Olcott was finished, but Harry was not. He reiterated his assertion from his initial interview: "I am a loyal Union man." That apparently was helpful to his cause, for the next day Olcott recommended he be released, asking special investigator Foster why Harry had been incarcerated in the first place. Because, Foster shot back, in his initial interview with Wood, "Mr. H. C. Ford gave such unsatisfactory and apparently untrue answers that Colonel Wells directed his commitment. Since that time his memory has much improved."

The investigators seemed satisfied. Harry would be released within two days. In the meantime, he tried to remain positive. "The experience," he rosily reflected two decades later, "had its comic side. After that first week we had more liberty and really had a very jolly time."[6]

★ ★ ★

Actor John Mathews was picked up on Friday, April 21, a full week after the murder. His L Street boardinghouse room was searched, but nothing—even ashes—was discovered to tie him to the crime. That he was arrested suggests that someone had been keeping an eye on him backstage at Ford's. Brought to Old Capitol and set in front of Foster, Mathews proceeded to lie from the outset, insisting he had not seen Booth for several days before the assassination. In fact, he had only met Booth for the first time this past New Year's Eve, he said, when they casually exchanged season's greetings over a glass of eggnog. While acting in Baltimore last winter, he had only "met him casually from time to time, two or three times a week, or perhaps oftener."[7]

Understandably, Mathews omitted any mention of those leisurely afternoons in his rented room in the Petersen house with Booth and other actors, including John McCullough, a close mutual friend. In the past few weeks, Mathews had seen Booth, oh, "perhaps half a dozen times," just casually passing him on the street, but "never anywhere except on the street." Then, suddenly aware that someone may have seen them together on The Avenue or in front of Ford's that afternoon, he now recalled seeing Booth, but only for a moment, to exchange a few words, he on foot and Booth on horseback. Wisely, Mathews made no mention of the letter Booth had handed him that he had burned.[8]

Now Mathews decided to get out in front of any evidence that may have surfaced regarding the box he had shipped to Baltimore at Booth's behest for the aborted kidnapping. It had merely been, he said, a present, "an empty box in which he used to carry his sword. He said he was not going to act any more so he presented it to me as a memento, that it was the last of his professional wardrobe and he had no use for it," because he was going into the oil business.[9]

Mathews's fears were justified. Actor Sam Chester, who had turned Booth down, had already reported to investigators Booth's attempt to coerce Mathews into participating in an abduction. Foster wanted to know all about that. "On my oath" Mathews denied any involvement in such a scheme. Sure, he was aware that Booth's sentiments were avowedly pro-Southern, but "I never heard [him] speak on politics." Rationalizing his association with Booth, Mathews argued that Booth was "a most winning, captivating man. That was the opinion of everyone who came into contact with him. It was reputed a man said he would be in love with him if he were a woman."[10]

Mathews had aroused the suspicions of a few other people as well; the following week the Judge Advocate General's office would receive a letter from a Boston man asserting that "Mathews of Ford's Theater is knowing to all of Booth's proceedings." Yet remarkably he was never arrested. It no doubt helped that Superintendent Wood had known him for many years. Other actors known to be close friends with Booth as well, notably John DeBonay and Ned Emerson, were never arrested or questioned—a major chance missed.[11]

★ ★ ★

By Saturday morning, April 22, the day Harry Ford was released, the arrests had tapered off. Gifford, though, was rearrested on Baker's orders. Something in the interrogations—perhaps Harry's disjointed connecting of Gifford with Spangler—had registered as suspicious. Gifford, observed Foster, "was quite intimate with Booth and considered to be disloyal in his sentiments." That morning, Gifford and Spangler were brought from their cells to Wood's office, where they were together identified by an army sergeant as having been seen together out on Tenth Street the night of the assassination. This identification was corroborated by an unnamed "witness" (which may have been Rittersbach) two days later in the prison exercise yard. No one else in the entire investigation ever placed Spangler out in front of the theatre with Carland, Gifford, and Hess that night, yet this identification became additional evidence against him. He and Gifford were unceremoniously returned to their rooms.[12]

★ ★ ★

A bizarre spectacle took place in the theatre Saturday afternoon: the reenactment of *Our American Cousin* up to the moment of the shot for the sole benefit of detectives and other investigators who formed its audience. It was organized by Lieutenant Simon P. Currier, of Colonel Ingraham's staff, who assembled with Wright and Phillips's help as many actors from the cast as could be located in the city (with the likely addition of others brought down from Baltimore to fill in for the absent Keene, Dyott, and Hawk).

They performed in street clothes since the soldiers had impounded their costumes and props. Their collective fear and grief can only be imagined as they uttered each comic line and pantomimed each piece of comic business out into a stony silence. The express purpose of this charade was to determine whether or not Booth might have had assistance backstage, particularly in keeping the wings clear to facilitate his escape. At the close of each scene, before the scenery could be shifted, everyone on stage stood in place while the investigators measured various distances, especially the width of the stage right passageway Booth had used. Currier created a scale drawing and marked where personnel had been standing when the president was shot.

Despite the earnest testimony provided by the Fords and others over the past week about the mechanics of scene shifting and the need to keep the wings clear for actresses with wide skirts, Currier concluded that Booth had had accomplices: "The carpenters and property man have it in their power to obstruct or keep clear the passage.... It appears to me that this passage was kept, to say the least, remarkably clear."[13]

Currier's sketch and conclusions would carry considerable weight in the trial of the conspirators, counting heavily against Spangler. By the end of the week, enough evidence had been compiled to warrant his being charged as an accomplice. At midnight on Saturday he was awakened by guards and brought, disoriented, down to Wood's office. There, a detective stood over him and informed him that he had "some jewelry" to put on him. The forlorn stagehand's arms were pinioned before him and forced into brutally restrictive Lilly irons that kept his hands ten inches apart. Leg irons were applied that restricted his shuffling gait to eight inches. Manhandled to the street, he was thrust into a curtained hack and conveyed to the Washington Navy Yard, where military guards took him on a small boat out to the ironclad monitor *Saugus*, anchored about a hundred yards offshore. Stanton intended to avoid any misguided vigilantism.[14]

★ ★ ★

More than a week after the president's death, like events in a typical melodrama, the darkly handsome villain was still at large, while desperate detectives rushed hither and yon chasing fresh leads and suspects.

On Sunday, April 23, Tom Raybold was brought from his home in Baltimore to Old Capitol for questioning in Wood's office by Foster, simply because he had been present when Booth had stopped by for his mail and in the box office when the assassination occurred. As a Union veteran, his loyalty was never in question and he was not held. He was unable to provide any new or helpful information, though, especially since his perception had been clouded that whole week by the pain in his jaw. His answers dealt perfunctorily with his duties at Ford's, the procedures for renting out boxes, and who had been present the afternoon of April 14. He recalled an occasion in November when Booth had spoken disparagingly about the emancipation of slaves, but that was nothing new.

On Monday Foster had Peanut John brought in for questioning. The youth had been engaged by Gifford to care for Booth's horse because of his knowledge of horses and his ability with them. He now proceeded to describe in detail Booth's light bay mare, using proper equine terminology (fetlock, hock, etc.), appraising her as "very spirited, very uneasy [and] blind in one eye."[15]

Foster pressed him about the atmosphere backstage, and Peanut shared definite feelings about Gifford and Spangler. The former, he said, assigned him his duties, paid him for the horse's feed, and decided who should be admitted at the stage door. In fact, Gifford had specifically told him to admit Booth that Friday, and Spangler had ordered him to hold Booth's horse. He hadn't wanted to, but Spangler had said if there was anything wrong "to blame it on to him." Spangler had provided the harness for Booth's horse—harness that Booth had told them to leave on when they stabled the horse, as "he intended to use it that night." Peanut had stood there that afternoon and heard it all clearly. He would be a surprisingly effective witness at trial, if they could just keep track of his whereabouts for the next month.[16]

Later that afternoon orders came down from Stanton to Foster: find out who knew the most about the process of renting out the boxes and arrest him. That turned out to be the hapless Harry Ford, who had already testified to Olcott on that subject, but who was rearrested that evening as a result. This would be another dead end.[17]

Actress May Hart had dutifully remained in Washington and on Tuesday was summoned to the Judge Advocate's office for more questioning. Still frightened from her ordeal at Old Capitol, she could only repeat what she had already told Baker and Wood: she barely knew who Booth was. She had seen him only twice, the first time about three years ago in Baltimore, and then briefly and in profile one time two weeks ago as he crossed the stage toward the greenroom. She had had to ask someone who he was. She would be useless as a trial witness—more energy wasted—and was sent away, catching the first train back to Baltimore.[18]

★ ★ ★

Meanwhile, John Ford fretted in Carroll Annex, albeit in less restrictive quarters. Wood had moved him to one of two conjoined rooms, with a few more amenities. Among his cellmates now were the three southern governors, whose penniless and downcast plight led Ford to share his reading material and whiskey obtained from the prison sutler (although this act of friendship tainted him as a southern sympathizer). His brother Harry, between arrests, had brought over clean clothes, but Edith was still prohibited from visiting her husband, despite continued overtures to Stanton and others. At the same time, public officials and private citizens in Baltimore advocated for his release.

He still could not get an explanation from Stanton or anyone else for why he and his brothers were being held. From supporters he could readily produce at least five hundred thousand dollars for his bond, he told them, but received no reply. He wrote to Holliday Street stage manager Tom Hall to retain as counsel for him Baltimore lawyer and former Congressman Henry Winter Davis, and to contact other public figures who could provide his bail. His instructions, though, met with a reprimand from Wood, who inspected nearly every piece of incoming and outgoing mail for possible espionage or escape attempts: "You should not mention names of other persons you wish the influence of," he told Ford. "Confine yourself to your *own* family affairs strictly."[19]

Ford was rewarded for his efforts with promises of support from the Maryland governor, governor-elect, Baltimore mayor, both Maryland senators, several Maryland congressmen, and *Intelligencer* editor Coyle. Even Maryland Provost Marshal McPhail urged parole for Ford, attesting to his good character. Many of these men had enjoyed performances at his theatres and stood willing to assist him. Even the insurer of Ford's Theatre wrote to General Augur expressing his fear for the building's safety while it stood vacant and unused, appending a testimonial to Ford's character. Over one million dollars was collected by the citizens of Baltimore and was proffered as bail.

Harry Ford, too, had been active on John's behalf, intervening with Judge Advocate Levi C. Turner, before being rearrested. Inexplicably, at Augur's order Harry was released again after only one day's detention. Still, the incarceration would not be his last.

All of these efforts yielded nothing. Stanton was adamant: Ford and his brothers were to be held without bail. Yet every day that they were incarcerated cost Ford financially. Hall worked tirelessly to keep the Holliday Street going, and the two men remained hopeful that performances might resume at a reopened Ford's Theatre in Washington (although Edith was opposed to reopening while her husband remained imprisoned). Hall made near-daily trips between the two cities, looked in often on Edith, and even traveled to Tudor Hall in Bel Air to see if he could learn anything about Booth's whereabouts. Ford's extant letters to Hall from prison are detailed and focused, indicating a man in full command of theatre operations and the legal and financial mechanics of his release. He relied completely on Hall: "I am anxious about my family and business. The one I must leave to Providence and the other to you."[20]

But day by day, business fell off at all of Ford's theatres. Hall was forced to cancel their leases in Cumberland and Philadelphia. Yet all he could do was counsel Ford to "make up your mind to wait patiently as possible." "Mrs. Ford," he reported, "bears her trouble very well, though I feared for her at first." By contrast, Ford's former stage manager, John Wright, remained immobilized, offering no help. Never questioned despite having been in complete charge of backstage operations, he received permission by the end of April to move back to Allston, Massachusetts, which remained his home for the rest of his life.[21]

★ ★ ★

On Wednesday morning, April 26, as the Lincoln funeral train chugged inexorably toward Springfield, and Confederate General Joseph E. Johnston surrendered his army of 89,000 men to Union General William T. Sherman in North Carolina, John Wilkes Booth was run to ground and fatally shot in a burning tobacco barn outside Port Royal, Virginia. Late that night his body was brought to the Navy Yard and arrayed on a carpenter's bench on the deck of the monitor *Montauk*.

Among those brought to identify the body before its autopsy Thursday morning was Edwin Brink, the former Union Navy paymaster who had spent time with him the evening of the murder. Brink asserted without hesitation that the body was Booth's. Despite the slain assassin's misguided sympathies and rash act, Brink still evinced a strange admiration for his late friend: "He died like a brave man, as I knew he would."[22]

With the tacit approval of the guards, various crewmen aboard the *Montauk* crept forward to snip souvenir locks of hair from the head of the half-bare body and stare at its twisted leg and its arm tattooed "J. W. B." Also present, crowding in for a closer look, was Navy Yard carpenter John Buckingham, the erstwhile Ford's Theatre doorkeeper (who had quickly found evening employment taking tickets at other Washington theatres). "All I wanted," he said, "was to see the mouth of the person lying before me covered with a white cloth, and one of the soldiers lifting the cover, I saw instantly that they had the right man.... I had no difficulty identifying the deceased as John Wilkes Booth. He had a peculiar sarcastic curl to his lips that was present even when his features were in repose, and which even death failed to obliterate."[23]

★ ★ ★

On Friday the twenty-eighth—two weeks after the murder—property man Jimmie Maddox was brought down from his cell for another round of questioning by Olcott. This would not be a dead end and would not be polite. Too many suspicions had been raised about Maddox's loyalty and his close association with Booth. John Miles had denounced him, and Harry Ford had provided at best a lukewarm endorsement: "I do not know ... whether he is a Union man or a Secessionist. Kind of both.... He might be a 'little on the Secesh,' but very little." Maddox, he tacked on, was "what we call a very nice fellow ... Drinks pretty freely though. Is always a straightforward, honest man."[24]

Maddox's own demeanor in this session did nothing to help him. As Olcott reported afterward, "Maddox, property man at the theatre, presented himself before me in a state of great trepidation, trembling violently when the examination commenced." Maddox's rambling answers certainly conveyed rising fear. He had met Booth only two years before, he insisted, when he did props for him during Booth's tenure as actor-manager at the Washington Theatre. After that, he had seen Booth only briefly in performances at Ford's. When Booth had asked about a horse and stable, Maddox had referred him to Gifford. In fact, beyond an occasional drink, "I never had five minutes conversation with Mr. Booth in my life without someone was by. I never was upon the street with him." Yes, once he had asked to accompany Booth on his tours as his personal dresser, but "that was the most conversation I ever had with him, except about his horse and such things. I am as innocent of knowing anything about this so help me God, as my Mother. I wish to God I had known for it would not have disgrace upon our country [sic]."[25]

The day of the murder, Maddox maintained, he had only spoken to Booth once or twice, out in the yard by the stable, and then joined him for a quick glass of ale. That night, he had been preoccupied with Selecman's errand to the druggist: "He was so long about it I had rushed to the door, and my boy and I came in through the alleyway; I met [Booth] outside of the door in front of the theatre" (a perfect excuse for his being out in front). Yes, he had seen Booth come in the stage door earlier, but had been in such a hurry he didn't look to see where he had gone. What about Booth's horse? "I did not know the horse was there until the excitement was over," protested Maddox. Only much later had he heard that Spangler had gone to hold the horse.[26]

When he had heard the shot, Maddox asserted, "I looked out and caught a glimpse of the back of the man." He had then run out on stage to bring a pitcher of water to be handed up to the wounded president. "That is all I know about the affair." Olcott bore in, asking about the extent of Maddox's foreknowledge of the assassination, and about his political sympathies. Maddox babbled even more erratically: "I take my oath to Almighty God that I never knew a word about [it]. I know nothing about politics. Since I have been a voter I have always voted the Union ticket. I voted for [Mayor] Wallach. I have never been a Copperhead or a Secessionist. My Mother knows I am a Union man. I am sure no one in the world believes I am secessionist. I would make some remark when Mr. Raybold was about to hear a good argument. I could argue. I am twenty-six years of age this month."[27]

Olcott duly noted Maddox's denial of having had [transcript underlining] "the remotest suspicion of what was to occur.... His protestations of innocence were numerous and emphatic." But unless the testimony of numerous previous witnesses "shall be set aside," Olcott decided, "I think his case is a bad one."[28]

Oddly, this conclusion ran counter to Foster's: despite Maddox's having been repeatedly seen with Booth, and "heard to utter extremely disloyal sentiments, [and] in the habit of allowing Booth access to the theatre at all times," Foster wrote, "there are no very strong circumstances showing that he was knowing to the murder prior to its commission." Apparently, like Spangler, Maddox had still believed that the evening was to have produced an abduction and not a murder. Yet Spangler was in irons and Maddox, while terrified, was only in Old Capitol.[29]

Scenic artist James Lamb narrowly avoided the fate of both of them. Although "clearly an accessory before the fact," Olcott had had trouble pinning anything on him. Two boys who hung around the theatre had overheard Booth convey the news of Richmond's fall to Lamb on the Monday prior to the assassination. The artist, they said, "seemed to be as bitter toward Mr. Lincoln as Booth"; they had heard him express his willingness to "shoot the President the first chance he had." On the night of the capital's celebratory illumination, Lamb had reportedly exhibited bitterness about the rejoicing, causing one of the boys to tell his father, "that man is a rebel." Olcott sought Lamb's arrest, but neither of the boys could quote Lamb precisely enough to provide testimony that could be used in a trial. Hence, he was never even questioned. Another dead end.[30]

Next, Olcott decided to see what more he could obtain from John Ford. Once again, the tone of the interview was muted and Ford was treated more as a consultant than a suspect. Olcott wanted his assessment of Maddox, Gifford, and Spangler. Ford knew little of Maddox except his backstage responsibilities, but praised Gifford's expertise and noted his hatred of the Booths. He pronounced Spangler "a half worthless man. He drinks. He seems to work hard, but there is no pride in him." Ford said he had never heard Spangler discuss politics, but then, he had not been in the theatre since early March, leaving its operation to his brothers. This prevented him from knowing anything about the stable behind the theatre or any other favors the carpenter might have done for Booth.[31]

Ford acknowledged knowing Booth for sixteen years, but had learned to discount most of the brash young actor's secessionist prattle and his boasts of making a fortune in oil speculation: "He could not really tell what was right." In fact, "he was the last man I would have suspected." Asked about the wide, clear passage in the wings backstage that had been so carefully measured during Saturday's reenactment, Ford reminded Olcott that many actors, including women wearing wide hoop skirts, had to enter and exit through that area. He had insisted it be kept free of furniture or scenery.[32]

Olcott pressed a little harder. What were Ford's own political leanings? Omitting any mention of his earlier involvement with the nativist "Know-Nothing" party in Baltimore, he claimed Whig and Republican loyalty, and "never voted a Democratic ticket." As for the war, he had remained above it all: "In a city like Baltimore where parties are divided, I have taken no part as I have a place of public amusement." Not only that, he had "subscribed liberally to every charitable affair got up for the soldiers." He had pointedly not done so for "the other side," despite having "married in Richmond, a poor milliner girl." He certainly had had no involvement with Secessionists, much less any conspiracy, he declared.[33]

Ford's discretion was well-advised. Baltimore still seethed with leftover Southern sympathy, despite the war's end and the president's assassination. Commanding General Lew Wallace, who held jurisdiction over the city and who would sit on the commission trying the conspirators, repeatedly had to admonish Baltimore clergy not to stir up rebellious sentiments in their April sermons, nor permit expression of it by their parishioners. "You know that what I thus request I have the power to enforce," he warned. "If you feel that you cannot yourself comply, [it would be better to] close the doors of your church for a season."[34]

Olcott's report on Ford struck a solicitous tone: the manager held Booth "in small esteem. He was annoyed at his frequent visits to his

Washington theatre, but tolerated him because of his business relations with [his] brothers Junius and Edwin. He feels outraged that his theater should have been chosen for the scene of such a tragedy, and that a stigma must rest upon his name for ever, although innocent of even a suspicion of the approaching catastrophe."[35]

Ford's demeanor "under examination was quiet, dignified and exceedingly proper," recorded Olcott. "He seems to feel as if smitten with a great calamity." Ford had also succeeded in muffling his outrage at being kept in Old Capitol, for Olcott was under the impression that he "regards his incarceration as perhaps a natural consequence of the event's having transpired in his theater." Olcott was convinced that Ford was in no way complicit: "Neither at this examination, nor during the progress of our whole investigation, have I found the slightest suspicion to Jno. [sic] T. Ford; and I, therefore, respectfully recommend his release without condition." This, however, was not granted, likely at the insistence of the secretary of war.[36]

★ ★ ★

On Thursday, April 27, Ford was moved again, to Room 33, a large communal room fronting on the Capitol, which represented "a vast improvement," even with its vermin and heat. (He recorded with some bitterness that only wealthy internees were housed in the cooler lower rooms.) His agitation at what he regarded as the deprivation of his constitutional rights grew by the day. Despite persistent efforts to gain a hearing, he and attorney Davis had met with deaf ears at the War Department. Davis had gone in person to see Stanton, carrying an impassioned appeal outlining the Ford family's suffering, but he, too, was coldly rebuffed. For over a week Edith was denied permission to visit her husband. She, too, had tried to see Stanton, only to be "brutally repulsed." When she was finally allowed to see John, the visit was brief and overseen by guards.[37]

Now, clutching a plebeian pencil, Ford wrote letter after letter—to Stanton, to Assistant Secretary of War Charles A. Dana, to Judge Advocate General Joseph Holt—seeking bail or at least specific charges. His continued imprisonment, he wrote, "cannot serve any public good, while it brings ruin and suffering" to his family, including his six young children and wife, who was "in very delicate health." He reminded the authorities that he could readily post any amount of bail they named. His letters went unanswered.[38]

To help investigators understand the layout of his theatre, he sketched its floor plan. To channel his outrage, he drafted a manifesto for publication. Ultimately never distributed, it stated his principles—echoing that of many Marylanders—opposed to the heavy hand of federal oppression, and excoriated Stanton. Worst of all, during all of this he had to watch the mental and physical deterioration of his brother Dick, who slipped at times into convulsions, alarming his brothers greatly. Dick, too, tried to keep a prison journal, but barely filled a page.[39]

★ ★ ★

Heading into May the investigation ground on with little progress to show in terms of any employees of the theatre. On Thursday, May 4, the day of Lincoln's funeral in Springfield, Illinois, costumer Louis Carland was brought to the War Department, to the office of Solicitor William Whiting. Tag-teaming with Baker, Whiting grilled him about his membership in a subversive organization known as the Knights of the Blue Gauntlet, a clone of the more widespread Knights of the Golden Circle. Actor Sam Chester had told detectives about acting in Richmond with Booth, who had been a member, as had Carland been as recently as last winter. Making matters worse for the costumer, Baker had a few days ago discovered a letter in Ford's Theatre addressed to Carland from the Philadelphia chapter of the Knights, ironically expelling him from the organization. Its ominous tone, wording, and use of a numbered row of stars to identify its sender—typical of such groups—lent it credibility.[40]

Carland had spent the 1858–59 season with Booth in Richmond and 1862–63 at Philadelphia's Arch Street Theatre, where Booth had played an engagement, but he insisted now that he had known Booth only professionally, "by seeing him almost every day in the theatre." Under heated questioning, he admitted being in Philadelphia as recently as two weeks before the assassination. Seeking desperately to put the onus on someone else, he swore that the last time he had seen Booth was the afternoon of April 14, when Mathews had walked up Tenth Street arm in arm with Booth, deep in conversation. As for the Knights, "I never belonged to any secret organization."[41]

But Baker had not shown him the letter, only alluded to it. Carland's improvisational skills failed him utterly when Baker brought it out. Carland launched into an improbable tale about its being nothing more than a request for books, sent to him in Philadelphia by an acquaintance whose name he could not quite remember. Then why did the letter refer specifically to his ejection from the Knights of the Blue Gauntlet? Oh, that? That was "nothing but skylarking." Then he veered into a different excuse: the letter was from a friend who "wanted some old postage stamps." This was frantic, implausible rambling. And so, like the others, Carland was promptly remanded to Old Capitol.[42]

★ ★ ★

Harry Ford, who must have spent nights waiting for the next knock on the door, was arrested for a third time on Saturday, May 6, and brought back to Old Capitol, this time by the zealous Baker "by order of the Secretary of War." Yet, true to form, he was not questioned, just thrust into the cell with his brothers and told he would be needed as a material witness. They could fulminate against whomever they wished, but they would be held until the trial. The interrogation of the owner of

Ford's Theatre and nine of his employees, including a lengthy session with his brother, had yielded little information except the arrest of Ned Spangler, and that was based almost entirely on the testimony of one man, Jake Rittersbach. Several of the others, notably Gifford and Carland, looked guilty, but if flipped could provide incriminating testimony.

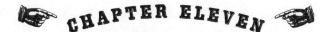

CHAPTER ELEVEN

"IGNORANCE AND INNOCENCE"

A S THE TRIAL NEARED, lead prosecutor Judge Advocate General Joseph Holt assembled a cadre of reliable, cooperative material witnesses. As little as high-strung Jimmie Maddox fit that description, even he was considered. Brought down from his cell on Sunday, May 7, he was questioned yet again by Wood. Back and forth they went over the same ground, Maddox still trembling: his duties backstage, his whereabouts on the day of the murder, and his close acquaintance with Booth. He admitted eating and drinking with Booth upon occasion, but vigorously maintained his "ignorance and innocence of all matters relating to the assassination." It remained unclear how much help he would be at trial. Wood sent him back to his cell.[1]

On Monday, with the start of the trial only two days away, the prepping of witnesses began in earnest. Tom Raybold had a wealth of information he was eager to share. So far, he asserted, he had not been asked "the most important questions, especially about the screws in the door of the President's box." When he mentioned Peanut John's presence during the decoration of the box, detectives spent several hours tracking the boy down, once again finding him wandering the streets of Washington. For the next two weeks, at least, patrolmen would need to keep better track of his whereabouts.[2]

They also scooped up Maddox's young assistant, John Selecman. The youth had already demonstrated his mettle and loyalty by reporting all he knew of the atmosphere backstage at Ford's to restaurateur James Ferguson, who had taken it directly to the investigators. Selecman's fear, though, was the possibility that he himself might be implicated, having been seen with Booth the afternoon of the assassination.[3]

★ ★ ★

One day that week John Ford overheard an egregious instance of "witness preparation" in the prison yard: Baker going at Rittersbach, putting words in his mouth. Whereas Rittersbach had actually heard Ned Spangler that night say, "Hush your mouth! You don't know whether it's Booth or not," Baker now told him to add that Spangler had slapped him across the face and warned, "For God's sake, shut up! And don't say which way he went." If Rittersbach would not so testify, Baker threatened, he would be thrown indefinitely into the general prison population at Old Capitol. This approach by Baker, Ford believed, would unnerve anyone, "and cause him to *think* he believed he heard what he did *not*." Even though Rittersbach was self-motivated to testify and required little prodding, he was hailed before Colonel Burnett on the eve of the trial for another conversation. No notes exist of its nature.[4]

Ford, his brother Harry, and Gifford witnessed the same sort of pressure brought to bear within the prison on a terrified Louis Weichmann, a Booth associate who had boarded at Mrs. Surratt's. Weichmann would in due course provide exceedingly incriminating testimony, which led directly to the conviction and execution of several of the conspirators. A day later, Maddox, Gifford, and Carland overheard an officer in Old Capitol tell Weichmann "if he didn't swear to more than he had told he would be hung." (Weichmann shortly after the trial would confess to Carland that he had perjured himself to save his skin, and tell Gifford "I'd give a million dollars if I had had nothing to do with it.") As John Ford recorded in his ever-lengthening jail house manifesto, "Another damnable feature in this prison is that if [underlining his] a prisoner will not or cannot give such information as may be demanded of him he is ordered to his room or cell and handcuffed and tortured into a more complaisant witness or informer."[5]

It would take Selecman six days to decide to testify as required; Maddox, ten (with a final personal "appeal" by Holt, who up to that point kept Maddox on his list of conspirators to indict); and Gifford, eleven; but they, too, would come around to provide testimony for the prosecution and be unconditionally freed. John and Harry Ford, along with Carland, would testify only for the defense in an effort to spare Ned Spangler. They would continue to pay a price for their intransigence.[6]

★ ★ ★

Spangler, charged as a conspirator, faced conditions far worse than any in Old Capitol. Held below deck on the *Saugus* in a cramped storage room, its meager air rank from overflowing water closets on either side, Spangler remained chained at the waist among filthy blankets and life preservers, unable even to recline. Two Marines guarded his door at all times. Rocking at anchor in the Eastern Branch of the Potomac River, the sound of its wash loud against the iron hull, the monitor also absorbed the full brunt of the sun, raising the daytime temperature below deck to an unbearable level. The only fresh air and sunlight Spangler experienced came on April 25 when he was dragged up on deck, still in leg irons and manacled, to be photographed against the *Saugus*'s armor-plated turret by Mathew Brady's associate Alexander Gardner.

One evening the captain of the guard approached Spangler: "I am going to tell you something, but don't get scared. They are going to place a bag on your head. It is the orders from the Secretary of War and I must obey it." Several hours later two guards forced a heavy canvas hood over his head, its thick cotton wadding covering his eyes, pressing them into his head. Cords through its sleeves drew it mercilessly tight around his neck. Forced to wear it day and night, unable to eat with his hands manacled and only a small hole in the hood for the intake of air and food, Spangler was saved by two guards who took pity on him, one feeding him while the other stood watch. He was kept in this inhumane condition for the rest of the week, his face bloating and his hands and legs increasingly swollen and purple from the tightly applied irons.[7]

At Stanton's order, around midnight on Saturday, April 29, amid a downpour, Marines came aboard the *Saugus* and roughly shook the nearly comatose stagehand awake. One jerked the cords of his hood sadistically tight, telling the other not to let him sleep, adding menacingly, "We are going to take him and hang him directly." Spangler, choking, confused, and terrified, heard chains rattling on the deck overhead and grew alarmed, certain that he was to be executed before ever being brought to trial. No one would tell him anything. Still hooded and in irons, he was manhandled up to and across the slick deck by two marines, who then forced him onto a gunboat, which carried them a mile down the Potomac.[8]

In the heavy rain, they rounded Greenleaf Point at the confluence of the Potomac and its Eastern Branch (now called the Anacostia River) and tied up at the Federal Arsenal (today, Fort Lesley McNair occupies the site). Spangler was pulled off the boat and forced to shuffle in irons about two hundred yards, inside the twenty-foot-high brick walls surrounding the complex. He was shoved up three flights of stairs to what had been the female cellblock on the top floor of the arsenal's brick penitentiary. Hit on the head and pushed drenched and semi-conscious into a dark, tiny cell (7' x 3½' x 7'), he collapsed onto its fetid corn shuck mattress.

For over a week he remained there, in cell number 184, its eighteen-inch masonry walls locking in the spring sun's heat, all the while hooded and manacled, before being briefly removed to be readied for trial. Two armed sentinels stood outside his door at all times, their bayonets visible through its grate. The cell on either side held no prisoner, to thwart communication.

No one tried to visit him. He may or may not have ever been shown the plaintive, semi-literate appeal written to him sometime in April by his father in York, suffering from chronic rheumatism. "Let me no the truth," he wrote, "about this murder of the Chief President... and The reason of your name in Almost everey paper in the Country.... I want to no wat you no about it.... My hand is so lame that I can scarcely hold the pen. Dear Son Do answer this Imediatly. From your Affectionate father God bee with you. W<u>m</u> Spangler. [sic]"[9]

Throughout Spangler's imprisonment, his warden was Special Provost Marshal Brevet Major General John Frederick Hartranft, an exacting yet humane officer, at whose direction the cells were swept by soldiers and the prisoners inspected twice a day by Dr. George Loring Porter. But Porter was forbidden to converse with the prisoners on any matter save their health. This he assiduously monitored, recommending that their bedding be changed regularly and the upper row of glass panes be removed from their cells' small windows to allow ventilation. Although hooded day and night, Spangler through his window on some days could hear the bells of ships on the river striking watches, the calls of men and the clank of machinery in the encampment surrounding the prison, and the sounds of cattle, pigs, and dogs that roamed its grounds.

From his years of working backstage in the dark, he was also able to distinguish his various guards by their voices, but his attempts at conversation when they brought his meals or came in to sweep out his cell and air his bedding were unsuccessful. Following orders forbidding conversation, the soldiers consistently—often rudely—rebuffed Spangler's efforts. A handful, kinder than the rest, did assist him with eating through the limited aperture in his hood.

His daily fare rarely varied: a breakfast of bread, salt pork, or boiled meat and cold coffee; a dinner of bread, meat, and water; and a supper of bread (occasionally with beef broth) and coffee. This food Dr. Porter adjudged "good and abundant" and was about what Spangler had consumed while in Old Capitol, having had no funds to purchase anything additional. No utensils were provided—fingers had to suffice—and after each meal his bowl was promptly removed.

Finally, on May 5, he was provided with clean underclothes, and the heavy canvas hood was removed long enough for him to be shaved. His skin had become bloated, purplish, and raw from the tightly cinched cords of the hood, the manacles on his wrists, and the iron ball and chains on his legs. He was now permitted, at Porter's insistence, to wash once a week, but under the guards' supervision and with ice-cold water.

Starved for human interaction, he knew nothing of the legal proceedings swirling around him until Hartranft appeared in his cell on Monday evening, May 8. Directing the guards to remove Spangler's hood, Hartranft read aloud by lantern light the charges against him pursuant to General Court Martial Order 356: "maliciously, unlawfully and traitorously" aiding and assisting Booth to obtain entrance to the president's box, obstruct the door of the box, and escape after the assassination.

On the eve of the trial, Spangler still lacked legal counsel. He would be tried on these charges far more quickly than would be imaginable today. On May 1 President Johnson had ordered the convening of "nine competent military officers" to serve as a trial commission for the accused assassination conspirators.

Eight days later the officers assembled for the first time in a large room in the northeast corner of the third floor of the Arsenal penitentiary. Roughly thirty by fifty feet, it had been the deputy warden's office. Its bare, whitewashed walls gave it a garret-like feeling, compounded by the shifting patterns of light falling through its four tall, heavily grated windows and from the gas lighting installed for evening sessions. A doorway from the cellblock had been cut through into the southwest corner of the room, and a massive, iron bolt-studded door installed through which the defendants would be brought each morning without risk of contact with the public, reporters, witnesses, or trial commissioners, who entered through a narrow sliding door in the northeast corner after ascending a newly built stairway from the waiting area below.

The officers assembled each day around a long baize-covered table across from a central witness stand, court recorder, and evidence table. Farthest from the defendants was presiding officer Major General David Hunter. Nearest them stood Holt, a staunch Unionist despite his southern birth, in civilian attire. Utterly convinced that Confederate President Jefferson Davis and elements of his government had had a hand in Lincoln's murder, Holt would prosecute these alleged conspirators with vigor and determination.

Like some ritualized Kabuki drama, the trial played out with a stagecraft understood by almost all its participants. Its audience—the government, the journalists, and the public—manifested clear expectations for its process and outcome; its actors—the tribunal, the witnesses, the attorneys, and their clients—understood (or were made to understand) the roles they were to play and the lines they were to deliver; its themes—of infamy, vindication, and revenge—were evident at every turn. The ceremonial scenes unfolded, as everyone on some level knew they would, and the denouement was preordained as the gods decreed. There would be no comic relief.

★ ★ ★

At 11:00 a.m. on Tuesday, May 10, the day that Jefferson Davis was finally run to ground in Georgia and taken to Fortress Monroe, the defendants shuffled into the courtroom for the first time, under heavy guard. Their hoods were removed, but they remained manacled hand and foot, sitting each day along the room's west side on a foot-high elevated platform fronted by a four-foot-high railing, a guard between each of them. Spangler occupied the fifth chair from the left, with actor Sam Arnold in the first seat and Dr. Samuel Mudd in the third. On Spangler's right were Michael O'Laughlen, George Atzerodt, Lewis Powell (alias Paine), David Herold, and Mary Surratt.

First, each of the accused was asked how he pleaded. Each responded "not guilty." After Johnson's order for the trial was read aloud, each was asked if he had any objection to any member of the commission. Spangler, still without representation, had no idea who any of them were and thus had no reason to object to anyone. He remained largely unconscious of anything going on around him, disoriented by the sudden stimuli after weeks of sensory deprivation. His lack of previous exposure to courtroom proceedings, the droning voices, their formal, indecipherable words, the glittering, clanking uniforms, the iron restraints on his body, and the room's oppressive heat (which worsened as the trial dragged on), combined to produce a surreal stupefaction that precluded comprehension. Sometimes he just put his head down on the rail in front of him, concentrating vaguely on his blue woolen shirt, and tried to block it all out.

This state of mind was not lost on court observers. Although one kindly writer thought Spangler had "a simple and pleading face, and there is something genial in his great, incoherent countenance," he was most commonly described to readers across the nation as "unintelligent" or downright "stupid." References abounded to his manifesting the effects of alcohol; in one exaggerated report, Spangler "had seldom drawn a sober breath and on the very day on which the assassination occurred had been very drunk." He was also "rough looking," "bloated," and "slovenly"—certainly understandable by now. "The heavy, purple-hued face of Spangler affords no clue to his thoughts, if he thinks at all," derided one reporter. A sketch of Spangler by trial commissioner General Lew Wallace portrays just such a man, with drooping shoulders, a bullet-shaped head and a dopey, bewildered expression. The journal of the era's pseudoscientific fad of phrenology concluded from Spangler's "unsymmetrical" thin head and "long face" that he had "a mild disposition easily controlled by others.... His face lacks a forehead. [It is] a brute face. We have seen cows and oxen with countenances very much like that of poor Spangler. He looks the picture of distress."[10]

It is likely accurate, as others wrote, that Spangler "looked by turns indifferent and apprehensive" and had "an expression of being frightened nearly out of his wits at the prospect before him." "The poor creature, more than any other, appeared to be under the influence of imminent bodily fear.... His hands were incessantly moving along his legs from knee to thigh, his bony fingers traveling back and forth like spiders, as he sat with his eyes fixed on each witness." Summed up the *New York Times*: "The poor man seems to have left only enough sensibility to understand that he has got into a very uncomfortable situation somehow or other."[11]

★ ★ ★

From his cell in Old Capitol, John Ford was not unaware of Spangler's plight. He was simply unable, despite a belief in the stagehand's innocence, to do much to help him. One thing in which he did succeed was securing legal representation for Spangler. Brevet Major General Thomas Ewing Jr., already representing two other defendants, Mudd and Arnold, agreed at Ford's request to add Spangler's case. Ford would pay all costs. Brother-in-law to General William T. Sherman, Ewing came with impeccable credentials as the son of a United States senator and Treasury secretary, having served with distinction in Missouri during the war. Prior to that, he had been private secretary to President Zachary Taylor and risen to become the first chief justice of the Kansas Supreme Court.

As a bonus, as Ford saw it, there was no love lost between Ewing and Stanton. For several weeks a bitter war of words, much of it public, had been conducted between the supporters of Stanton and of Sherman over the latter's conduct of the war's denouement. Ewing let it be known that the vilest of the attacks on his brother-in-law, which included "egregious falsehoods" and "flagrant lies," had emanated from one source: "the whole of these assaults may be imputed to Stanton."[12]

Ewing's representation of the feckless Spangler came just in time. On Friday, May 12, as the commission began hearing testimony, he stepped forward to represent this newest client, despite having had no opportunity to confer with him. Ewing met with Spangler for the first time on Monday evening, May 15, in the courtroom following adjournment, but could converse with him for less than twenty minutes, under the watchful eye of Colonel Levi Dodd, commander of the prison's guard detachment. Ewing was further hampered by having no copy of the specific charges against his clients, no list of prosecution witnesses—and thus any opportunity to assess their credibility—and no opportunity for his defendants to take the witness stand in their own behalf. Such limitations were standard procedures in a military trial in 1865.

★ ★ ★

Starting on Saturday, May 13, when they were first admitted, a throng of reporters and curiosity-seeking civilians jammed shoulder to shoulder daily along the wall opposite the commissioners. Most appeared mesmerized by the wretched collection of defendants and awed by the military assemblage who, they were certain, would administer justice and retribution.

Within the first few days of testimony, trial procedures settled into a proper military routine, convening each day at 10:00 a.m. with the prisoners in the dock, their hoods removed. The previous day's testimony was read aloud, sometimes taking as long as two or three hours. An hour's break was taken for dinner, during which the prisoners were returned to their cells, and adjournment came anywhere between 5:00 and 6:30. Attorneys' consultations with their clients took place in the courtroom in the hour after adjournment or in the prisoners' cells during the dinner hour.

Spangler soon became vaguely aware that he was a lower priority to the commission than most of his fellow defendants, if only because his name, or that of anyone he knew from the theatre, came up less frequently than that of Booth, Atzerodt, Powell, Herold, or Surratt. He recognized, and tried to focus on, the first Ford's Theatre employee called to testify that Monday afternoon: genial doorkeeper John Buckingham. Holt steered Buck through the daily operation of the theatre, as well as the sequence of events on Friday, April 14, including Booth's comings and goings in the lobby that night and his leap onto the stage.

Since an earlier witness had reported a "stout, ruffianly" man with a mustache talking with Booth out in front of the theatre that night, Ewing on cross-examination prodded Buck to clarify that Spangler never wore one, nor could he have been out front, as he was needed almost constantly backstage.[13]

Stepping confidently into the raised witness box after Buck was conductor Billy Withers, who testified with self-assured phrasing why he had been up on the stage at the moment of the shot. He described Booth's mad crossing of the stage, slashing Withers twice as he passed. Booth had then exited through what Withers considered an unusually wide-open wing space. Expressing an opinion he would hold onto steadfastly until his death, Withers insisted that normally "the stage and passageway would have been somewhat obstructed by some of the scene-shifters and the actors in waiting." Sometimes, in fact, there were so many people there "that you cannot pass. But that night everything seemed to be clear."[14]

So the careful measurements taken during the eerie reenactment of *Our American Cousin* had resonated with the prosecution; Withers's testimony now validated them. Ewing's cross-examination failed to shake the conductor's hidebound certainty that someone must have helped assure a clear path of escape for the assassin. Again, Ewing elicited the fact that Spangler never sported a mustache.

Next up were two stagehands, completely out of place in this august assembly but willing to do their duty. First, Joe Simms established Spangler's close bond with Booth, including their frequent drinking sessions, notably one late on the afternoon of April 14. He recounted Booth's arrival on horseback that night and Spangler's scurrying to attend to him, as well as hearing the shot and seeing Booth run across the stage holding a Bowie knife.

John Miles then corroborated Simms's testimony regarding Spangler's attention to Booth's horse, placing Maddox there as well. Miles, too, had heard the shot and seen Booth run off, but now contributed a more damning detail: after Booth had fled, Miles had confronted a "very much excited" Spangler just outside the alley door and been told, "Hush! Don't say anything about it." And no, neither Simms nor Miles could recall a mustache on Spangler.

Both men, identified as "colored" in the trial transcript, were questioned respectfully by prosecution and defense attorneys alike and accorded credibility as reliable witnesses who could connect Spangler to Booth and clarify backstage procedures at Ford's. Their initial statements, given only days after the assassination, had been taken seriously.[15]

Following them was John Selecman, who had been brought over from Old Capitol under guard in an army ambulance, a squad of soldiers posted at each intersection—a procedure Stanton had ordered for the transport of all material witnesses for the duration of the trial. There would be no getting cold feet. On the stand, Selecman's unswerving theme was *distance*—from any suspicious events and from anyone suspected of complicity. He too described Booth's arrival on horseback but was careful to portray himself not as a participant, but rather as a mere observer. In fact, he had stood so far away, "I do not know whether Booth saw me." He judiciously placed Booth and Spangler a good eight feet away from himself, but close to each other. Still, he had distinctly heard Booth request, "Ned, you'll help me all you can, won't you?" and Spangler reply, "Oh, yes." "Those," Selecman stated, "were the first words that I heard," as if he had merely stumbled onto an ongoing conversation.[16]

Likewise, rather than having a drink with Booth that afternoon, he had merely noticed Booth in the saloon when he went looking for Maddox, finding him there drinking with Spangler and Peanut John. Spangler, he opined, "is a drinking man," but he could not tell "whether he was in liquor that night." Booth, he said, had been exceptionally familiar with the theatre and its actors, managers, and stagehands. Cross-examined by Ewing, Selecman admitted that right after the fatal shot and Booth's escape, he saw Spangler standing in the wings, very pale, holding a white handkerchief, and possibly crying.[17]

Withers's testimony about the stage right wing space apparently played to Holt's intent, for at the close of that afternoon's session he announced that the trial commission would assemble the following morning at the site of the murder. He wished the officers to gain a clearer understanding of the layout of the premises. Their primary focus would be the wings.

★ ★ ★

Amid a crowd of gawkers, the commissioners stepped out of army ambulances at 9:30 on Tuesday morning in front of Ford's Theatre and strode up the stairs past the sentries and into the gloomy lobby. Accompanied by a handful of reporters but no theatre employees, they moved down the aisle of the parquette, where heavy dust already coated the seats and furnishings. On the stage, the scenery of Act Three, Scene Two of *Our American Cousin* still stood where it had been left from the restaging and photographing three weeks before.

The officers and reporters worked their way into the stage right wings, one correspondent pointing out an ironic label on the back of one piece of scenery identifying it as used in a production of *The Rebel Chieftain*. The wing space and rear exit to the alley appeared as unobstructed as the men had anticipated. When they stepped through the alley door Booth had used to escape, soldiers lounging on what remained of Peanut John's bench jumped to attention.

Re-entering the theatre's dim interior and ascending the lobby stairs to the dress circle, the commissioners proceeded to examine the reception lounge on its far side, looking for possible alternative entrances that accomplices might have used. That room's elegance was by now marred by the soot, grime, and mud generated by its employment for a month as a guard encampment. The commissioners found the large presidential box undisturbed except for the removal of the rocking chair in which Lincoln had sat. As had been the case on the day of Stanton's visit, they paid particular attention to the mortised niche in the wall of the passageway outside the box.

Returning to their ambulances and thence to the penitentiary grounds, the officers proceeded promptly to their third-floor courtroom, where they found the prisoners already arrayed along the wall with their hoods removed. Testimony began immediately.

★ ★ ★

Shortly after 2:00 that afternoon, the prosecution called Peanut John, who spoke with uncharacteristic assurance, using a mature vocabulary and sentence structure—hardly the slow-witted creature that some contemporaries as well as later historians have described. First, he summarized his duties around the theatre, including helping to arrange the presidential box on April 14. Spangler was doubtless disheartened now hearing Peanut repeat his words damning the president and General Grant as they had worked together in the box.

Next, Peanut related Booth's actions that afternoon and evening and explained how—at Spangler's behest—he had ended up holding the reins until Booth rushed out and grabbed them, knocking him down. Cross-examined by Ewing, Peanut elaborated on the duties of various backstage personnel and underscored Booth's familiarity with, and acceptance by, nearly all of them. Like everyone before him, Peanut had never seen Spangler with a mustache.

Much of what Peanut said was reinforced by the next two witnesses, women who lived behind the theatre. Just as disconcerting to Spangler was hearing them both identify him by name as the one person most helpful to Booth. Worse, they both said—with strikingly similar wording, as if they had been coached—that they had later confronted Spangler about his involvement with Booth and been repeatedly told that they were mistaken, that he knew nothing about Booth or tending to his horse. One of the women repeated her erroneous observation that it had been Booth standing in the alley earlier in the afternoon with a lady—testimony that had imperiled May Hart. But neither Holt nor Ewing pursued that, nor did either follow up on the women's assertion that Maddox had also been present.

All this talk of backstage goings-on, coupled with the transcripts he had read of interrogations of the Ford's Theatre staff, especially Judge Olin's report on James Gifford's demeanor, reminded Holt that he had suspicions about that man. If Gifford had not been directly involved in the conspiracy, he had at least allowed a climate to flourish in which secessionist sentiments could be openly expressed. These suspicions had been compounded by testimony a few days before by saloonkeeper James Ferguson, who repeated Gifford's disgruntled words the morning after the assassination.

Consequently, after the court's adjournment on Thursday, Holt had Gifford brought to his office. Neither man spoke later about their conversation nor left evidence of its content, but Gifford the next afternoon dutifully appeared in the witness box to testify for the prosecution. Torn between his regard for his abject subordinate on trial and Holt's stern countenance in front of him, he measured his words carefully.

First, he described the setting up of the presidential box that Friday afternoon, including specifics about its furniture, then speculated on the design and purpose of the peephole in the door to the box and the niche in the wall outside it. He spoke little of Spangler other than to clarify that his assistant was merely "a sort of drudge for Booth," who was as friendly to Spangler as he was with "everybody about the house, actors and all," with "access to the theatre by all entrances." But Spangler, he said, was too busy with his duties backstage that night to provide Booth with any special help; his presence close to the scenery "would have been indispensable to the performance." Gifford refuted Withers's testimony about the abnormally clear wing space, asserting that such an area, less than three feet across, would never have been obstructed during a performance. In the long run, whatever Holt may have said to Gifford the night before paid no great dividend. He was as much help to the defense, if not more so, than to the prosecution and was returned directly to his cell.[18]

Jake Rittersbach, who followed Gifford to the stand, established that he knew Spangler well, having slept in the same room at the theatre and boarded with him at Mrs. Scott's, where Spangler kept his valise. This Rittersbach had handed to the detectives who arrested Spangler, establishing its evidentiary connection to the case, although Rittersbach professed ignorance about its contents (the length of rope). Brought to the stand, the detectives quickly verified the essential details of Rittersbach's account. Immediately upon completion of his testimony, Rittersbach was released unconditionally, on Stanton's orders, "having given his testimony satisfactorily." He would return to the stand in two weeks and again perform as required.[19]

★ ★ ★

The afternoon session on Monday, May 22, brought to the stand the perpetually addled Maddox, questioned specifically about Spangler. Like Gifford, he had also been summoned to Holt's office, but likewise provided little help to the prosecution. While not portraying himself as quite the innocent bystander Selecman had made himself out to be, Maddox implied that he was nevertheless little more than an intermediary—someone who collected stable rent from Booth and delivered it to its owner. He was unfamiliar with anything that might have transpired while the box was being decorated. The only people he could remember seeing that afternoon were Harry Ford and Joe Simms, for a moment each.

Ewing cross-examined Maddox more persistently than any other Ford's employee, perhaps out of pique for his having been flipped by the government. He elicited from Maddox what appeared to be a genuine desire to help clear Spangler's name, clarifying in considerable detail his own responsibilities backstage as property master, notably including keeping the wing space clear. In fact, Maddox insisted, it would have been unusually clear during *Our American Cousin*, since that was "a heavy piece" requiring a lot of furniture to be rushed on and off the stage for its many short scenes. Spangler had been diligently at his post "during nearly every scene," he maintained. "If he had not been at his place, I should certainly have missed him. If he had missed running off a single scene, I should have known it."[20]

Maddox described learning about the president's visit that morning from Harry Ford and explained where he had been during each act of the performance, especially the necessity of his being out in front of the theatre during Act Two and returning to the stage during intermission. At the moment of the shot he had stood stage left and observed Spangler at his post. When Booth ran by, Maddox had caught only a glimpse of him, then turned his attention to providing the pitcher of water. And like the others before him, no, he had never seen Spangler wear a mustache. A visibly relieved Maddox stepped down and was conveyed back to Old Capitol.

After the dinner break Holt recalled Peanut to explain how Spangler had modified the stable behind the theatre for Booth, then sold Booth's horse and buggy. Spangler, he said, had acted at the direction of Booth and Gifford. Peanut then stepped out of the witness box and out of the pages of history. Any number of theories and stories, most likely apocryphal, about Peanut's identity and life after the trial have emerged over the intervening century and a half, including a statement by Harry Hawk in 1909 that Peanut was alive and well and selling cough drops on the streets of Washington. Newspaper articles about various "Peanut Johns" living well into the twentieth century in New York and Massachusetts cropped up from time to time, but no concrete evidence to support any of them has ever surfaced.

★ ★ ★

On Tuesday, May 30, amid a heat wave that would sap the energy of everyone in the courtroom for the next month, Holt wrapped up his case against Spangler. Its keystone was additional testimony by Rittersbach, which proved to be exceptionally damaging. Rittersbach asserted that he had vainly pursued Booth that night—an action no one else ever reported seeing—only to be driven back at knifepoint. He had been the first to reach the alley door, with Major Stewart close behind him, and had wrenched it open in time to see Booth ride off. Returning to the stage, he had confronted Spangler, who "hit me on the face with the back of his hand, and he said, 'Don't say which way he went.' I asked him what he meant by slapping me in the mouth, and he said, 'For God's sake, shut up.'"[21]

On cross-examination Ewing probed for holes in Rittersbach's claims. Who else had seen or heard the confrontation with Spangler? "Some of the actors," the stagehand replied, including "one they called Jenny [sic]," who had been only a few feet away. Perhaps realizing immediately that Jeannie Gourlay would not corroborate this—as she in fact never did—Rittersbach added, "I do not know whether she heard what he said; he did not say it so very loud."[22]

Next came an outright lie: he denied telling anyone but Gifford (while they were together in Old Capitol) and a detective what Spangler had said and done. This despite having cornered Carland, Lamb, and Selecman within hours of the event, and Withers a day later, to make sure they knew of it. He repeated, "I have no recollection of telling anyone else." Questioned further, Rittersbach acknowledged that he had not seen Booth's face clearly enough to recognize him. And he remembered returning to the center of the stage to find Spangler "kind of scared, and as if he had been crying." But without warning, Spangler had lashed out at him.[23]

The detective to whom Rittersbach had told his story was identified only as "one of Colonel Baker's men." Baker had taken a personal interest in Rittersbach, keeping investigators Wells and Burnett, who reported directly to Stanton, informed of his whereabouts. Immediately after his release that afternoon, Rittersbach returned to Ford's Theatre with one of Burnett's officers to try to locate his carpentry tools, which had disappeared while he had been in Old Capitol. He was not successful. At some point that year, he was granted United States citizenship. As much tabloid attention as Rittersbach would have received today for his damning testimony, no picture of him survives.[24]

Having done his duty, Selecman was unconditionally freed on May 26, as were Gifford and Maddox the following day. Either because so many public figures had advocated for John Ford's release or because the prosecution no longer had any use for him, he, too, was at last freed, on Saturday, May 27. But his two brothers, along with Louis Carland, would be held another week.

When Ford reached Baltimore, a crowd of well-wishers awaited him at the train station, some accompanying him to his home on Gilmor Street. There, surrounded by his family, he perused a pile of congratulatory letters. Their common theme was indignation at his "confinement for an act in which you were in no wise responsible [despite] those who are eager to implicate everybody connected with your theatre." Many expressed optimism about his being allowed to reopen his Washington theatre.[25]

Without delay Ford released a statement thanking these "many kind and earnest friends for their unwavering confidence [which] half made prison life endurable." He was especially relieved that "the most complete and rigid investigation ever known in this country" had failed to implicate anyone connected with his theatres other than Spangler.[26]

That unfortunate man's exoneration became his next task.

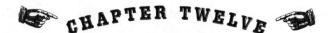

CHAPTER TWELVE

"GOOD BYE. SOMETIMES THINK OF ME."

FOR THE NEXT MONTH Ford alternated his days between Baltimore and Washington, renting a room in the National Hotel and working long hours in Ewing's Capitol Hill law office. He hired young Will Ferguson, his erstwhile prompter, to copy out briefs and trial testimony. Together they also created a more polished version in color of the floor plan Ford had sketched out while in prison, for Ewing's use during the trial.

To prove Spangler's innocence, Ford and Ewing necessarily focused first on refuting points established by the prosecution, especially those bolstered by Rittersbach's questionable testimony. As he had done in prison, Ford filled page after page with notes, including extensive marginalia. He went one morning with Tom Raybold back into the theatre to examine the door to the box and make sure he understood Raybold's explanation of its broken lock: a few weeks before the murder a late-arriving party had needed entry to the box after the usher who held its keys had gone home. Raybold had forced the lock, stripping the threads of its screws. The peephole in the door Ford attributed to Booth, citing an auger that had been found in Booth's trunk. All of this Ford outlined for Ewing, along with what he knew of the sequence of events of April 14.

Ewing had his work cut out for him. Not only did he have to damage Rittersbach's credibility, he had to provide convincing witnesses of his own. Foremost among these would be Ford. When it became apparent, though, that he would be testifying for the defense, Ford sensed a sea change in the attitude of the courtroom spectators and commissioners: "A witness for the defense was generally viewed and treated with undisguised contumely, and at times with abuse and assault [whereas] witnesses for the prosecution were to a certain extent petted and rewarded." This, he said, "intimidated some from performing a hopeless duty to the parties arraigned, and encouraged other unscrupulous parties to be swift and eager volunteer witnesses, supplying links of evidence with avidity if not with integrity."[1]

The most serious allegation against Spangler was the supposed atypically cleared wing space that had allowed Booth to escape unhindered. Withers's testimony had hurt, as had that of Captain Bell of the 24th V.R.C. occupying the theatre, based on Currier's reenactment sketches. Bell maintained that at the time of the murder, the stage right wing space was "less obstructed by the presence of the employees of the Theater than at most other portions of the play." Currier's measurements "strongly favor the belief that the precise moment of the assassination was premeditated."[2]

Public perception, as well as that of the trial commissioners, had to be overcome. To Ford's chagrin, even the theatre-friendly *Clipper* implied that his theatre had been a less-than-loyal house [italics theirs]: "Yet why [Booth] should be thus confident, *unless he had accomplices on that stage*, is difficult to discern. [Why] was there no fear of his being interrupted [by] people whose presence is required upon the stage?" Not all of the stagehands, it averred, were "good, loyal men."[3]

On Ford's advice, Ewing planned a full-scale attack on the notion that a theatre employee would have cleared an otherwise cluttered wing space. Keeping it clear was common practice; not to do so "would be as suicidal as obstructing the front passage whilst the patrons of the theatre were entering." Furthermore, argued Ford, the actresses that night were "in full dress and they could not go on or off the stage to their dressing rooms or to the Green room without using this passageway."[4]

Plus, Spangler could not have been the one who kept it clear; he could never have left his place during the third act due to its frequent shifts of scenery. Ford urged Ewing to portray Spangler simply as "a good natured drudge ... an industrious, yet drinking man." Anyone that "unlettered and ignorant" would readily have fallen under the sway of someone as charismatic and manipulative as Booth, whose "graciousness to that class was proverbial and unstinted."[5]

Another defense point was to be Spangler's remaining in the theatre in the days following the assassination, "bitterly lamenting he did not know Booth's intent or his crime until after his escape." At no point, even between his two arrests, had he attempted to leave the city. To humanize the poor carpenter, they would introduce his fondness for dogs, horses, fishing, and crabbing, explaining away the length of rope found in his trunk as nothing more than a crab line.[6]

Ford's motivation was fueled in part by another desperate letter from Spangler's father: "There is so many reports about him that we dont no wat is true. And _if_ you pleas or dare to let me no the facts bad as they may bee.... Our famaley is so much distrest about Edman & we have no use off ackwantance now no scarciley one man in your Cittey. I would wright more but I am so much confused that I can scarcely no wat to wright. From your friend Wm Spanlger. [sic]"[7]

Ford realized, too, that he would have to establish his own *bona fides* on the witness stand. He planned to articulate the damage Booth's crime had done to his business: "The ruin and suffering it has brought to my door must be apparent to any sensible or fair man." He would also cite occasions on which he had helped Union soldiers in the field and their families on the home front. To boot, every year he had promptly paid his full share of taxes without complaint. Yet his recompense for all of this, he would argue, had been imprisonment with his brothers, one of them acutely ill, for over a month without being charged with any crime.[8]

★ ★ ★

Ewing opened his defense on Tuesday, May 30. Harry and Dick Ford, brought over under guard from Old Capitol, joined John in the courtroom. Spangler, they were happy to see, appeared "infinitely brighter and cleaner than heretofore. He shows more sensibility in countenance." According to the *Washington Star*, Spangler was hopeful, asserting, "God is the best judge of my innocence," with the afterthought, "I wish I were better acquainted with him" (the paper's wording; his actual utterance was likely less eloquent.)[9]

Dick became the first of eleven theatre employees to testify in Spangler's defense, and despite his weakened condition he spoke clearly and forcefully. He established that Booth had not learned of the president's visit until around noon on April 14, and thus had had little time to make any plans specific to Ford's Theatre.

Next, aiming to impeach Rittersbach's credibility, Ewing called Gifford to the stand concerning Rittersbach's imparting to him in prison Spangler's supposedly incriminating words and slap. Gifford, trapped between the government's threats and a genuine desire to help Spangler, denied hearing this. In fact, Rittersbach had come to him about three weeks ago saying he needed to "amend his statement, [as] he was scared and could not tell what he was doing.... He seemed to be troubled about it." Gifford had told him to simply stick to the truth. Asked about the broken lock, Gifford professed ignorance: that was the responsibility of the ushers. As for Spangler's rope, it was just the sort of line the stage-hands regularly used for crabbing.[10]

★ ★ ★

On Wednesday Ewing called Dwight Hess, Leonard Grover's partner, to establish that the distance from the box down to the stage was less at Ford's Theatre than at Grover's, and thus Booth may have chosen the former site for reasons other than its personnel who might assist him.

Then it was Harry Ford's turn. The boyish treasurer, guided by Ewing, walked the commissioners through the events of April 14. He reinforced Dick's testimony about Booth's noontime learning of Lincoln's visit, describing this as a regular occurrence, while emphasizing how busy the afternoon's preparations had kept Spangler. And no, Harry too had never seen Spangler wearing a mustache.

Cross-examined by the commissioners, Harry clarified the procedures by which boxes were rented out and professed ignorance about the mortised niche, the peephole, and the broken lock. He created an image of a backstage environment where nothing that day was amiss or abnormal, with all hands preparing conscientiously for a presidential visit as they had done on numerous prior occasions.

Following his brother, John Ford struck a defiant stance. He had clearly rehearsed from his notes and adhered closely to their logic: Each person backstage fulfilled a vital function to the smooth running of a production; Spangler's presence at his duty post backstage could not have been spared for a minute, especially during a production as complex as *Our American Cousin*; and the failure to keep the wings clear would be ruinous to a production. This last point he stressed strongly: as owner of the theatre, "my positive orders are to keep it always clear and in the best order," especially stage right, being nearest the dressing rooms and thus used at least three times as much as stage left. His stage manager, John Wright, had made certain his orders were followed.[11]

As planned, Ford tried to humanize Spangler, stressing his love of crabbing and the recent loss of his wife. Booth, he said, was an irresistible, fascinating figure who "controlled the lower class of people such as Spangler belonged to." Beyond this, he could not speculate, having been in Richmond the night of the murder tending to his aged, ailing uncle. He as well had "never known Spangler to wear a mustache."[12]

Cross-examined, Ford adjudged it would not have been a difficult feat for Booth to vault out of the box: "I have seen him make a similar leap without any hesitation." Nor would he have needed rehearsal, being "a very bold, fearless man [who] excelled in all manly sports." Using eight lengthy sentences, he stressed that Booth would not have needed assistance, but even if he *had* sought any, Spangler was not unique; there were other likely possibilities, such as actors Sam Chester, who had turned Booth down cold, and John McCullough. Ford concluded with a reminder of Booth's *carte blanche* presence: "I seldom visited the theatre but what I found him about or near it, during the day," often just to pick up his mail.[13]

McCullough may have been more involved than anyone at the time or since has ever established. Although married, he and Booth had drunk and womanized together, using code names like "Jack" and "Bob" in telegrams for women with whom they were conducting dalliances. When in Washington, he had often hung out with Booth and Mathews, and had been present in Mathews's room at Petersen's in March when Booth had relaxed and smoked a cigar on the bed where Lincoln would die. Touring for years with Edwin Forrest, McCullough would have received a steady diet of that actor's anti-Lincoln sentiments. Once, a Union Army sergeant had heard McCullough, in Booth's presence, speak openly against the

North, damn Lincoln, and assert that "he would never fight against the South, that, if drafted, would die first; those who were fighting in the Union cause were damned fools and men of no brains." Lincoln, McCullough had asserted, was "too ignorant for the position and should be put out of the way." He "praised those of the South and said the North never would conquer them."[14]

Ford was so certain that McCullough was somehow complicit that he telegraphed him shortly after his release from Old Capitol to see what McCullough knew about the assassination. The actor, he learned, had left Washington five days before it had occurred, then fled to Montreal where he remained, away from suspicion, for months.[15]

★ ★ ★

Later that day Ewing called stagehand Henry James, who spoke enthusiastically in support of Spangler. He had worked closely with Spangler the entire evening of April 14 and had never seen him stray from his duty post. Furthermore, he had watched as Spangler applauded the president's arrival "with both hands and feet" (which admittedly could have been glee at the arrival of the planned abductee). Refuting Rittersbach, James insisted he never saw the man anywhere near Spangler the entire night.[16]

Next up was young prompter-actor John DeBonay, whose Confederate service and disloyal remarks to saloonkeeper James Ferguson had curiously not led to any interrogation or arrest. Having relayed Booth's request for someone to come hold his horse, he now explained how Peanut John had attended to that task; Spangler had been too busy. Like James, he had never seen Spangler leave his post. He stressed that Booth's brisk transit of the stage, which he had witnessed, was assisted by no one. To a final question, DeBonay equivocated: although he had stood among the men surrounding Booth on the steps outside the theatre around noon that day, he now denied seeing Booth there.

Recalling prosecution witness Withers, Ewing asked what he had seen that night. Tersely, the conductor described Booth's flight and slashing of him, but said nothing to implicate anyone else in assisting Booth.

★ ★ ★

On Friday, June 2, Ewing called Rittersbach, who predictably proved unhelpful, sticking to his story that Spangler had slapped him and said, "Shut up. Don't say which way he went." When he contradicted his own previous testimony by stating that he had reported this soon afterward to Carland, Ewing failed to pursue it. Asked about the afternoon, Rittersbach could only recall seeing a mysterious man with a mustache in the theatre, smoking a cigar in the dress circle after nearly everyone else had left, and Spangler's going up to the man and speaking with him.

Scenic artist James Lamb, next to testify, convincingly refuted almost everything Rittersbach had said. He related Rittersbach's trolling the story of Spangler's slap to anyone who would listen, and swore that nothing along the lines of "Don't say anything" was ever part of the story. Lamb asserted that Rittersbach had absolutely known who Booth was and had loudly identified him backstage afterward. In an attempt to restore Rittersbach's credibility, prosecutor John Bingham persistently cross-examined Lamb, badgering him with no fewer than eighteen variations of the same questions about his testimony, trying to trip him up. But Lamb would not be shaken, concluding brusquely, "That is what I have stated."[17]

Ewing's next witness, Tom Raybold, had trouble remembering the events of April 14 due to his facial pain that day. He explained his forcing open the door to the box in March, stripping out its screws, which he had forgotten to report to Gifford. He summarized the process of renting out the boxes, mentioning two occasions when Booth had reserved one, then narrated the Lincolns' reserving of the box, its decoration, and handing Booth his mail around noon. None of this exonerated Spangler, but did establish a typical, uneventful day of preparation for a presidential visit, with no one demonstrating any unusual or suspicious behavior.[18]

Asked about Spangler's rope, Raybold believed it to be the same sort used widely around the theatre—nothing out of the ordinary. Cross-examined by Bingham, he acknowledged that it was a bit improper for it to be found "in a carpet-sack half a mile off." As for the anomalies in the door to the box, Raybold stated that he had gone inside it so infrequently, especially on that day, being ill, that he had not noticed anything amiss. Asked to speculate how Spangler might have obtained the rope, he had no idea.[19]

During Friday's dinner break, Raybold, at Ewing's urging, went back to the theatre and examined the broken lock more carefully. Returning to the arsenal, he was recalled to the stand, where he explained again why it was broken. It was his effort, and his alone, he said, that was responsible. His own shouldering of the door had caused cruder damage than might have been accomplished by carpentry tools; thus, it was not something Spangler might have done.

★ ★ ★

On Saturday Ewing called ticket agent Joe Sessford and chief usher James R. O'Bryon. Sessford established with one sentence that no other boxes had been rented for the night of April 14, and O'Bryon succinctly confirmed Raybold's testimony about the broken lock.

Later that day, Secretary Stanton ordered Harry and Dick Ford's release after they took loyalty oaths. Allowed access to their rooms above the Star Saloon to retrieve their clothing and personal property, they were instructed to find lodging elsewhere. What they saw upon their return appalled them. All areas of both buildings had fallen into grime and disrepair, and the occupying soldiers' detritus lay everywhere. Worse, Dick realized that their rooms had been vandalized and nearly five hundred dollars worth of jewelry had been stolen from a locked drawer. He began an immediate if quixotic campaign to identify the thief and have the items returned.

An immediate letter to Stanton was passed down the chain of command to Captain Bell, who had requisitioned the brothers' rooms for his quarters while occupying the theatre. Within a week he conducted a thorough investigation and issued a report that made its way back up the chain. Upon taking command at Ford's, he said, he had noticed the rooms had been broken into, and posted guards there. But any theft must have occurred right after the assassination, "during the excitement and bustle" when many people roamed freely through the theatre. He was "truly grieved by the reflection (though indirectly) cast upon my honor by Mr. J. R. Ford before he has taken the pains to inquire into the facts of the case." Moreover, "my duties at this post have been very unpleasant indeed." In other words: I did all that I could, it was gone before I got there, and it is I who am the aggrieved party. There is no record of any further action, so presumably no compensation to Ford was forthcoming.[20]

★ ★ ★

For the rest of the next week Ewing turned his attention to defending Arnold and Mudd. But on Friday, June 9, he recalled John Ford, who tried to further humanize Spangler "as a very good-natured, kind, willing man [whose] only fault was in occasionally drinking more liquor than he should." He was never violent, was always "willing to do anything, and was a very good, efficient drudge." Spangler, he said, had little self-esteem, kept to himself, and humbly slept on the floor in the theatre. As for disloyal thoughts, Ford had never heard him utter any "expression of partisan or political feeling."[21]

The following Monday, in a sweltering courtroom, Ewing called Louis Carland, who continued the assault on Rittersbach's credibility. Yet knowing he himself had been under suspicion for the "Knights of the

Blue Gauntlet" letter, he weighed his words carefully. Having been held over a month in Old Capitol, he had no wish to return. He had heard Weichmann being threatened.[22]

On the stand he related the Spangler-slap story Rittersbach had been peddling, emphasizing that at no point had he reported Spangler saying anything like "Don't say which way he went." He summarized Spangler's fearfully uncertain status following the assassination, still returning each night to sleep in the theatre instead of trying to run off. The rope found in his room was easily explained: he, Spangler, and Rittersbach regularly used such ropes to haul lumber up outside the theatre to the scene shop on the third floor. Aggressively cross-examined by Bingham, Carland stuck firmly to his testimony.[23]

On Tuesday the prosecution put DeBonay back on the stand, the last Ford's Theatre employee to testify. In an attempt to discredit defense witnesses who had poked holes in Rittersbach's testimony, DeBonay was asked to retell his version of the shooting. He gave the prosecution nothing, wavering little from his testimony of two weeks before: Booth had asked for Spangler to hold the horse, but Spangler had been needed backstage and told Peanut John to do it. Spangler had stayed at his post as Booth had leapt to the stage and fled.

★ ★ ★

The courtroom and cells had by now become ovens. The insufferable heat and humidity overcame some of the hooded and manacled prisoners, especially Spangler, whose mind began to wander. Dr. Porter, aware that he alone was responsible for their physical and mental health and that "the attention of the civilized world" was focused on their condition, became alarmed. Worst were the hoods, which acted "as sweating baths to the head, caus[ing] symptoms of mental trouble" in prisoners "already debilitated by the nervous tension" of their situation. He insisted that Stanton order the hoods be removed and two to three hours of exercise in the open air be permitted each day. Otherwise, he said, the Secretary of War "would have a lot of lunatics on his hands."[24]

Porter also believed his prisoners' minds craved stimulation and so recommended reading material be provided to them. Hartranft concurred on all counts. After inspecting each prisoner, he approved the removal of their hoods and a daily opportunity for exercise, but only for thirty to sixty minutes, and mandated the continued use of manacles and irons in their cells. He disallowed any reading matter from the last thirty years, so Porter improbably provided the prisoners, including the semi-literate Spangler, with early novels of Cooper and Dickens. With this relief granted, "they all behaved well and gave no trouble," recorded Porter. Their health improved noticeably, especially Spangler's, as he was allowed exercise twice a day. One afternoon he even pitched a game of quoits in the arsenal yard, a few feet from its soon-to-be-used scaffold.[25]

★ ★ ★

On Tuesday, June 20, Ewing summarized his case for Spangler's innocence, sticking to fundamental points: the man's character was fundamentally sound—that of a good-natured, willing drudge who was only one of many captivated by a charismatic star who had free access to the theatre; Booth could have carried out his deed at a theatre other than Ford's; the preparations for the president's visit had been routine; the box's broken lock and peephole, however created, could not be linked to Spangler; Spangler had remained at his duty post all evening, and no one except for Rittersbach ever witnessed him doing or saying anything incriminating; his behavior in the days after the assassination had been irreproachable; and the rope found in his bag could easily be explained.

Furthermore, Spangler could not have been part of any conspiracy, since no one had connected him to any kidnapping or assassination plot, and no one had seen him assist Booth in gaining access to the box or fleeing afterward. There was "not the slightest indication that Spangler ever met Booth except in and around the theatre," or ever associated with any of the other defendants. As for Spangler being Booth's accomplice, "not only does it not appear he *had* one, but also that it *does* appear he did not *need* one." (A statement by conspirator Davey Herold indicated that even Booth as he fled was pained by accounts he read of Spangler's troubles.) Finally, as must have become abundantly clear by this point, Spangler was not the man with the mustache seen conferring with Booth outside the theatre.[26]

Ewing had every right to feel confident. He had mounted a solid, persuasive defense. The strongest testimony against Spangler—the words of Jake Rittersbach—no one else reported hearing. There remained no other aspect of the prosecution's case to rebut. His final act on his clients' behalf was questioning, on June 23, the court's jurisdiction, a crucial aspect of the trial still debated today. His contention was summarily rejected.

John Ford knew better than to be hopeful, though, having experienced his own unsuccessful two-month campaign against Stanton. By now, too, public opinion, shaped by newspaper coverage of the trial, favored universal conviction. The *New York World* expressed the prevailing sentiment: "evidence taken in the first three or four days was sufficient to justify the conviction of all."[27]

To this Ford strenuously objected, crafting a corrosive rebuttal. "Against Spangler," he wrote, the evidence was "not sufficient to hang a dog." Much of it "was rendered doubtful if not positively false by subsequent evidence and [by witnesses] eager to escape consequences." At least, rejoiced the *Star*, "there is not a scintilla of evidence to connect [Ford] or any of his associates or employees, with the possible exception of Spangler, with the remotest knowledge of Booth's devilish purpose."[28]

Even some of the commissioners were initially sympathetic to Spangler. General August V. Kautz believed that "Spangler does not seem to have been a conspirator knowingly. He was simply a tool of Booth's.... His greatest crime was his ignorance, and that he did not see the ends to which he was being used." General Lew Wallace wrote to his wife as the trial closed that he anticipated deliberating only a few hours to derive a verdict, one which would acquit "three, if not four, of the eight."[29]

It was not to be. The verdict, decided on June 30 and immediately endorsed by President Johnson—but not conveyed to the prisoners until July 6—was only a partial victory for Ewing: his three clients, while found guilty, were among the four spared execution. Spangler, acquitted on the charge of conspiracy to murder, was convicted of aiding and abetting Booth's escape. He was sentenced to six years' hard labor in federal prison.

Rittersbach's words had carried weight.

★ ★ ★

When the sentences were read to the condemned on July 6, Spangler was kept ignorant of his fate. For the next twenty-four hours, he later told one of his guards, he was "in hell. I heard the condemned pass my cell; then my heart stopped beating, for I expected to be called next. I heard the drop fall, and my agony was terrible. I had no relief until suppertime, when I couldn't eat, and this hurt me worse than anything else." Over the next few days, though, as the realization sank in that he had indeed escaped the hangman's noose, he regained his appetite. He was, reported Ewing to Ford with understatement, "in high spirits and rejoices at not being hung." Looking to the future, Spangler even asked Ford to send him his Bible and his little dog. Unable to comply with either request, Ford must have chuckled at the latter item.[30]

Amid relaxed vigilance in the prison yard, Spangler now exercised and chatted cheerfully with anyone who passed, even in the shadow of the gallows. To his guards he seemed "a harmless fellow, a big coward.... He was always hungry and could eat anything that was placed before him." Unbeknownst to him, one of those executed, George

Atzerodt, had the night before his hanging confessed to what had been an abduction plan and declared Spangler to be innocent. Booth had told Atzerodt that someone else, "an actor," would help him escape by turning off the theatre's gaslights. Whether this was Mathews or DeBonay or who—or merely unfilled braggadocio on Booth's part—is pure speculation.[31]

Nine days after the executions, on Sunday, July 16, Hartranft assembled the remaining guilty conspirators in the prison yard and read them their sentences: Spangler would serve his six years at hard labor, and the other three—Mudd, Arnold, and O'Laughlen—their life sentences, at the federal penitentiary in Albany, New York. At 10:00 the next morning, the four men were manacled and marched, shuffling in leg irons, between a double row of guards commanded by now-Brevet Brig. General Dodd to the arsenal wharf and onto the steamer *State of Maine*. Porter accompanied them to ensure their continued health.

At 2:00 a.m. on Tuesday, the *State of Maine* cast off and headed down the Potomac toward Fortress Monroe. It was too late for Spangler to receive an anguished letter from his sister in York dated July 16, and its presence in Hartranft's papers today suggests it was never conveyed to Spangler. She pleaded for a chance to see Ned before he was sent away: "He has not herd from home since his confinement. I am a feared he thinks we have forgotten him, no never he is my brother." She was certain "he would never harm any one." But she knew he drank too much, and now believed his sentence was "a judgement from heavan to stop him in his sins [sic]."[32]

Once underway, Dodd ordered the prisoners' manacles removed. Spangler's spirits lifted in the morning sunlight as he passed the time on deck playing backgammon with Mudd. Around 4:00 that afternoon, they docked at Fortress Monroe and the four prisoners were immediately transferred to the larger side-wheel steamer *Florida*. Ascending its ladder in leg irons with only eight inches of chain proved especially grueling.

Within hours they cast off again. Kept in the *Florida*'s hold overnight, the prisoners were subjected to stifling heat and foul odors, but each morning they hobbled up the ladder into sunlight and fresh air. Spangler boyishly even tried once to ascend several steps at a time despite his leg irons. He played checkers and remained as talkative as ever, sometimes even joking. He insisted to all who would listen that he was innocent—he had had absolutely no inkling of Booth's intentions. Naïvely, he said he could not understand how men he knew could have lied on the witness stand or how the commission could have taken their word over others, such as John Ford, who had spoken the truth. He wished he had been able to think more clearly during the trial, he said, so he could have helped Ewing understand what had been misrepresented. His offer to help Booth "all I can," he lamented, had been twisted out of context and spoken days before the murder. But, he now pronounced, as long as he had enough to eat and work to keep him busy, he was satisfied: "I'll come out all right. Six years is not such a long time after all."[33]

The *Florida*'s paymaster deemed him "a coarse, rough, uneducated, unprincipled man. His bull neck, bullet head and brutish features mark a villain, but without sufficient nerve and steadiness to carry out the villainy his heart would prompt.... He protests with any amount of profanity his entire innocence of the charge but he admits that he has committed crime enough of other kinds to merit the punishment so that his sentence is not undeserved."[34]

Rounding Cape Hatteras, the *Florida* encountered heavy swells, causing seasickness among both prisoners and guards. Yet Spangler mischievously turned his condition to his advantage, eliciting a daily ration of medicinal brandy from Porter, even after he had recovered. As the ship departed from a coaling stop at Port Royal, South Carolina, the prisoners began to have serious doubts as to their destination: they realized they were heading south, not north, the climate was growing hotter and more humid, and they saw sizable piles of provisions stacked onboard—more than would be needed for a trip to Albany. But only Dodd and the ship's captain knew their true destination.

Now they unsealed their orders, and Dodd read them to the prisoners. A week earlier President Johnson, at Stanton's urging, had decided to remove the four men to a military prison far beyond the reach of potential civil *habeas corpus* proceedings; their destination was Fort Jefferson in the Dry Tortugas, seventy miles off the coast of Key West, Florida.

Until they learned more, they had no idea what this switch meant, but Spangler, at least for now, rejoiced in simply being alive, taking a childlike pleasure in watching the porpoises, sharks, and sea turtles that came near the ship. The mounting heat led the guards, at Porter's suggestion, to bring the prisoners' beds topside at night and remove their leg irons during the day, so Spangler was as comfortable as he had any right to expect. Arnold and Mudd were less sanguine. At Dry Tortugas, Mudd bemoaned, "None of us will live more than two years." He spoke of suicide and announced that he planned to take any chance he could to try to escape.[35]

By the twenty-third, Porter noticed that even "Spangler's goodness seems to have vanished." A maudlin letter from Spangler onboard the *Florida* to a barkeep in Washington, probably Peter Taltavul, was likely drafted by Arnold, as its theatrically florid passages resembled in no way the semi-literate letters Spangler later wrote to John Ford—but do resemble the rhetorical flourishes in Arnold's own letters—and it was erroneously signed "Edward Spangler." In it, Spangler found himself "thinking of old times, and wishing I was seated in your saloon.... The last drink I had was [there] and you may put it down as a settled fact that it will be the last for six long years to come.... When joy shall swell your heart.... stop for a moment to cast a lingering but bright thought upon [me], and I will feel happy in my exile—banished and in a burning clime.... Good bye. Sometimes think of me."[36]

After a brief stop at Key West, the *Florida* reached Fort Jefferson around noon on the twenty-fifth, and the prisoners' spirits lifted. Freed from their leg irons upon transfer to the fort, they thanked their guards for the kind treatment they had received en route, hoping for the same from the fort's garrison of the 110th New York Regiment, commanded by Colonel Charles Hamilton. Porter opined that that would be the case if they exhibited good behavior. Hamilton warned them, however, that any infraction of prison rules or attempt to escape would have them back in irons and placed in the fort's dungeon. Spangler duly became prisoner number 1526.[37]

Covering seventeen of the twenty-two acres of Garden Key, the hexagonal Fort Jefferson was the third largest in the nation. Despite nearly thirty years of construction incorporating over sixteen million bricks, it never saw completion and saw no action during the Civil War. "Every species of malefactor was represented" among its 550 prisoners, described a guard captain, but the majority were bounty jumpers and deserters. It stood "like a vessel riding at anchor. No other land is anywhere visible excepting a few small coral reefs.... No sound is heard except that of the waves beating against the stone breakwater.... On every side is a broad expanse of green ocean.... Never was jail more jail-like." Another soldier wrote to his wife, "If there is a Hell.... I don't believe it is much hotter than Tortugas."[38]

But as desolate as it was, sea breezes ameliorated the scorching summer heat, and the availability of productive work assured that the new arrivals would not lack for exercise. Watching other inmates shingling a roof, Spangler requested a carpentry assignment, which was readily granted. Arnold was allowed to work as a clerk due to his exquisite penmanship, and Mudd became an assistant to the fort's doctor, duty that would within the coming years prove invaluable.

The four convicted conspirators shared reasonable quarters in a boarded-in casemate directly above the fort's sally port (entryway), its three narrow windows perched above the fort's drawbridge across a fifty-foot moat that contained a few sharks. Sleeping on straw mattresses on the cell's dirt floor, they appreciated Mudd's idea of creating a ditch (still there today) to drain the rainwater that came in during tropical storms.[39]

Arnold, the eternal pessimist, bleakly proclaimed the fort "without exception the most horrible place the eye of man ever rested upon, where every day the miserable existence was being dragged out." He had some cause for this assessment. Cruel punishments were meted out daily to intractable prisoners, and their diet consisted of greasy coffee, rancid meat and fish, and hard, dry bread suffused with worms.[40]

Spangler, stoically serving out his sentence, avoided reprimands and remained optimistic. A newspaper correspondent reported the former stagehand to be "feeling more cheerful since learning that he is to have pure air to breathe and plenty to eat, with accompanying manual employment." Another described him as "robust and jolly, a physical condition he attributes, however, solely to his being innocent." To his guard captain he was "a German, fat and jolly. I think I never saw him when he had not a smile on his broad face. He seemed to treat the whole affair as a joke, and went about his work with as good a stomach as any free artisan working for top wages."[41]

Spangler's carpentry skills proved to be an asset for the fort's ongoing construction and a godsend for his three cellmates, yielding various items of furniture, including canvas-covered wooden bedsteads. Taking on odd jobs and selling handcrafted wooden items to the soldiers, he earned a modest income, occasionally making more than he had at Ford's. Called one day to complete some repairs on the home of the fort's doctor, he told the man's wife that even though his sentence was a mistake and that he had had nothing to do with the assassination, "I suppose I have done enough in my life to deserve this, so I will make the best of it." Except for one or two brief spells in the fort's hospital (perhaps seeking the same medicinal alcohol he had discovered aboard the *Florida*) he remained in good health.[42]

In September he wrote to a "gentleman in Baltimore" (likely Ford) who was savvy enough to have the letter published in local newspapers. Its rough-hewn diction, spelling, and punctuation are a far cry from the sentimental style of his letter aboard the *Florida*. "This is a purty hard place to live," he began. Describing his meager diet, he asked to be sent some fish hooks to supplement it. While he accepted his sentence, he was resolute that it was unjust: "Before God who I know will find me accountable if I lie I knieu nothing or herd nothing about the existence of eany such a thing until after the assassination." He had merely tried to help a friend who "asked me to see to his horses wich I did he said that he would make me a hansome presen, wich he did, six years on the Iland of Dry Tortugas." He would derive comfort in the days ahead from one thought: "All the evidence in my case is known I leave it to all honest and unprudical people to judge of my innocence or guilt. Grate injustice has been done me by some false witnesses [sic]."[43]

An amateurish escape attempt later that month by Mudd—stowing away on an outbound steamer, but discovered even before it cast off—changed everything for the four conspirators. They were clapped into irons and moved from their quarters above the sally port to a ground-level gunroom in the bastion at the south end of the fort. This was the dungeon Colonel Hamilton had warned of. Its two small portholes above the moat's water line admitted no fresh air and nearly no sunlight, and its brick walls remained perpetually slimy. The fort's sewage, which emptied into its moat, occasionally surged back into the cell, its noxious fumes unavoidable day and night. A massive hurricane struck the fort in October, flooding their compartment. As soon as it passed, Spangler was put to work six days a week on repairs to the fort, in irons with an armed guard standing over him.[44]

Not surprisingly, his "jolly" demeanor disappeared.

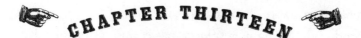

CHAPTER THIRTEEN

"ACTORS, IN ORDER TO LIVE, MUST GO ON WITH THEIR BUSINESS"

F OR THE ACTORS OF Ford's Theatre, every day that passed now
was a day of unemployment. As haphazardly as they had come
together to support Laura Keene that night, their paths now
diverged in equally random directions.

But the ground had shifted beneath them, and certain factors beyond
their control made theirs an increasingly uncertain world. The long-
accepted declamatory style of acting under which many of them had
trained and performed, in which melodramatic posturing and stentorian
vocal delivery "made points" with the audience, was losing ground to
demands for more realistic acting that mirrored real-life emotions and
behavior.

Public tastes were changing, too, in terms of the plays being written and produced. Daring new subject matter and scripts blended comedy and tragedy, calling for more nuanced interpretations of playwrights' carefully-crafted lines. Actors could no longer rely on suspenseful twists of plot in predictable melodramas to cover inadequacies of talent. They were increasingly being cast as multi-dimensional characters, rather than being able to take comfort in the relative job security of the "lines of business" they had always known. No longer could an actor hover onstage on the periphery of a star who monopolized the audience's attention. More often now, each had to function as a member of an ensemble interacting to create the illusion of a room full of real people in a real dramatic situation.

Added to all this would be the exploding popularity in the coming decade of a new American art form called the "musical." Within a year it would burst onto the scene with William Wheatley's smash Broadway hit, *The Black Crook*, the product of his inspired integration of an abandoned French ballet troupe, their talent and endowments exhibited in flesh-colored tights that simulated near-nudity, into what had been an ordinary melodrama. The result would be months of sell-out crowds (unsurprisingly, mostly men). Soon, actors would have to develop an ability to sing and dance or be left behind. And for the handful who lived into the twentieth century, the embryonic film industry would bring an entirely different set of demands.

Perhaps most threatening of all to those still employed in stock companies would be the rise in the 1870s of "combination companies." The precursors of twentieth-century touring companies, or "road shows," these were packaged touring productions of only one or a few scripts, with all cast and technical elements intact, crisscrossing the nation on its ever-expanding network of rail lines. No longer would a theatre maintain a stock company on salary, but now could merely provide an empty stage and a skeleton stage crew. In 1860 the theatregoing public across the country had supported sixty stock companies. By the mid-'70s this would shrink below fifty, as thirty combinations came on the scene; by 1880 only seven stock companies would be left to compete with 176 combinations; by 1890 even those seven would be gone, as the number of combinations approached three hundred.

True, this meant that residents of smaller cities could enjoy Broadway-quality shows, but it forced actors to be away from home and family for greater periods of time. While this remains a consideration today, actors of 1865 lacked our modern means of cheap, rapid communication with those left behind.

Only a few of the assassination-night actors felt any particular loyalty to the Fords, despite John Ford's nurturing of their careers and abiding concern for their welfare. But whereas no particular *esprit de corps* had existed among them before, a perverse connectedness began to emerge now from their shared experience of simply having been together backstage that night. Booth's deed was an added onus as they tried to move forward. As they traveled, they constantly wondered: How would they be regarded in each new city by each new audience? Would anyone realize they had been there "that night"? Would newspaper reviews dredge up that event? Should they give interviews about it? Or—the ultimate question—should they even stay in the profession?

In each case—and no two were alike—they had to find a way to put the trauma of April 14 behind them and move forward. They had been warned not to leave the city, and the stigma of their association with Ford's precluded their being hired at Grover's. "Probably no class of our citizens have made more sacrifices or suffered more pecuniary loss, in consequence of the assassination," noted the *Washington Chronicle*, "than the actors and managers of the theatres." The *Intelligencer*, too, encouraged the public to remember "actors, in order to live, must go on with their business like other men."[1]

But venturing out could be dangerous. For weeks after the assassination, reported the *Chronicle*, "so thoroughly was the national vigilance aroused ... that no man who bore a remote resemblance to the doomed assassin could safely venture beyond the precincts of his immediate home." Ned Emerson's resemblance was more than "remote," making him hesitate to seek employment, despite the spreading news of the assassin's capture and death. But he had to work. So, scaling back his ambitions, he accepted a contract at the newly opened Oxford Music Hall on the unsavory lower side of Pennsylvania Avenue, and thus became the first of the Ford's Theatre actors to regain employment. He opened there on April 24 in *Fanchon*, supporting Nellie Whitney, a local actress.[2]

Conductor Withers and acting manager Phillips came up with a short-term solution. They formed a new company to hire as many of the Ford's actors as feasible, leasing the old, unused Washington Theatre on Eleventh Street, which Withers remembered from two seasons there between his enlistments. But previous managements there by Ford, Keene, Booth, and Withers himself had all failed. It sat in the same unattractive part of town as the Oxford, had barely adequate acoustics, and remained impervious to the efforts of even the brightest stage lights to cheer up its interior. It was, said one actor, "a most miserable-looking place, the worst I met with in the country." Plus, it was small, seating only seven hundred. "The audience," said the *Chronicle*, "could almost inhale the gin toddy that Richard or Macbeth had taken previous to the murder of Old King Henry or white-haired Duncan.... When Othello fell head foremost it was a mercy that he did not kill the whole orchestra, or kick smothered Desdemona out the back door."[3]

But it could be had cheaply. Withers and Phillips's leading lady would be Jeannie Gourlay, whose April 15 benefit had been sidelined by the assassination. Withers had another reason to feature her: they had impulsively married on April 25, having become engaged within twenty-four hours of the assassination. Her sympathy for his jilted plight, along with his stabilizing presence through the weekend's horrible uncertainty, had kept her by his side. The marriage, however, would be short-lived.

Leading male roles would be played by Phillips or actors from the Holliday Street Theatre; Mrs. Muzzy would play the Old Woman parts, and George Spear the Old Men. John Mathews was again to be the Heavy. Soubrettes would be Helen Truman and Maggie Gourlay, who was briefly engaged to Mathews. The company would be rounded out with utility players Tom Gourlay, George Parkhurst, C. V. Hess, and Will Ferguson (still doubling as callboy/ prompter).

Before this could be undertaken, though, they had to extract their wardrobes, scripts, and instruments from the padlocked Ford's Theatre. They pleaded for access from Colonel Burnett, who, at Stanton's order, had carefully logged each backstage item, prop by prop and costume by costume, even confiscating Gorman's gas bags and hoses. By the end of April, their efforts began to bear fruit, although the complete process—understandably a low priority of the War Department that month—took weeks. Ironically, one of the first trunks released was Parkhurst's, which he had obtained from Booth (although it was several decades before he admitted the identity of his benefactor), now conveniently delivered to him by one of the V.R.C. guards.

Withers and Phillips faced considerable competition: the city's Oxford and Canterbury Music Halls were already playing to good houses, and a remodeled Grover's was slated to reopen in early May. So, on Monday night, May 1, they opened their Washington Theatre, relying for the time being on whatever costumes, properties and scenery they could scrounge. To save rehearsal time, they presented plays the actors already knew— shopworn scripts that Washingtonians unfortunately had tired of: comedies such as J. B. Buckstone's *Married Life* (their initial production) and Tom Taylor's *Still Waters Run Deep*, and sentimentalized dramas like Bulwer-Lytton's *Lady of Lyons* and *Richelieu* and—a true chestnut—an English translation of Kotzebue's *The Stranger*. Each evening's performance also included a farce and Withers's sister Charlotte, age twelve, singing the postponed "Honor to Our Soldiers."

Meanwhile, their competitors were mounting productions of colossal hits like *Aladdin* (at Grover's, where its highly successful run had been interrupted by the assassination), *The Sea of Ice*, and *Uncle Tom's Cabin* (which by mid-May was filling houses nightly at all three other theatres). Newspapers in the capital for the most part supported Withers and Phillips's efforts, but for two weeks, initially meager box office declined a little more each day.

Mathews lasted for only a few performances. Toward the end of April, still afraid of being caught up in the investigative net, he had sought out a trusted friend from his days at St. Mary's, Father Francis Edward Boyle, now pastor at St. Peter's Church on Capitol Hill, and confessed to him his knowledge of the contents of Booth's letter. Boyle, a popular, charismatic figure with strong ties to Washingtonians of all faiths, could easily read the city's mood that spring and advised Mathews to flee to Canada. So, less than a week into the new theatre's season, Mathews heeded the advice and was gone. He may or may not have told his momentary fiancée Maggie he was leaving; neither ever said.[4]

John DeBonay opted out of the new venture entirely, going instead to one of Ford's two remaining venues, the Alexandria Theatre. There, under the management of Ford proxy Joseph Parker, he played supporting roles in light comedies and otherwise tried to keep a low profile.

By May 15, the day Withers testified in the trial of the conspirators, business at his and Phillips's new theatre began to pick up, due to warmer weather and the massive influx of veterans gathering for a Grand Review of the Troops. By the following week their new company was playing to overflowing houses.

On the eighteenth they brought out their heavy artillery: their unrivaled star attraction, Miss Major Pauline Cushman. Virtually unknown before the war, this strikingly beautiful, raven-haired, black-eyed thirty-year-old had been performing in Union-occupied Louisville, Kentucky, early in 1863 when she became friendly with some nearby rebel officers who dared her to toast Jefferson Davis and the Confederacy from the stage one night. Accepting the dare led to her arrest, but before doing so she had obtained the permission of the Union provost marshal, who enlisted her as a spy.

Twice arrested by the Confederates in Tennessee, Cushman escaped both times, but was less fortunate the third time, when she was sentenced to death and kept under close guard. Feigning illness to buy time, she was rescued at the last minute by Union forces. Ironically, it had been Phillips who terminated her contract in Louisville when she made her infamous toast. Now, he had to add a hundred chairs each night to accommodate her fans, many of whom were starstruck Union officers.

On May 29 dozens of actors from all Washington theatres participated in a colossal benefit at Grover's to raise funds for a Lincoln monument. Their combined orchestras played, along with three regimental bands, but Withers was not chosen to conduct.

By mid-June, Withers and Phillips found themselves competing with Grover's opportunistic staging of *Our American Cousin*, the city's continued oppressive heat, and its rapid depletion of soldiers. Except for Cushman, the venture had been a disappointment, and the two men announced a closing-night benefit on July 5. But it, too, was poorly attended, with reviewers perceiving their company as "rundown." Once again, the actors were stranded.

Eighteen-year-old May Hart, with scant experience in minor roles that required her to look pretty more than demonstrate histrionic ability, performed for a few weeks in May at the unsavory Canterbury. In June she accepted a better offer from John T. Raymond, who had taken over Ford's lease on Belvidere Hall in Cumberland. There, within weeks she married fellow company member John G. Saville, twenty-four. The new couple, playing leads in reliable scripts like *Uncle Tom's Cabin* and *Ticket of Leave Man*, quickly proved popular.

One of the first actors to put the assassination completely behind him was John Dyott, who never mentioned it again and granted no interviews on the subject. When he left Laura Keene's tour at the last minute before that April 22 performance in Cincinnati, he walked into a lucrative contract with the management of New York's Winter Garden Theatre to play featured roles opposite major stars.

Keene, too, refused to discuss the assassination after issuing an initial statement on April 29, which was printed in the *Clipper* and other newspapers. In it, she restricted herself to narrating her own actions that evening: waiting near the prompter's desk to go on stage when the shot rang out, and being struck by Booth as he rushed by holding an enormous knife. She had walked to the front of the stage, tried to quiet the audience, heard a call for water, and then made her way with it by the "rather circuitous" backstairs route to the president's box, remaining with him until he was carried out. She contradicted callboy Will Ferguson's statement that he had also been in the box, saying he was out calling actors.[5]

Continuing the pattern of short-lived relationships among the Ford's Theatre actors, the May–December Brinks marriage was in trouble by summer (they would divorce in the mid-1870s). Still, they kept their fortunes hitched together and left Washington in June for Richmond. There they performed under the management of a newly-circumspect D'Orsey Ogden at the struggling Richmond Theatre that Ford had revisited in April. Edwin took walking gentleman roles and Kittie assayed her first acting in small general utility parts.

Had Dyott not taken the Murcott role in *Our American Cousin* at Ford's Theatre on the fatal night, Brink would have performed it; his night off had enabled him to walk to the theatre with Booth. Now, in Richmond, he reclaimed the role, and Kittie played Sharp, the maid. Still holding a morbid fascination for theatregoers, the play attracted good audiences. Praised for his "masterly manner," Brink was soon playing leading roles, including the title role in *Othello*. Ogden retained both Brinks for his coming season in Richmond, but reserved the lead roles for himself. Edwin played everything from improbably juvenile parts to major roles (e.g., Macduff to Ogden's Macbeth); Kittie continued with general business (e.g., the Player Queen in *Hamlet* and a witch in *Macbeth*).[6]

Johnny and Kate Evans also left town, passing up Withers and Phillips's offer. In June they headed for the Pennsylvania oil boom towns of Meadville and Pithole City, a hundred miles north of Pittsburgh, which they likely had learned about from Booth, who had invested in oil wells there. They joined the McFarland Dramatic Company, whose new theatre in Meadville had just opened, and after that, the company of the new 1,100-seat Murphy's theatre in Pithole. Johnny played minor roles and leads in farcical afterpieces, and Kate played general utility roles. The ubiquitous *Clipper* covered these performances, deeming Kate "among those especially deserving mention."[7]

Their close-to-capacity audiences were as unsophisticated as anything encountered by actors out West during the Gold Rush and Silver Fever years. "The simple clapping of the hands," finger-wagged the nearby *Titusville Herald,* "is sufficient to express the most exquisite delight and satisfaction with the performance ... but rude boisterous stomping and screaming so often, yes invariably witnessed in our public gathering, is absolutely disgraceful."[8]

Pithole City epitomized "boom town." Two oil strikes there in January 1865 had started a town that by September sported a population of fifteen thousand, increasing by December to at least twenty thousand. It had more than fifty hotels, three churches, a daily newspaper, the third-busiest post office in the state, and a flourishing red-light district. But the dearth of other strikes and the discovery of oil elsewhere dropped its population to two thousand by the close of 1866 and to 237 by 1870. Nothing remains there today but tall grass.[9]

★ ★ ★

After the trial of the conspirators, John Ford turned his attention to retaking full operational control of his Washington Theatre so he could begin to repay his sizable debts. He still owed Ewing $1,200 for Spangler's defense and estimated that the loss of box office revenue so far had cost him over ten thousand dollars (nearly $150,000 today). Yet he faced his current situation with a certain gallows humor: Before he was thirty-six years old, he would later joke, he "had had two theatres burned out and one shot out" from under him.[10]

His Alexandria theatre was thriving under Parker's management, and Ned Emerson was justifying there the promise Ford had seen in him. Emerson had come down from the Oxford Theatre with co-star Whitney and they were filling houses nightly. Ford's Holliday Street Theatre, too, did well that summer.

In mid-June, Ford wrote to his *bête noir*, Stanton, and to Captain Bell to complain about the deplorable neglect of his theatre's furnishings, scenery, and costumes, with "many articles of value carried off while in military possession." A *New York Times* reporter concurred: "the building has been roughly used." Ford asked Stanton to at least allow Gifford and Carland to enter the still-occupied theatre to assess the state of things and pack up and protect scenery and costumes. It angered Ford, too, that Withers and Phillips had been permitted during his imprisonment to cart off costumes, drapes, and scenery for their theatre. No record exists of Bell's or Stanton's response, but there is no indication that Ford was any more successful with them than his brother had been recovering his purloined jewelry.[11]

Then, abruptly on June 22, the heretofore intransigent Stanton relented, ordering the theatre to be returned to Ford. At 2:00 that afternoon the guard company withdrew, handing the keys over to Gifford. Sensitive to the hallowed aura now surrounding his theatre, Ford's initial response was to put it up for sale, so its purchaser could properly consecrate it as a memorial to the slain president. Several religious organizations came forward, among them the Young Men's Christian Association and the nearby Methodist Episcopal Church. Both intended that the edifice never again be used as a theatre. Even the nearly assassinated secretary of state, William H. Seward, weighed in with a proposal to use it for religious purposes. A secular proposal being bruited about was to turn it into a "Lincoln Institute" similar to the Smithsonian—a concept that only in 2012 came to pass in an educational facility across the street from the theatre.

The YMCA's offer of one hundred thousand dollars met with Ford's approval, and a down payment of ten thousand dollars was to seal the deal. So, one morning in late June, the Fords and a few employees began packing all of the theatre's equipment and furnishings for removal to

Baltimore and Alexandria. By the end of the month, piles of furniture, backdrops, curtains, and costumes competed with curious onlookers and souvenir hunters—no longer held at bay by soldiers—for space on the stage.

Yet the deal fell through. The YMCA failed to raise even the down payment and backed out, as did all other organizations. Now, out of financial necessity Ford had no other option but to reopen his theatre. On July 3 he acknowledged the public's "desire to change the character of this property" and the prevailing "religious sentiment," but stated his intention to resume business "at the earliest practicable moment."[12]

His first production would be *The Octoroon*, which had been scheduled for April 15. He telegraphed as many of his former actors as he could, but not all were available on short notice. He signed up Emerson, Spear, Ferguson, Parkhurst, and Carland, but notably absent was Jeannie Gourlay, along with her father and sister. The rest of the cast he filled out with actors from the Holliday Street. He wrote to former stage manager John Wright in Boston about the reopening, adding [underlining his] "I will want you." But Wright, about to start work at Wallack's Theatre in New York, declined, and Ford again turned to the stalwart Tom Hall. With the obvious exception of Spangler—and most likely Rittersbach, who would have known after his testimony not to return—most of Ford's other staff were readily available. Former acting manager Phillips, realizing he was *persona non grata*, stayed away, instead booking Grover's empty theatre to stage musical variety shows (Grover having taken his management skills to Philadelphia and New York).[13]

Opening night would be Monday, July 10, amply publicized across the city. But the main topic swirling through Washington the week before was the impending July 7 execution by hanging of the four assassination conspirators who had been found guilty. This represented another crusade for Ford: although he had never met the condemned Mary Surratt prior to their incarceration together in Old Capitol, he was utterly convinced of her innocence, largely based on a series of encounters he had had there with Louis Weichmann, her primary accuser. Weichmann had as much as confessed to Ford that he had been browbeaten by Stanton into testifying, and had sought Ford's advice. Mrs. Surratt, Weichmann had said, had been like a mother to him, truly "the most exemplary of women." Ford had advised him to simply tell the truth.[14]

Now Ford swung into action. He worked late into the night of July 5, composing a fervent letter to President Johnson urging clemency. At 3:00 a.m. he left Baltimore by train for Washington, letter in hand, arriving at 6:00 and going directly to the home of former Postmaster General Montgomery Blair, who he knew had the president's ear. Yet that effort and various other attempts to approach Johnson were rebuffed as harshly as his previous attempts to reason with Stanton had been. "Mrs. Surratt," he accepted gloomily, was "a dangling corpse before I turned homeward."[15]

The hangings, carried out under a blazing sun, provided a measure of retribution in Washington and beyond. But Ford's timing in reopening his theatre the following Monday could prove dangerous, attorney Ewing warned him. This was based on a tip from the ever-loyal Spangler, who had heard his guards muttering about the upcoming reopening, insinuating there might be a riot. "You had better get a special guard," Ewing advised Ford. "I understand *soldiers* well enough to believe it not unlikely they would attempt to lock up the performance and even destroy the building, or gut it, and *authorities* well enough to believe they might wink at it."[16]

★ ★ ★

The morning after the executions, the new *Octoroon* cast assembled on the stage of Ford's for a lengthy, productive rehearsal. By midday on Monday, it began to feel like old times backstage as the staff toiled at preparations for the evening's opening. Scenery was pulled into place, costumes were dusted off, and Hall oversaw the actors' lines and movement. The backstage and front office crews worked through their dinner break to refurbish the theatre after its ruinous occupation. Doorkeeper Buck thoughtfully draped the presidential box with black crepe, then hurried home to change. Ticket sales had been brisk, with equal numbers of strangers and former patrons reserving seats, and he wanted to be ready.

But once again Stanton intervened. Based on real or perceived rumors of rioting, he ordered the theatre shut down, preventing any performance. Shortly before 5:30 p.m., a detachment of soldiers marched up Tenth Street, stacked arms, and took up stations around and inside the theatre. Its captain announced that he was taking possession of the theatre "in the name of the Government of the United States," informed Ford that he was not to open, and ordered him to report to Stanton within twenty-four hours. The soldiers posted large notices on the doors reading "Closed by Order of the War Department," and cavalry stood by to intercede if necessary.[17]

By 7:00 several hundred patrons began to arrive, but quickly appraised the situation and turned back. Well past the scheduled 7:45 curtain time, up until almost 9:00, a few bands of theatregoers milled around out front, either hoping for a reversal of policy or itching for trouble. But nothing untoward materialized, and around 10:00 the majority of the guard was withdrawn. For the thoroughly dejected cast and crew inside the guarded theatre, an eerie evocation of the night of April 14 was inescapable.

The next morning Ford stormed into Stanton's office, only to be coldly informed that the seizure of his theatre had resulted from fears of rioting; its disposition would be brought up later that day in a cabinet meeting. But, Ford argued, he had received assurances from the city's mayor and police superintendent that *they* had entertained no such fears. He got nowhere. Stanton remained resolutely opposed to the building ever again being used as a theatre. In his mind Ford was only trying to "make money from the tragedy, by drawing crowds to the place where

Lincoln was slain." He had it within his power to seize any building he wished and intended to do so now.[18]

But Ford could be just as tenacious. Three days later he returned to Stanton's office to again press his case, only to be told that President Johnson had now intervened and ordered that the theatre remain closed. Ford argued that his "duty to creditors and dependant people compelled me to make a legitimate use of it." Stanton had nothing to say and showed Ford the door.[19]

By now, Ford's determination to reopen had also ignited a theological firestorm. Leading the torch and pitchfork brigade was the Reverend Dr. B. H. Nadal, pastor of Wesley Chapel of the same Methodist Episcopal Church that had sought unsuccessfully to purchase the theatre. Within days Nadal alleged publicly that Ford "did not appreciate the national feeling and the national conscience." His theatre promoted "profanity and pollution.... Such an idea could only be agreeable to the enemies of the cause in which Mr. Lincoln fell." To reopen would be "a sacrilege."[20]

Ford's response was eloquent and swift. Published in several Washington and New York newspapers, it reminded Nadal that he had offered the building for sale and found no takers. Furthermore, "the late President Lincoln was alike my friend, my patron, and my benefactor.... Cheap lip service is distasteful to me [and] I begin to doubt the sincerity of those who question my motives." His efforts to reopen were not for his own gratification, but "on behalf of my helpless and unemployed company."[21]

Public opinion remained divided, but more than a few newspapers backed Nadal and Stanton. One asserted that the theatre was "not a fitting place for a good or a great man." Another was more pointed, decrying "the possibility that the place in which the great martyr had spoken his last conscious words would echo with the coarse laugh and ribald jeer of men not too far removed from the great crime."[22]

It was time for Ford to retain legal counsel. Henry Winter Davis once again agreed to represent him. Together they informed Stanton in person that unless the building was rightfully returned to its owners they would initiate legal proceedings. Stanton countered that he had been acting at the express direction of the president.

But Ford and Davis stood their ground. As Ford said later, "It was an interesting scene. Violent as Stanton was, he was no match for Davis, who was as brave as a lion, and who could talk just as well as Stanton." The parties hammered out an agreement on the spot for the federal government to purchase the theatre for one hundred thousand dollars and to rent it for $1,500 a month until Congress approved the sale. The building would be considered government property as of July 24, to be converted into a three-level storehouse for records of the late war, to be called the Bureau of Rebel Archives and Relics. The partition, door, and furniture of the presidential box were to be carefully removed and preserved.[23]

Stanton, confident of Congress's approval, began with a relish in October to gut the building, farming out its renovation to his brother-in-law. Ford saved the stage's proscenium arch and other furnishings for his other theatres and took the door from the box to his home in Baltimore; his brother Dick retained the portrait of George Washington, its frame chipped from Booth's spur. Gifford, overseeing the transition for Ford, quit the property in disgust soon after the renovations began, over the shoddy workmanship and cheap materials he saw being used. This cutting of corners would have dire consequences several decades later.

The settlement could not have come soon enough for Ford, who now owed Davis on top of Ewing, plus outstanding notes due to star performers such as Edwin Forrest. Complicating the picture were letters from former actors plaintively seeking charity or back wages, or both. He hoped "to get them all paid before Christmas."[24]

★ ★ ★

By the start of the next theatrical season in late August, the actors had dispersed widely. Withers and his new bride Jeannie Gourlay (still her stage name) headed to Memphis. She would be First Walking Lady and he (as "Professor" William Withers, the prevailing nomenclature of the day) as Music Director.

Within months of the Union occupation of that city in June 1862, its New Memphis Theatre had reopened following an extensive renovation and was thriving, attracting equal numbers of local citizens and Union officers (enlisted men seldom possessing the pocket change or the aesthetic inclination to attend). Like Washington, Memphis had enjoyed a population boom during the war, exploding from three thousand in 1860 to twenty thousand now. The city had been shaken, though, by the nearby explosion and sinking in late April of the steamship *Sultana*, and on August 17, just before Withers and Gourlay arrived, by one of the largest earthquakes in its history, wreaking widespread devastation.

Young Will Ferguson, perhaps persuaded by Withers, announced that he, too, would be joining that company, as a walking gentleman. But at the last minute, partially because Ford was still paying him to perform clerical duties, he stayed in the capital, acting and prompting in Alexandria and Baltimore, until March 1866, when he joined a third-rate touring company playing small towns in central Pennsylvania.

New Memphis Theatre manager W. C. Thompson could have used him that season; as of late August he was still advertising for actors. Actresses were in even shorter supply, due in part to the tainted reputation the profession still held. Certainly not helping was the September 1864 decree by the Memphis mayor: in an effort to eradicate immoral activities and social diseases, all single women in his city had to register with him weekly, refrain from wearing "showy, flashy or immodest dress in public [or visiting] the public square or the New Memphis Theatre." Jeannie Gourlay must have been less than thrilled.[25]

Playing leading roles in melodramas, she proved popular with Memphians. Reviewers praised her "modesty, sweet simplicity and womanly tenderness," saying she "ruled by enchantment." The orchestra, no less, "discoursed most eloquent music." Withers came to realize quickly, though, the true sentiments of his Southern audience: patriotic airs like "The Star-Spangled Banner" and "Yankee Doodle" were hissed, while Confederate songs were applauded. By mid-season this had gotten so bad that the occupying Union general threatened to intervene. Manager Thompson appeared to be complicit, conducting benefits for Confederate veterans' causes. Despite a successful benefit for Withers, by the end of the season he was writing to John Wright in Boston, seeking a position there. Worst of all for Withers, around the same time, Jeannie left him, returning to the Northeast where she initiated divorce proceedings, citing irreconcilable differences.[26]

In July 1865 her parents suffered the death of another baby, which they took home to Brooklyn for burial. Maggie went with them, and Jeannie joined them at the close of the Memphis season. Only their father, Tom, was able to find work in New York, joining the company of Lucy Rushton's Theatre. This brand-new Manhattan venue had been converted from a church for Rushton by her benefactor, a wealthy department store magnate, in little over two weeks. But Rushton's limited talent and mismanagement led to its closing in five months.

John Mathews, still fearing the long arm of Washington justice, achieved some measure of success that fall in Montreal. By December he risked returning to the United States to accept a modest contract with the manager of the Rochester Opera House in New York. With each passing day he felt slightly safer, especially as news reached him that the trial of the conspirators had ended with no mention made of the potentially incriminating letter Booth had entrusted to him. The strain was beginning to tell on him, though. Friends observed that he "has never been quite himself" again, that he was "ever after very eccentric," and sank into an increasingly deep depression from which he never fully recovered. His stooped posture and deflated demeanor led to his being hailed at age thirty by the *Clipper* in December as "one of the best old men in the profession."[27]

★ ★ ★

By fall some opportunities opened up for the actors in Washington. May Hart Saville and her new husband drifted back from Cumberland to join the company of the Washington Theatre, now under new management. Helen Muzzy acted there, too, as well as at Grover's, where Parkhurst and Phillips were in the company; they were among the cast of a memorable January 1866 production of *Fanchon* starring Maggie Mitchell. Phillips flourished, playing First Old Man roles to glowing reviews. His benefits were well attended, and by summer 1866 he was managing Grover's touring company.

A few remained with Ford. Acting with Emerson in Alexandria, Ferguson was promoted by Parker to walking gentleman. He began a ten-year apprenticeship there and at the Holliday Street, playing a variety of roles from comedian to villain and studying pantomime, elocution, and even fencing. John DeBonay and Helen Truman, near the start of their careers with little else available to them, took minor roles at the Holliday Street for the next two seasons.

★ ★ ★

The beleaguered star the night of the assassination, Laura Keene, had ended the spring of 1865 season early and returned to her new forty-acre estate, Riverside Lawn, on the Acushnet River in New Bedford, Massachusetts, to recuperate. That fall she plunged into another round of touring, attended by her faithful dresser, Billy Otis, with Harry Hawk back playing comic leads opposite her.

New Hampshire native Otis, twenty-nine, whose real name was Otis Reed, had been waiting tables in Boston when he had been discovered by actor-manager E. L. Davenport, who prepared him for the stage with particular emphasis on elocution. Keene had picked him up two years ago in a swing through New England. Now, Otis earnestly sought an acting career of his own and treasured every tip and small part she gave him, striving diligently to improve his craft.

Keene toured that 1865–66 season in a lesser orbit—cities such as Milwaukee, Detroit, Louisville, and Providence—with one-week stands instead of the previous two, and the same tired repertory of plays—a major miscalculation. She also found herself in a legal brawl over the rights to *Our American Cousin*. Despite her fervent belief that she controlled sole rights to perform it, calling it one of her "most valuable possessions," John Sleeper Clarke, husband of Booth's sister Asia, announced his intention to perform it in New York at the Winter Garden. Worse, that theatre was owned by another Booth brother, Edwin (who had not returned to the stage himself out of shame). Worst of all, Clarke had made his announcement while the trial of the conspirators was still going on, then topped that by casting John Dyott as Murcott, the role he had played for Keene. (Although it must have given Dyott pause each night as he readied himself to play Act Three, Scene Three, which he had never gotten to perform on April 14.)

With her husband's help, Keene published an open letter to Clarke in several newspapers in September. It dripped with vituperative allusions: "If you steal the property of a woman [it] is not far from shooting a man behind his back…. The bad taste of seeking to deprive me of the use of this play is only equaled by your ever appearing in a comedy which ought to have only a memory of shame and sorrow for you and every member of your family, [a] cloud which has lately fallen upon our whole profession."[28]

Keene had already sued Clarke once, in 1858, when he had first tried this piracy, and had won. Now she sought an injunction in New York Superior Court against him, with damages. The case of this already-infamous script became a *cause célèbre*. This time the judges decided in favor of Clarke, on the basis that playwright Tom Taylor had sold another version of the play to a now-deceased comedian whose widow had sold the rights to Clarke. In rendering their decision, they denounced Keene and Lutz for their "coarse, malignant, vulgar libel" of Edwin Booth, which had contained "the most cowardly allusions to an event which has clouded all his present, and cast a pall of death over his future."[29]

An unrepentant Keene continued her tour, but box office receipts declined and reviews were tepid. A December stop in New Orleans was especially disappointing, with unseasonably cold weather and actors who didn't know their lines. In a Christmas Day letter, she lamented the long hours of fruitless rehearsals that yielded meager audiences. In Chicago in January, she and Hawk met with withering reviews. In *The Sea of Ice*, her performance slipped "over the edge of the super-pathetic and border[ed] on the ludicrous."[30]

Hawk was castigated for ad libbing (a perennial fault) that included profanity, a transgression particularly embarrassing to Keene, who prided herself on above-board backstage and onstage morality. He was, however, "a great favorite" in Milwaukee and later capitalized on his popularity in the area by buying property in Minneapolis. By the end of April, though, after playing Springfield, Massachusetts, and Hartford, Connecticut, he and Keene parted ways and he moved on to Boston to support his antebellum role model, John E. Owens. After a few more New England towns, Keene retreated once more to Riverside Lawn to absorb the realization that she was no longer a star of the first magnitude.[31]

Her other erstwhile touring partner, John Dyott, was enjoying his last hurrah at fifty-four at New York's Winter Garden. In addition to Clarke's *Our American Cousin*, this engagement included on January 3, 1866, the profoundly emotional return to the stage of Edwin Booth, who had chosen for the event his most famous role, Hamlet; Dyott was Polonius.

Extra police stood on duty outside the theatre that night to control the anticipated violent response to the re-emergence in the public eye of this brother of an assassin. Yet when the lights came up on the second scene, revealing Booth seated among the Danish court—rather than making a triumphant stage entrance—the crowd went wild with cheers of approbation. "Surely such a scene was never before witnessed in a theatre," professed the *New York World*. "The applause burst spontaneously from every part of the house. The men stamped, clapped their hands, and hurrahed continuously; the ladies rose in their seats and waved a thousand handkerchiefs; and for full five minutes a scene of wild excitement forbade the progress of the play."[32]

Booth was overcome and stood with his head lowered, his body shaking with emotion. Dyott, standing among the court, had a close view of the tears of gratitude flowing down Booth's face as he rose and crossed to the footlights, bowing deeply and repeatedly to acknowledge this heartfelt tribute. It was not until well into the second act that he fully regained his composure.

When Dyott took his own benefit night in February, the *Clipper* hailed him as "an artist in every sense of the word, and an old New York favorite." He stayed on to support Booth through mid-March, then played a few weeks at the Academy of Music in Brooklyn, where he enacted King Henry IV opposite James H. Hackett's Falstaff. Returning to the Winter Garden to support comedians Mr. and Mrs. Barney Williams, he may have been influenced by their goofy antics, or was simply weary of the demands of the profession, but he succumbed at some point to Hawk's bugaboo: ad libbing and "introducing stupid 'gags.'" This led to a contretemps with the critic for the *Chicago Tribune*, who deplored these variations from the script and asserted that Dyott did not know his lines. Dyott furiously defended his performance and threatened legal action. The next night the paper sent a shorthand reporter to record his performance verbatim, comparing it to the play's printed text. The result, the *Tribune* crowed, was damning to Dyott and effectively ended his career in New York.[33]

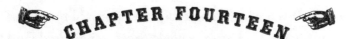

CHAPTER FOURTEEN

"TO OPEN ALL MY WOUNDS AFRESH"

B Y 1866 THE ASSASSINATION had receded slightly in the public consciousness, its perpetrators duly tried and punished, and Andrew Johnson presided over a nation turning its attention to the thorny issues of Reconstruction. By any measure, it would seem that everyone connected with Ford's Theatre could begin to embrace the future. Yet within two years, its former managers and employees would be dragged back into court to relive the awful events of April 14, 1865.

The central figure in the continuing saga was still John Ford. His hope to repay all creditors lay unfulfilled; if anything, his debts had grown. Knowing his settlement with the federal government was imminent, he stalled for time, joking to Ewing in January that he would pay him "in a few more days (I mean days as lawyers mean words when they say 'one word more')." Even when Congress finally approved the sale of Ford's theatre in February, after its shareholders were reimbursed Ford barely broke even on his three-year Washington investment.[1]

Having sold his theatre only reluctantly, he redoubled his efforts to command the theatre scene in Baltimore and Washington. When his Alexandria Theatre unexpectedly failed, he abandoned it, owing more than two thousand dollars in rent. But he leased a second theatre in Baltimore, the Front Street, which he planned to use for staging "grand, sensational" productions, while keeping the Holliday Street for legitimate drama. He booked for it some of the biggest names on the American stage, such as Forrest (although hardly the draw he used to be), Owens, and Edwin Booth. Unwisely, Ford kept the old model of a stock company, including Ned Emerson, in whom he still saw star potential.

In June 1866, Ford leased Washington's National Theatre—the old Grover's—and undertook a massive renovation to accommodate larger "spectacular" productions. James Lamb created elaborate new backdrops and a new act curtain. For stage manager, Ford hired Tom Hall, who had been so helpful during Ford's incarceration. To mollify Wright, he told the former manager, "Should I lose him, you would be the first I should think of to fill his place," and promised to arrange for Wright to manage Forrest's upcoming tour.[2]

Ford's heavy investment in the two cities was risky, but not uncharacteristic. He envisioned increased audiences in the Baltimore-Washington area and figured that by booking the right stars and promoting them properly, the market would reward him. What he didn't count on was a postwar recession that would hurt all entertainment business. After losing considerable money with the National, he quit the capital for another five years.

★ ★ ★

Having finally settled his legal fees, Ford began in late 1866 to incur more, aiming for a new civil trial or a pardon for Spangler. He was "determined to leave nothing undone to release Spangler, if it costs $5,000." He remained in contact with that former employee, telling Ewing in January 1867 that Spangler was "doing well and is a general favorite" at Fort Jefferson. Ford sent newspapers and shipments of food to Spangler, who reciprocated with gifts of handcrafted cribbage boards, an inlaid chess table, and a lady's writing desk for Edith.[3]

Heartened by the United States Supreme Court's 1866 decision in *Ex parte Milligan* that the military trial of civilians was unconstitutional, Ford asked Ewing, along with Maryland Senator Reverdy Johnson, to draft a writ of *habeas corpus* on Spangler's behalf. To assist them, Ford crafted a lengthy account of Spangler's arrest and imprisonment in Washington, the anomalies of his trial, and the conditions of his incarceration now. The three men appealed directly to President Johnson, but were rebuffed. "In the present state of political excitement" the chief executive "did not think it prudent ... to take any action" regarding Spangler.[4]

Apparently, the nation's emotional wound was still raw. A soured Ford wrote to Ewing melodramatically, "Alas our poor country—she bleeds at every vein." He looked "with fear to the future and entertain a vague regret that I am father to children who may only inherit the wreck of our once proud country."[5]

Ford's patriotism was tested again in spring 1867 when the Judiciary Committee of the United States House of Representatives began hearings exploring possible grounds for impeachment of the president. Spearheaded by newly elected radical Republican Congressman and former Union General Benjamin Butler, an unrelenting critic of Johnson's Reconstruction policies, the hearings dredged up aspects of the assassination that focused on Johnson's interaction with various figures in its subsequent investigation and trial.

Judge Advocate General Joseph Holt, the assassination trial's lead prosecutor, testified before the committee about the contents of Booth's diary, taken from him when he was killed. In the process, Holt read aloud several passages from it that alluded to the letter Booth had written justifying his actions, intended for publication in the *National Intelligencer*—the letter that John Mathews had destroyed. The secret was out.

In late May, Old Capitol Prison Superintendent William Wood, following Holt, identified Mathews as the letter's recipient. He had learned of its existence from John Ford who, he said, "can tell you more about it, [that] this man Mathews had the letter and had destroyed it, and that he had told some priest about it." Wood downplayed Mathews's complicity, though, saying the actor was only one of "thirty or forty other persons from Maryland who were suspected of having aided Booth."[6]

Three days later, Ford himself was hauled before the committee and grilled about Mathews and the letter. He reported running into Mathews, whom he identified as a warm friend of Booth's in those days, just after his release from Old Capitol. It was then that he learned from Mathews about the letter and its delivery, contents, and destruction. Mathews, he said, had moved to Rochester, but last winter had written to him in search of employment. Ford may not have known, or chose not to say, that Mathews was by then back in Washington acting for a competitor, Wall's Opera House.[7]

It took the committee another five weeks to get around to bringing in Mathews, who explained to them that his training as an actor had enabled him to memorize the letter from several re-readings before burning it. He said he had been able to associate the various names in the letter with real-life circumstances, an actor's trick. Given some strong similarities in phrasing between that letter and a manifesto Booth had written in 1864 and left with his sister Asia, and Mathews being a close friend of the Booths, he likely mingled the contents of the two.

Now, he narrated for the committee in lengthy, precise detail his encounter with Booth on Pennsylvania Avenue, including Booth's specific words and manner, especially his nervousness and urgency. He verified that the letter had been in Booth's handwriting and that it had been addressed to *Intelligencer* editor Coyle, whom he had told about the letter before he left for Canada; yes, John Ford had been present. The only other persons with whom he had discussed it, he said, were an attorney and a priest [Father Boyle].

Butler's search for inculpating evidence against Johnson reached as far as Fort Jefferson. Spangler and Mudd, having been returned to their previous quarters from the "dungeon" and freed from their irons following repeated complaints to the president by Mudd's wife, were visited in mid-November 1867 by Florida notary William H. Gleason. He had been sent by Butler to obtain statements about possible complicity in the conspiracy by the then vice president.

Spangler and Mudd saw no reason to cooperate and refused to provide any statement. For two weeks Gleason worked on them, threatening them with return to their dungeon and a diet of bread and water if they did not cooperate, and finally secured lengthy sworn statements. Spangler's described his limited acquaintance with Booth, primarily concerning the horse and stable, yielding nothing remotely helpful to the House committee.[8]

★ ★ ★

The impeachment hearings did not end the Sisyphean testimony about the assassination by former Ford's Theatre employees. News had reached Washington in November 1866 that Mary Surratt's fugitive son, John, whom Stanton had mistakenly thought could be smoked out of hiding by the threat of his mother's execution, had been captured in Egypt. Brought back in irons to the Washington Navy Yard in February 1867,

Surratt was to be tried, but in a civilian court, the new Supreme Court for the District of Columbia.

The trial, Judge George Fisher presiding, commenced on June 10. John, Harry, and Dick Ford, property man Jimmie Maddox, stage carpenter James Gifford, costumer Louis Carland, house manager Tom Raybold, and actors Mathews and C. V. Hess all received subpoenas. Thus, each was yet again compelled to relive the traumatic events of April 14, 1865, now more than two years in the past, and relate any number of details about it as if still fresh in their minds. Most had to travel to do so, having moved away from Washington as another means of putting it all behind them. Two would again be impressed into testifying for the prosecution.

Maddox, who would have been glad to permanently turn his back on the city that had terrified him so thoroughly, had lived since August 1865 on High Street in Baltimore with his wife, Maggie, continuing to work at the Holliday Street Theatre, where she played small parts. Now, recalled to Washington, he was put forth by the prosecution on June 22 to describe the basic events of the fatal night.

He stuck to simple facts about Booth's use of the stable and movements that day. Again, he described hearing the pistol shot and providing the pitcher of water. Again, he described Spangler's remaining at his duty post all night. No, Maddox said, he did not know John Surratt, nor had he ever seen him before. Surratt's defense attorney, Joseph Bradley, saw no need to cross-examine him.

Four days later Gifford was similarly summoned to attest to the same general facts he had supplied in the original trial. Clearly, a central aspect of the prosecution's strategy was the recreation in jurors' minds of the horrific events of two years ago and to imbue them with an immediacy sufficient to find Surratt guilty by association with Booth. Gifford complied, providing a carpenter's knowledge of the gimlet hole in the door to the box and the piece of wood used to wedge it shut. He, too, knew

Spangler well, and had seen him on duty backstage all evening. An unstated implication was that Surratt, not Spangler, may have been the mysterious man seen out on Tenth Street with Booth shortly before the assassination.

In early July, Bradley opened Surratt's defense. The first theatre figure he called, on Monday, July 8, was John Ford, who explained with his diagram the layout of his theatre and its basic operation. He was unable to be more specific about the events of the fatal night, however, as he had been in Richmond. He acknowledged knowing Booth since childhood and Booth's father before him and affirmed Booth's physical characteristics, charisma, and agility.

Harry Ford followed his brother, elaborating on procedures of the theatre, particularly those of that day's rehearsal, and described the process of assigning and decorating the presidential box. Spangler and Rittersbach, he said, had assisted him, but he made no mention of any disloyal comments or disagreement. As with Bradley's questioning of John Ford, Surratt's name never arose.

Right after them, Gifford returned, questioned both by Bradley and his associate, Richard Merrick. Here the focus moved to events that had transpired out on Tenth Street during the second and third acts of *Our American Cousin*, particularly Hess's noting of the time of 10:10 p.m. After relating his whereabouts throughout the day in question, Gifford maintained he had at no time during the evening encountered Booth, and thus could certainly not have seen anyone with him, either inside the theatre or out in front of it.[9]

Some of Gifford's answers were testy, such as his response to repeated questions about preparations for Lincoln's visit that had occurred while he had been out to dinner: "How can I tell you what was done when I was not there to see it?" When Bradley persisted in questioning Gifford's never having seen Booth out in front of the theatre at any time during the third act, he would only concede, "There was a great deal of confusion at the time." He concluded by summarizing his and Carland's actions backstage in the hours after the shot.[10]

Hess, who had moved to Philadelphia to act at the Walnut Street Theatre, was called back to Washington to testify after Gifford. He described his preparing to sing "Honor to Our Soldiers," backed by the entire cast, at the conclusion of *Our American Cousin*. Walking to the theatre, he had stopped for a cigar, then encountered Gifford and Carland out front. He had asked the time (10:10) in a pleasant—not furtive—tone and then gone backstage to don his black suit. Except for Lincoln's driver, he had seen no one else on the street, especially not Booth, and did not know Surratt.

That afternoon's session ended with Carland, brought down from Boston, where he had moved to get far away from Washington, Baltimore, or—still gun shy from the "Knights of the Blue Gauntlet" episode—Philadelphia. Since he had been inside Ford's Theatre most of the day in question, he was asked to describe the rehearsal that had taken place and the noontime gathering on the steps outside. He described his own actions on the fatal night, along with what he knew of Gifford's, Raybold's, and Hess's. Carland acknowledged having known Booth, but had never seen Surratt before the defendant was pointed out to him now.

The next morning, Bradley called Dick Ford, who similarly reviewed his actions that day. Asked about an evening several weeks before that when Booth had attended a performance at Ford's, Dick stated categorically that Surratt had not been present. At this point prosecutor Edwards Pierrepont abruptly questioned Dick's loyalty during the recent war, musing that he "probably should ask several other [witnesses] the same question." Something about Gifford, Hess, and Carland's demeanor troubled him. Ordered by the court to reply, Dick invoked the Fifth Amendment and was excused. Later that morning he asked to return to the stand, explaining that he had declined to answer because he "did not see what bearing it had on this case." As a matter of fact, he asserted, "I

was always a thoroughly loyal man, was always on the side of the government ... in sympathy with the North against the South."[11]

On Wednesday morning Raybold was the first defense witness. He, too, narrated the events of April 14, including his early arrival at the theatre, receiving news that the president would attend, letting Lutz in to help guide rehearsal, and then selling tickets. He explained how he had broken the latch into the box, and provided information about the theatre's various doors, footlights, and scenery. Asked about his service in the war, Raybold readily complied.

As in the 1865 trial, the prosecution relied now on the testimony of Louis Weichmann, the long-term tenant of Surratt's mother who had drawn a clear connection between Surratt and Booth. To impugn Weichmann's credibility based on encounters they had had with him during the earlier trial, Bradley recalled Carland, Gifford, and John Ford on July 16. All testified that Weichmann had admitted to them that his testimony in that trial had been suborned and that he was thus not to be believed now.

Carland described Weichmann's declaration on a street in Washington in July 1865 that he had lied on the witness stand, having been threatened with death by Stanton and Burnett, leading him to seek Carland's advice. Severe guilt over the impending execution of Mrs. Surratt, largely on the basis of his testimony, was destroying him, Weichmann had said, comparing his torment to that of Shakespeare's Hamlet. His testimony in 1865, he asserted, had actually been written out for him in advance by a detective embedded in Old Capitol. Carland, a fellow Catholic, had counseled confession and walked Weichmann to the nearest church, urging him as well to swear out a public statement about his testimony being coerced. Weichmann agreed to the confession, but refused to make any statement, as it might lead to his conviction for perjury. Since then, Carland testified, he had made it a point to shun Weichmann, even to the point of moving away from Washington within the month. Now, he expressed his dismay at this perversion of justice.

On cross-examination, Pierrepont's attempt to impugn Carland's loyalty during the war was met with a stony response: "I did not sympathize with either [side]. I was doing a business with a mixed population and I kept myself neutral." Pierrepont hammered away, repeating the same question a dozen different ways, eliciting the same answer in increasingly haughty tones. The outcome of the war, retorted Carland, was "an indifferent matter to me." Asked if he didn't care, then, if the Union Army "was slaughtered," he asserted, "I am opposed to war." Pierrepont attacked Carland's Canadian birth, declaring that he was less believable because he was "a foreigner," and reminded the jury that Carland knew Weichmann from their being in prison together.[12]

Gifford followed Carland and hammered another nail into the credibility of Weichmann, who was present in the courtroom. Gifford swore that he had heard detectives threaten Weichmann in prison; Maddox and John Ford had also been present. The next day, Ford and Maddox verified all of this, explaining that the conversation had occurred in Old Capitol in May 1865. They each pointed directly at Weichmann, identifying him as the perjurer.

Now it was Mathews's turn to testify, only two weeks after his appearance on Capitol Hill. The defense hoped to elicit from him the fact that the letter given to him by Booth contained the names of his co-conspirators, names that did not include Surratt. Yet after some preliminary information about the circumstances by which Mathews obtained the letter, the prosecution objected and, after deliberation that lasted until the next morning, Judge Fisher declared Mathews's testimony about the letter inadmissible.

Cross-examining Mathews, Pierrepont attempted to damage his credibility, questioning first his loyalty during the war and then his memory about the events of April 1865. Mathews maintained his allegiance to the Union and rebutted the latter implication: "I think anything as impressive as all the circumstances connected with the assassination would be

as deeply impressed upon my memory when I was 100 years old, as it would be an hour afterwards."[13]

But Pierrepont then brought out a transcript of Mathews's interrogation by Colonel Foster on April 21, 1865, on which occasion Mathews had lied about his acquaintance with Booth. As Pierrepont pointed out inconsistencies between things which Mathews had said at that time and those he stated now, Mathews turned circumspect, hedging defensively on dates and splitting hairs on words. At which time was he mistaken, Pierrepont asked, then or now? "I do not know whether I am most likely to be mistaken, or the man who wrote down the examination," Mathews tried. "I am not sure that that is my examination correctly reported." The rest of his answers were variations of "That happened too long before the interview," "I do not remember," and "It is possible I did say that then, but was mistaken." Finally, he blurted, "I did not wish to have it understood that I had been with him that day, because I had understood that persons who had been seen speaking with him on that day had been interrogated."[14]

Luckily, the focus of the trial was on John Surratt and not John Mathews, so he was excused and the matter dropped. Mathews's last word on the subject was a letter to the editor in the next day's *Intelligencer*, apparently at Coyle's request, to say that the paper had never actually received the letter and thus could not be accused of suppressing it. That day, Mathews recited the contents of the letter to Coyle, and it was printed "verbatim" by the paper on July 18.

Eventually, Mathews developed the story that he had withheld the existence and contents of the letter in 1865 not out of guilt but out of concern for Edwin Booth, who was a dear friend, and for Booth's mother, whose death it would likely have caused. Doubtless he wished he had never mentioned the letter to anyone at all.

The final testimony by any Ford's Theatre employee in any trial related to the assassination came on July 24, when Hess was recalled so the jury could assess his resemblance to Surratt. That was minimal, consisting primarily of having dark hair and a mustache; his darker complexion and shorter stature were considerably at odds with Surratt's. Bradley, in his summation, dwelt on this only briefly, making a much stronger case for Surratt's not having been anywhere near Ford's Theatre the night of the assassination. This was compounded by the dubious testimony of a chief prosecution witness, Weichmann. The proof of the defense team's effectiveness came on August 10, when the jury deadlocked. After an abortive attempt at a retrial, Surratt was freed.

In denouncing Weichmann, Bradley had also rhetorically asked, "Who impeaches Carland? Nobody.... I challenge an impeachment of him." Ironically, Carland's honor *had* been impugned twice, once officially in 1865—the Blue Gauntlet letter—and a second time a year after that in print. Carland had teamed up with Keene protégé Billy Otis, advertising their availability for acting and costuming engagements. But they apparently skipped out on a contract, leading a pair of theatrical managers in Mobile, Alabama, to take out a public notice in the *Clipper* in September 1866 warning other managers nationwide not to hire them.[15]

★ ★ ★

By the time these trials had ended, a wave of mortality had broken over the actors, managers, and stagehands of Ford's Theatre. Of the forty-six people backstage that night, ten would die within a decade, some of them key figures in the performance.

The first to go was actor **Johnny Evans**, who had been performing in fall 1865 with his wife Kate in Pithole City, Pennsylvania. For months he had had little stamina, having suffered a stroke while pushing an overweight fellow actor uphill in a wheelbarrow, compounded by contracting consumption (tuberculosis). Not yet thirty years old, he succumbed on December 6, 1865, leaving Kate to raise two young children alone. Before that evening's performance at the Murphy Theatre, the manager stepped to the footlights and delivered a brief tribute to the deceased. The local newspaper was less laudatory, noting of his passing that Johnny was "not one of the greatest stars in the theatrical firmament."[16]

The life of **Maggie Gourlay** was cut short as well. In late summer 1866, Leonard Grover had brought her to New York as a dancer at his Olympic Theatre (probably hoping her more talented sister Jeannie would follow). At that time, such girls were often easy prey for wealthy men about town, and enough instances of such "patronage" occurred to give the "girls of the ballet" a less-than-pristine reputation. Maggie, who had just turned eighteen, must have been disillusioned or of insufficient talent, for she was gone after one season.

In February 1867, as Jeannie's divorce from Withers was being finalized in Connecticut, new men appeared for both of them. Jeannie had been touring New England towns in a company that included thirty-one year-old Glasgow-born upholsterer-turned-actor Robert Struthers, with whom she, now twenty-one, became romantically involved. He became her manager, promoting her at every opportunity as she played the title role in *Fanchon*—Maggie Mitchell's signature role—and Ophelia in *Hamlet*.

While performing in New York in August 1867, Jeannie realized that one of the actors in a different company, another Scotsman, W. D. Shiels, would be perfect for Maggie. Within a month Shiels and Maggie had married, and by January 1868 were expecting their first child. Maggie went to stay with her parents at their farm in Lumberland in southeastern New York, and Jeannie interrupted a Canadian tour to help care for her in her confinement. The love letters Jeannie and Struthers exchanged during this period—he remaining in New York City to promote her career—convey a poignant blend of romance and practicality. They married in Montreal in August 1868, and by fall she resumed acting.

In late September, Maggie delivered a healthy baby boy but contracted puerperal fever and ten days later was dead at age twenty. She was buried near Lumberland. Jeannie again cut short her touring to return to the farm to comfort her parents and help care for the baby.[17]

Property man **Jimmie Maddox** likewise never lived to see thirty. He died suddenly in Baltimore on February 19, 1868, still working for Ford, who uncharacteristically never spoke of him afterward, despite giving any number of interviews. If the pressures of the past three years led Maddox to commit suicide, no one knows for sure; his death certificate has not survived. Baltimore obituaries barely gave him a line, although the *Sun* did reference his joviality: "To know him was to love him."[18]

Were it not for his one rash deed, the same epitaph might have been accorded John Wilkes Booth, whose ignominious burial in the corner of an ammunition storeroom in the Washington Arsenal penitentiary had deeply troubled his family, especially his mother, Mary Ann. This disposition of his remains also came to involve Ford, whose help in reclaiming the body was sought by Edwin Booth.

Having twice unsuccessfully petitioned President Johnson and now Secretary of War Ulysses S. Grant for permission to retrieve his brother's remains, Edwin turned to Ford, promising, "I shall not forget it. Any reference to this fearful subject being to open all my wounds afresh—and God knows the shower of horrors heaped upon my family is enough already.... Anything that can be done to lessen this agony should—from humanity's sake—be done."[19]

Edwin, overwhelmed by worsening business at his theatre in New York, arranged for Baltimore undertaker John Weaver to visit Johnson, carrying a letter from Booth assuring that they would "observe the strictest secrecy in this matter—and you may rest assured that none of my family desire its publicity." On February 12, 1869, Johnson granted Edwin and Ford an audience.[20]

Three days later, strictly admonishing that no publicity and no monument were to mark the reburial, Johnson released the body to them. Ford returned to Baltimore, and Edwin to New York, confident in Ford's handling of all arrangements. That very afternoon, with the assistance of a few trusted arsenal soldiers and a Washington undertaker (whose enterprise backed up to the alley behind Ford's Theatre through which the assassin had escaped), Weaver exhumed the pine musket case that held Booth's body wrapped in rotting army blankets. Atop the case were black block letters clearly identifying its contents as the remains of John Wilkes Booth.

The undertakers brought the pine box to the alley, ironically placing it in the very stable Spangler had built four years before for Booth's horse and carriage. Waiting there was Booth's youngest brother, Joseph, a doctor, who definitively identified the body as his brother's. Confirming that identification was a Baltimore dentist who had worked on Booth's teeth, which resided now in a head detached from its body since its autopsy on the *Montauk*. Transferred to a larger, sturdier pine coffin, the remains, accompanied by Joseph, were conveyed by train to Baltimore, arriving later that night at Weaver's Fayette Street establishment, behind Ford's Holliday Street Theatre. Meeting Joseph at the train station to escort the body to Weaver's was Ford, who telegraphed its safe arrival to Edwin: "Successful and in our possession here."[21]

Two days later Ford quietly gathered the few friends and family who were to know of the reburial and walked them over to Weaver's from the Holliday Street. These included his brother Harry; two young actresses whose tour Ford was managing, Ella and Blanche Chapman; comedian Charles Bishop (a close friend of Edwin's); a profoundly grieving Mary Ann Booth and her children Joseph, Rosalie, and Asia; along with Asia's husband, John Sleeper Clarke.

All conclusively identified the body, despite its mummified skin, as John Wilkes's, noting its recognizable head, which was "passed around and looked upon," its profuse, wavy black hair, and fine teeth (Joseph and Bishop even extracted a "peculiarly plugged" one to be certain). John Ford observed that the handsome jaw line "bore resemblance to the living man," then turned back to the body, feeling along the left leg to locate the broken tibia. Blanche ceremoniously clipped locks of hair from the brow and distributed them, including one reserved for Maggie Mitchell, Booth's early co-star and possible lover. Mary Ann Booth moaned softly as she stroked the strands from the head of her favorite son.[22]

The next day, February 18, the body was placed by Weaver and his assistants in a receiving vault (due to the frozen ground) at Green Mount Cemetery, a mile and a half away. There, on the sunny afternoon of June 26, the two Ford brothers joined many of the same people as had gathered at Weaver's, with the addition of actor Junius Brutus Booth Jr., among a crowd of about fifty mourners, reporters, and curiosity-seekers, for the actual interment. John Wilkes Booth's handsome mahogany coffin was carried from vault to grave by pallbearers from the theatrical profession. Officiating was the Reverend Fleming James of St. Luke's Hospital in New York, who had been visiting a rector friend nearby. Despite not knowing whose service he would be conducting until his arrival at the cemetery, James was terminated from his position at the hospital for doing so.

★ ★ ★

Mortality also stalked the convicted conspirators at Fort Jefferson, in the form of yellow fever, which struck in August 1867. The first to succumb was Michael O'Laughlen, with **Ned Spangler** at his bedside, the next month. Dr. Mudd worked tirelessly to care for those stricken, finding comfort in the darkest days when "a hearty laugh was frequently indulged at the expense of our ready wit, Edward [sic] Spangler." Then Mudd, too, fell ill, and Spangler—his "faithful and ever solicitous roommate," nursed him through it while constructing coffins for those in the fort who died (thirty-seven of 280 guards and prisoners). Although Spangler "was not generally select in his epithets toward those whom he disliked," observed Mudd, "if he saw them in suffering, it excited the liveliest sympathy, and he would do anything that laid [sic] in his power for their relief."[23]

Continued petitions from Mudd's wife, coupled with renewed efforts by Ford and Ewing and reports of Mudd's heroic efforts to care for the yellow fever victims, led President Johnson on March 1, 1869—three days before his term expired—to pardon Spangler, Mudd, and Arnold. Three weeks later the pardon arrived at Dry Tortugas, and Spangler was released, dropped off at Key West to make his way home as best he could. He found passage—likely with funds from Ford—on a steamer to Baltimore, arriving on April 6. Appearing to be "in relatively good health and spirits," he answered questions readily, if occasionally profanely. His sense of innocence, he asserted, "kept him from utter despair."[24]

For four years he worked at Ford's Baltimore theatres, then accepted an offer from Mudd to live at his farm in Bryantown, Maryland. Arriving at night and frightened by the Mudds' dogs, he passed that first night perched in a tree. Mudd gave him five acres behind the house, and Spangler spent the next year and a half doing carpentry for him and various neighbors.

But caught in a chilling downpour the first week of February 1875, he fell ill, and his weakened resistance from exposure to yellow fever led to his death from a respiratory ailment, possibly tuberculosis, on the seventh. Having embraced Catholicism in his final years, he was buried in St. Peter's Cemetery near the Mudd farm. Mudd's daughter Nettie eulogized him in terms far different from those used to describe him at his 1865 trial. Ned Spangler, she said, was "a quiet, genial man, greatly respected by the members of our family and the people of the neighborhood. His greatest pleasure seemed to be found in extending kindness to others, and particularly to children, of whom he was very fond."[25]

★ ★ ★

The curtain came down as well on the lives of other Ford's Theatre figures around that time. Washington actress **Helen Muzzy,** who had played the imperious Mrs. Mountchessington that fatal night, died suddenly at fifty-nine from a heart attack on October 13, 1870. For several years she had been semi-retired, giving private lessons from her home on Fourteenth Street and acting only when "specially engaged" to play Old Fadet in *Fanchon* at the National Theatre, where she also served as wardrobe mistress. Her career had spanned more than forty years.

House Manager and "office factotum" **Tom Raybold,** who only a few years before had testified at the Surratt trial, passed away shortly after Muzzy. He had returned to his former career as a paper hanger in Baltimore when he suddenly died at age thirty-seven on April 7, 1871. He left behind a wife and young daughter, who were granted benefits from his army pension.

Perhaps the saddest post-assassination tale connected with Ford's Theatre was the slow, irreversible decline of **Laura Keene**'s career, reputation, and health. For the rest of her life, she could not "bear to hear the slightest allusion to that moment," observed Kate Reignolds, an actress who knew her well. "She had a frail physical constitution, which made the hard life of an actress a specially severe one to her, and her delicate temperament brought its usual penalty."[26]

Keene's energy dissipating, she insisted on continuing to tour in 1867, again employing Hawk and Otis. In place of Dyott, Keene had been grooming Otis and using stock company actors in whatever city she visited. But bookings became more difficult, the towns and theatres grew smaller and dingier, and the year brought only mixed results. Past the peak of her fame, she was unable to draw the crowds she had before and during the war. Even the boosterish *Clipper* observed this season "her powers are on the wane." One of the lowest points had come in Mobile, Alabama, where she was threatened with bodily harm and told to leave town for being "nothing else but a Yankee."[27]

The constant travel was grueling, and she struggled along from city to city, sometimes ill for weeks at a time. Desperately needing a vacation, she left for nine months in England, returning somewhat re-energized and looking for new scripts. With **John Lutz**'s help she arranged to perform in March 1869 at Wall's Opera House in Washington during President-elect Grant's inaugural festivities. Her engagement included four nights of *Our American Cousin*, which drew sizable crowds due to her not having played Florence there since the night of the assassination.

But Lutz's death in April robbed her of both her resurgent energy and the practical management of her career, despite the efforts of her daughter Emma to fill that role. Against her better instincts Keene tried during the 1869–70 season to tour with her familiar repertory while simultaneously leasing and managing Philadelphia's Chestnut Street Theatre. But it was in the midst of a renovation, and the season there proved short and financially disastrous.

She tried producing children's shows, but that, too, fared poorly. When Colonel T. Allston Brown, editor of the *Clipper*, told her he was forming a theatrical management agency to arrange performances in small towns, she signed on, leading to another exhausting tour to even lesser venues. Brief management attempts in Charleston and New York failed as well. Her resources dwindling, these efforts acquired an air of desperation. Still, Hawk and Otis stood by her for most of these ventures, the former filling in as tour manager.

By now, Keene had contracted tuberculosis and her performances resembled only faded copies of the compelling characters she had created in earlier years. Critic Laurence Hutton attended one in January 1871 in which she performed what had been one of her best roles, Lady Teazle in Sheridan's *School for Scandal*. He came away sadly disappointed: "Laura Keene is old, thin, haggard, scragged, horrid, her appearance is painful and made me think of some cartoon I've seen representing death in silks and satins dancing at a ball with youth and beauty. Never want to see Miss Keene in young parts again."[28]

She started a cultural magazine, but it, too, failed, due to her misreading her audience and the times, which had moved beyond the topics she covered and the aesthetic philosophies she espoused. Unfortunately, its production had been underwritten by a heavy mortgage on her Riverside Lawn estate, which she nearly lost. Trying with her last shred of energy to mount one final successful tour, she was performing in tiny Tidioute, Pennsylvania, on the Fourth of July, 1873, when she suffered a massive stroke. She recovered enough to arrange the disposition of her estate and belongings, including her "Lincoln dress" from the night of April 14, 1865; it would go to Emma. The sale of Riverside Lawn in the midst of the nation's financial panic of 1873 yielded little more than one thousand dollars.

She felt tired and alone. Lutz was gone, her mother had died the year before, and now, on November 4 at age forty-seven, she joined them. By the end she "was so emaciated that her many friends would scarcely have recognized her," noted a reporter. "She was painfully aware of her lost beauty—so much so that one of her last bequests was that her funeral should be strictly private."[29]

It was, and few in the theatrical profession even learned of her death until after her interment. Her fall from the heights of managing her own Broadway theatre, producing hit shows and selling out the best theatres in the biggest cities, to this unassuming final curtain was sadly typical of the fleeting fortunes of theatrical figures in that, or any, century. Yet, ultimately, the events of one night overshadowed all of her accomplishments; when she is remembered today, if at all, it is as "that actress who was performing at Ford's Theatre when Lincoln was shot."

Ever-loyal **Billy Otis** followed her closely even in death. Several times he tried striking out on his own as a light comedian for part of a season, but always seemed to come back to Keene. On these final tours she had awarded him prize roles like Dundreary in *Our American Cousin*, and he had gained experience and confidence. After her death, for a season or two, he began a modest touring career on his own as an "eccentric comedian," which apparently extended to his private behavior as well; he was known for touring with thirty pairs of pants, each with its own creative name.

An accomplished elocutionist, he toured New England towns reciting Shakespeare, *Lady of Lyons*, and *Our American Cousin*, taking special pride in reading in his hometown newspaper that Keene would have had "reason to be proud that she has furnished the artistic world such a son." Throughout, he made it a point to carry Keene's rectitude and religion with him, always whispering a prayer before going out on stage. When he died at thirty-eight of typhoid fever at his mother's home on October 10, 1875, it was said that he died with Keene's name on his lips.[30]

Just as Keene failed to adapt to changing public expectations, so, too, did **John Dyott** slip into the final days of his career, unable to adjust. His stiff, formal acting style and recent "gagging" and improvising had irreparably damaged his career in New York. Critics now hedged their praise of his performances: "Mr. Dyott, though somewhat deficient in person, inexpressive in feature, stiff and ungraceful in action, frequently inaccurate in memory, and never brilliant, has always marked his delineations with such correctness of conception and earnest identification of character, and so much genuine feeling, that he has until lately maintained his position as a leading serious actor."[31]

Dyott tried his luck for part of the 1867–68 season in New Orleans, but postwar civil strife and a wretched supporting company doomed the venture. Except for Dyott "to relieve the terrible dullness and inefficiency of the majority of the troupe," said one reviewer, "the performances would not be endurable." He returned that spring to New York, where, at the lavish new Pike's Opera House on Eighth Avenue, he ended his career performing in outdated melodramas, still trying to adjust to the demands of the new "sensational" dramas. No newspapers took notice except the *New York Times*, which observed, "John Dyott has disappeared, having been his own worst enemy."[32]

He and Henrietta moved to a small house in New Rochelle, New York, where he helped his brother run the town newspaper that consumed most of what little funds he had acquired. When she died in October 1876, it took the life out of him as well. They had been married, performing together, almost forty years, and he was rudderless. So great was his grief and depression that he stopped eating, appearing strikingly frail at her funeral. Little more than a month later he, too, died, on November 22 at age sixty-four and was buried next to Henrietta and their daughter in Green-Wood Cemetery in Brooklyn. Not a single actor attended the service.

His life, Dyott had said a few years before its close, was "full of adventure and singular incidents." His career bridged many of the sea changes in the American theatre of the nineteenth century and shared in some of its most emotional moments, including the Astor Place Riot, the Lincoln assassination, and Edwin Booth's return to the stage. Strewn about his room above the parlor of the small house in New Rochelle where his body had lain was a lifetime's accumulation of Shakespearean costumes, properties, and scripts. Among them was a playbill from the night of April 14, 1865, which Dyott maintained he had picked up from the floor of the fatal box, dropped from the slain president's hand. He had refused one hundred dollars for it while living, yet when his effects were auctioned, it went for $4.19.[33]

As he would have wished, none of his obituaries mentioned the assassination. The *Clipper* waxed nostalgic: "There are elders who, while smiling at the recollection of his textual vagaries, will with admiration recall his scholarly readings and the laborious methods by which he sought to make amends for an unreliable memory."[34]

An era, and a style of performance, had ended.

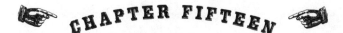

CHAPTER FIFTEEN

"THE MEREST SHADOWS OF TRUTH"

BY THE END OF the decade, Secretary Stanton and Lafayette Baker were dead as well. As zealous as their investigation had been, an easy but erroneous assumption would be that there were no loose ends, no unanswered questions. Yet, as with any conspiracy, more than a few still linger.

Perhaps the most pressing question relative to Ford's Theatre is: *Why did Stanton and his subordinates move so quickly to arrest and interrogate backstage workers*, while overlooking actors who might have provided information or insight to Booth's behavior prior to the assassination? Did these men have advance knowledge, gleaned from sources planted there ahead of time, that something subversive was imminent? Or did these arrests flow from simple deduction?

While Booth often graced stagehands with his presence (usually in a saloon), he spent many hours in the company of actors such as John Mathews and John McCullough, even trying to recruit the former to assist with his kidnapping scheme and later entrusting him with his manifesto. Nearly two dozen actors were never questioned, including some, like Ned Emerson, Johnny Evans, and Edwin Brink, who had known Booth for years. What did they know that they were never asked?

Was Union Navy veteran Brink staying close to Booth that night on someone's orders? To the end of his life Brink claimed, in addition to his navy service, to have served with "Baker's Rangers," formed by Lafayette Baker for the defense of Washington during the summer of 1863 but reassigned to other states' cavalry by January 1864. Baker was notorious for his monitoring and arrests of soldiers and civilians in the capital, with an extensive network of spies. But Brink had remained in the Navy, primarily on the armed ferryboat *Commodore Morris* out of Hampton Roads, Virginia, until November 1864. Was he involved with tasks for Baker after his return to acting? Or was his lifelong admiration for Booth—who, he said, "died like a brave man, as I knew he would"—an insurmountable hurdle to his being able to spy on such a "bosom friend"?[1]

What was it about Booth's friendship with the Evanses that triggered the prompt, massive searches of their house? How did the soldiers who conducted it know so quickly to look for Booth there? And why, as Kate Evans noted, did they make a special point of ransacking the room shared by Harry Hawk and John Dyott?

Among other overlooked actors were Dyott (whose whereabouts that night remain unknown), Helen Muzzy (a long-time Washingtonian of unimpeachable character who had recently acted with Booth and could readily have identified him), and Will Ferguson (who, although young, claimed to have seen Booth leap down from the box and make his escape). Apparently, maintaining the lowest of profiles was everyone's objective that night. "Suspicions were rife," observed Ferguson. "The merest shadows of truth were being materialized into incriminating facts."[2]

Why was Mathews never called to testify for either side in the trial of the conspirators? Was he never charged with complicity due to simple lack of evidence? For the rest of his life he continued to be dogged by Booth's letter, even after moving to New York City. Through twenty more years there, as he acted steadily, interviewers remained as interested in his ties to the assassination as they were to his performances. Again and again they questioned him about the letter and his friendship with Booth. "That tragedy has made me ten years older," he moaned at one point. But anyone found that night with that letter, he asserted, would have been hanged: "I get a touch of the throat disease whenever I think of it.... The Angel Gabriel himself ... wouldn't be safe at that time with that document." He didn't help his case by trying to protect Booth's image: "Do justice to poor John," he told one journalist. "He thought he was doing right.... He was a brave man. There was something exalted in his courage." Most reporters left their interviews thinking, as did the *New York Herald*'s, that Mathews "knew a great deal more about the subject than the keenest cross-examination could elicit—a great deal more than he will ever tell."[3]

For the rest of his life, the assassination confronted him wherever he turned. "He was afraid to pick up a daily paper for fear he should see his name in print," noted a friend, and "almost decided to change it." Walking near the Metropolitan Opera House one day, Mathews saw in the window of a memorabilia shop a playbill for the fatal night's performance of *Our American Cousin*, his name included; he panicked and scurried home. Once, when called up for jury duty, he asked to be excused when a bailiff brought up his connection to the assassination.[4]

Was it guilt that caused this man, who as a youth had considered the priesthood and sought advice from a priest just after the assassination, to turn to altruistic pursuits? He devoted the last fifteen years of his life to the Actors' Fund, providing assistance as an almoner to destitute actors, sometimes even sharing his meager fifteen-dollars-a-week salary with those in need.

Similarly, how much did Ned Emerson know that no investigator ever asked about? Harry Hawk insisted for decades that Emerson knew more than he let on, questioning in 1894 why Emerson "never answers enquiries on the subject of the assassination."[5]

★ ★ ★

And how much did the charged atmosphere backstage at Ford's Theatre contribute to, or foster, a conspiracy? Had men like Gifford, Maddox, and Spangler tacitly encouraged disloyal expression? Their openly secessionist words and their associations with Booth suggest complicity, at least in the abandoned kidnapping plot. Even though they were arrested and interrogated, and a strong case could be made for their involvement, except for Spangler they were never charged. Maddox and Gifford were both unconditionally released after testifying for the prosecution. The early death of the former precludes any look at how the whole affair affected his life, but Gifford must have carried forward some sense of responsibility for having been in charge backstage. He went on to help Ford build a new opera house in Washington in 1871 and remodel another a year later, followed by a third in Baltimore two years after that, yet by all indications their politics never affected the operation of these theatres.

Louis Carland, John DeBonay, and James Lamb, whose secessionist sentiments and/or service for the Confederacy might have entrapped them as it did the hapless Spangler, were released after testifying for his defense. Each resumed his career with modest success.

It's easy to imagine how stunned Spangler must have felt that night when he realized that whatever plot he had been privy to, to any degree, had suddenly become something far more terrible. Was he in the end a scapegoat for all of his backstage Confederates? Did Stanton think, "Someone at that theatre *has* to be held accountable, and this Spangler seems as good as anybody, perhaps better?" The Secretary's hostility and intransigence toward Ford and the theatre suggests more than a desire to honor the memory of his slain friend and chief executive. To what extent was he aware of the climate that existed backstage in the weeks leading up to the assassination?

Were any of the backstage staff actually complicit in Booth's aborted plans for abducting the president? Was the horse and buggy sold by Spangler at Gifford's order for Booth to have been part of the kidnap plot? Some vehicle would certainly have been needed. Were the stage wings kept clear for that eventuality after all? Who really was to have extinguished the lights?

And who was the man smoking a cigar in the theatre that afternoon, whose presence there Spangler casually dismissed? If it was Booth, and he did bore a peephole in the door to the presidential box, it goes against an assertion by Harry Ford's son, Frank, in 1962 that the hole had been bored earlier at his father's direction, to allow a guard to keep an eye on the president when he attended. Frank said his father would "blow his top" whenever "this historical absurdity" was recounted, quoting him as saying, "John Booth had too much to do that day other than to go around boring holes in theatre doors."[6]

Perhaps the largest unanswered question relating to backstage staff is the presence there of Union Army veteran Jake Rittersbach for a mere three weeks prior to the assassination. *Why his hidebound insistence from the outset that Spangler had slapped him and uttered incriminating words?* Rittersbach's testimony, bolstered only by Withers's insistence that someone had helped keep the aisle backstage abnormally clear, was a deciding factor in Spangler's conviction. Did he manufacture Spangler's words or parrot testimony fed him by authorities? Did he mishear Harry Hawk's "I won't tell" to H. B. Phillips backstage in the confusion after the shot, and later confuse the words and the speaker? Why was he so insistent in subsequent days on telling so many people what he had heard Spangler say? Why did no one—except John Miles, obliquely, but certainly not Jeannie Gourlay, who had stood nearby—ever corroborate his version?

Rittersbach's quick release on the morning following the murder, coupled with his presence later in Old Capitol, begs the question: *Was he placed there as he had been backstage, to spy on other stagehands?* Was it he who informed Provost Marshal's detective Charles Rosch within days that Spangler, "was on very intimate acquaintances with Booth," that "they were seen together on the afternoon of the murder," leading Rosch to become "fully convinced that some person or persons belonging to the theater were accomplices"? Rittersbach was the only Ford's Theatre employee to report directly to Judge Advocate General Holt in the days following the murder. *Why?*[7]

★ ★ ★

Another unanswered question is the extent of John (and perhaps Harry) Ford's latent secessionist sentiments in the wake of the assassination and the war. *How thoroughly did any investigator plumb the depth of the Ford brothers' ties to Baltimore*, a city whose population remained largely sympathetic to the Southern cause? Why was John Ford, although held in prison over a month, treated as a gentleman while Harry was questioned for hours and repeatedly arrested? Was John simply more established and respected in the theatrical fraternity? Even William Sinn, a partner of rival manager Leonard Grover, vouched for him, saying Ford, "knew no more about [the assassination plot] than a child."[8]

Even today, some question remains why Ford was in Richmond on the day of the assassination. However, he had applied for a pass to go there several days in advance, his relatives there would have been in dire straits amid the devastation in that city, and he left before anyone at his theatre knew that Lincoln would be attending that night.

Ever the pragmatist, Ford at least knew enough during the war to throttle his latent secessionism in the face of Union occupation of both cities in which he was trying to earn a living. But did any trace of his pro-Southern, states' rights attitude linger once the war was behind him? It was to the South that he turned to rebuild his financial empire after the war, leasing a theatre in Charleston and organizing a series of tours to southern cities like Savannah, Norfolk, Richmond, and Washington (in many ways still a "Southern town").

Did he not realize that Southern citizens had scant money for entertainment, and the Reconstruction racial climate would not be to his liking? The consequences of his refusal in Charleston to admit a Negro who held a valid ticket (purchased for him by a white man) must have brought him up short. Predictably, he was arrested and informed that the penalty, established by South Carolina's reconstructed legislature, could run as much as five thousand dollars and five years in prison. However, Ford sent "a polite note and a season's pass" to the prosecutor, and the charges were dropped; the Negro policeman who made the arrest and the original complainant were also generously provided for. Thereafter, all of Ford's tickets in that city contained the statement, "It is agreed, and this ticket is sold, with the understanding that the management shall have the right to refuse admission to the holder."[9]

His surprisingly profitable new theatres in Charleston, Washington, and Baltimore and his southern tours in the 1870s continued his pattern of featuring stars previously popular in the south, like John E. Owens, John McCullough, and the irrepressible Maggie Mitchell, as well as his latest discovery, a tall, beautiful seventeen-year-old Kentucky native named Mary Anderson. One exception was a tour featuring Edwin Booth, which was complicated by the star's refusing to ever set foot in

Washington; to his dying day if he had to travel south, he skirted the capital. Yet even Edwin Booth was forced in the Deep South to confront in a macabre way the legacy of his brother's deed. In Mobile, Alabama, he was approached for complimentary tickets by Sergeant Boston Corbett, who said, "I am sure you will not refuse ... when I tell you that I am the United States soldier that shot and killed your brother." Booth graciously provided the tickets.[10]

When Edwin died, an event in Washington the same morning as his funeral in New York, June 9, 1893, raised enough questions that a congressional investigation was launched. At nearly the exact hour of Edwin's burial, the edifice that had been Ford's Theatre, which the government had converted in 1866 into office space for army medical records, collapsed, killing twenty-five clerks and wounding more than a hundred others. (Ironically, its medical museum contained a bone from Booth's neck, flattened by the bullet that killed him.) Asked for comment, architect-builder James Gifford recalled the difficulty he had had in the building's initial construction trying to lay a foundation on "quicksand," with repeated cave-ins, as well as his disgust with the shoddy work done in the refitting by Edwin Stanton's brother-in-law. Why then, was work allowed to continue? The ensuing investigation mandated significant structural improvements before the building could be reopened for office and museum use. It would take another seventy years until live dramatic productions again graced the stage of Ford's Theatre.

★ ★ ★

Well into the twentieth century two questions appeared with regularity in newspapers in April, observing various anniversaries of the assassination: *Whose version of the event was the most accurate, and who still survived among the performers?*

Following Edwin Booth's death, a spate of interviews appeared with former Ford's theatre actors who had previously withheld their accounts of that night out of respect for him. Harry Hawk and Jeannie Gourlay, among others, shared their views, but the most rabid competition for the spotlight was that between conductor Billy Withers and callboy-turned-actor Will Ferguson.

Hawk's post-1893 interviews—some quite lengthy—provided unique and sought-after insights. High points were: the warm audience reception that night, his shock at seeing Booth appear with the knife, running from him (as any sane man would have done, he asserted), his identification of Booth as the assassin, and his own arrests in Washington and Harrisburg. He took issue with errors in the accounts by some of his contemporaries, who had only been backstage, not on it. In one of his last interviews, he revealed his post-assassination ploy of traveling under an assumed name, but refused to divulge it. His story remained remarkably consistent, integrating decades-old details about Keene, the Fords, and Mathews, but strangely omitting any mention of Dyott, with whom he had been touring.

Within weeks of Edwin Booth's death, Kate Evans, too, began to grant interviews. She spoke of everyone's reactions at the moment of the shot, and of seeing Lincoln carried out on a shutter. She focused on Phillips and Maddox's help later that night, on Harry Hawk, whom she knew the best, and on Spangler, for whom she felt the greatest sympathy. Sometimes she waxed nostalgic: "In those days, I wonder how we ever got along with coal oil lamps and gas."[11]

In 1894 doorkeeper Buckingham published his version, *Reminiscences and Souvenirs of the Assassination of Abraham Lincoln*, detailing Booth's nervously entering and exiting the theatre lobby, badgering him about the time, and the nightmarish chaos just after the shot. He maintained that Spangler was innocent.

Violating wait-until-Edwin-Booth-dies orthodoxy, Withers began in the 1880s touting his version of the assassination. In a series of self-aggrandizing accounts that became increasingly melodramatic as the years progressed, he told of becoming frustrated that night because his song kept being deferred. He had stormed up on stage to confront stage manager Wright, when he heard the shot—which he thought was a property man's firing a pistol backstage—as he stood in the stage right wings, and saw Lincoln lying on the floor of the box (impossible given the vertical sightline).

According to Withers, little Tad Lincoln, whom he had taught to play the drum, had spent the evening in the box with his father and had tragically witnessed the murder (untrue). Withers had then heroically wrangled with Spangler to prevent his turning "the crank" (actually eight-inch wheels) to shut off the gas to the house and stage lights (contradicting all testimony placing Spangler elsewhere). Next, he had confronted an enraged Booth, his eyes bulging cartoonishly from their sockets, and attempted to block his exit in an abnormally cleared passageway. But Booth had brutally stabbed ("almost murdered") him, cutting him to the bone; the Bowie knife "which he tried to plunge into my heart...buried itself in the back of my neck" (not only physically implausible, but rebutted by the Gourlays' relief immediately afterward that it was only his coat that was slashed, and his 1902 military disability physical reporting no visible scars).

At that point Withers (in one version) was accosted by the crowd—which "grabbed me and wanted to hang me right there, but some who knew me shouted that I was not the man"—and (in another) was grabbed by a detective who "arrested me as an accomplice" (of which no record exists). Withers was confident, though, that he had conducted himself nobly at the trial: "It was mainly on my testimony that the principals in the case were convicted." As for Spangler, Withers asserted that the stagehand "confessed that he was in the plot to assassinate the President" (witnessed by no one else and recorded nowhere). The entire experience either traumatized Withers for life ("To this day [1892] I can feel the dagger cutting through my clothes") or was nearly forgotten ("Why, I've never told about it except on the witness stand, and that a long, long time ago." [1911]).[12]

Ferguson, an increasingly successful actor on Broadway, gushed interviews for decades and authored numerous articles. Usually when asked about the events of that night, he would begin, "Oh, that's an old story. It's been in print a hundred times.... Well, if you want them, here are the details...." And he would be off, vigorously correcting errors in other survivors' versions—especially Withers's—in the process.

Many of the details in his accounts directly contradicted those of others. He asserted erroneously that Booth had not been seen near Ford's for months before the assassination, that he "never shouted '*Sic Semper Tyrannis*' or anything else," that the audience that night "seemed singularly unresponsive," that "I was the only one on the stage that night who was not called on to give testimony at the trial," that Lincoln was carried out of the box in his chair, and that Mathews was neither in the cast nor ever questioned about the letter Booth gave him. Much of Ferguson's energy was directed at specifically refuting Withers, with whom Ferguson disagreed on major particulars—especially Withers's claim to have heroically prevented Spangler from dousing the theatre lights—to the point that theirs assumed the air of a personal feud.[13]

By the 1920s, Ferguson began speaking before civic organizations about the assassination, increasing the frequency of his interviews, and publishing lengthy articles: "I Saw Lincoln Shot," in *American Magazine*—disingenuously described as "told now for the first time"—and "Lincoln's Death" for the *Saturday Evening Post*. These were largely autobiographical and paved the way for his 1930 book-length version entitled *I Saw Booth Shoot Lincoln*. All were told from a backstage perspective with remarkable (and sometimes imaginative) detail, considering the immense time that had elapsed.

Emerson, too, was eager to narrate his version of the assassination. In 1913, at age seventy-four, he was still "in full control of all his powers."

"It all seems to me as though it was last night," he reminisced. Nearly every detail of his version, though, is congruent with information provided previously by others. Several years after his death, his son discovered a more detailed account that Emerson had written decades before. It received moderate press coverage and revealed a few new details, including Booth's breaking the cane across Emerson's shoulders, Booth's learning of Lincoln's intended attendance that night by reading Harry Ford's posting of box occupants, and, like Kate Evans's recollection, the president's being carried out of the theatre on a shutter.[14]

By 1916 Jeannie Gourlay also emerged from her silence about the assassination. It was time, she said, that "I should give to the public my experience of the night of April 14, 1865," but repeatedly expressed a desire to avoid any notoriety. Her memories have provided assassination scholars with some of the most precise, vivid details about the sequence of events and actions of various figures at Ford's Theatre that night.[15]

Around the same time, Helen Truman provided an account that was unique for its identification of dates that Lincoln attended Ford's and its vivid description of the horror of the moments following the shot. In another round of interviews in 1923, she covered much of the same ground.[16]

So whose was the most accurate version of the assassination? The debate over the definitive account, as with any conspiracy, continues to this day. The truest picture emerges from a composite of all of the many versions related by actors as well as audience members, with preference customarily given to details recalled at the nearest remove from the event.

As with any conspiracy, countless questions remain unanswered.

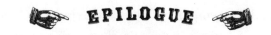

EPILOGUE

WALKING SHADOWS

R EGARDLESS OF WHERE THEIR lives had taken them, the actors, managers, and stagehands of Ford's Theatre the night of the assassination must have experienced a chilling sense of *déjà vu* on July 2, 1881. On that afternoon President James A. Garfield—another chief executive who loved the theatre, attending and critiquing it diligently—was shot by Charles Guiteau in Washington less than seven blocks from where they had stood the night Lincoln was killed. Worse, eighteen of them had to endure the news of yet another presidential assassination, that of William McKinley by Leon Czolgosz, in 1901. Unfortunately for historians, none of them recorded their reactions to these tragedies.

Those who did live into the 1890s saw tremendous changes in the theatres in which they worked: brighter illumination from electric lights; better safety due to asbestos curtains, steel construction, and stringent new fire laws; and more exciting scenic environments through the application of innovative stage machinery and special effects. For those employed in New York, the heart of Broadway was moving uptown, from Greenwich Village past Union Square, up into the Thirties. Burgeoning theatre attendance had been sparked by spectacular new escapist musicals and the phenomenal rise of vaudeville. Happily, too, by this time the stigma of their profession had lifted, evidenced by the 1882 attendance in New York at the first Actors' Fund Fair by the president of the United States, Grover Cleveland, who, prompted by his young wife, often attended the theatre.

The ensuing careers of actors and managers, whose names appeared in theatre programs, have proved easier to track than those of the stagehands, who, until well into the twentieth century, toiled in anonymity. Hence, many of the Ford's Theatre backstage personnel faded into (perhaps eagerly embraced) obscurity. In addition, their backstage skills were often transferable (for example, gasfitter Edward Gorman became a plumber, and ticket-seller Joseph Sessford and chief usher James O'Bryon became government clerks), allowing them to blend into the general working population. Also, being on average older than the cast, they had less of their careers ahead of them and may thus have retired earlier; their death in that era rarely merited an obituary. Some, like Gorman, O'Bryon, Selecman, and Lamb, can be tracked for awhile, but then disappear. Lost to history and even the most diligent search engines are stagehands Clark, "Skeggy," Henry James, John Miles, Joe Simms, and the ever-elusive Peanut John Burroughs.

★ ★ ★

Theatrical patriarch **Tom Gourlay** remained in Brooklyn with his wife, Margaret, and five of their remaining six children (Jeannie was touring) after Maggie's death. In 1880 he lost Margaret but the following summer remarried, to Lavinia Berner, a much younger singer. He passed away on Friday the Thirteenth of February 1885, at sixty-five, and is buried with Margaret in an Actors' Fund plot in Cypress Hills Cemetery, Brooklyn.

In 1867 at age nineteen, prompter-actor **John DeBonay** married Angela Sefton, an older (thirty-five), experienced, talented dancer, singer, pantomimist, violinist, pianist, fencer, and translator of French plays. They moved to New York, where he acted regularly at Wood's Theatre and dabbled in management and vaudeville. With Angela's help he translated French works, but ran into legal trouble over copyright issues. In May 1885 the *New York Mirror* reported that he "was found very ill in a room in University Place. He was unattended and without food." No mention was made of Angela, but when he died of tuberculosis on October 29, 1885, at thirty-seven, his death certificate stated, "married." His passing warranted no obituaries, even in New York papers.[1]

Courtland V. Hess, who never got to sing that night, remained in Philadelphia. He gave up acting to work as a telegraph operator (likely arranged by his brother), followed by stints as a salesman and a clerk. He died on February 21, 1887, at forty-eight and was buried in Laurel Hill Cemetery in Philadelphia.

One of the saddest victims of the assassination's aftermath was old **George Spear**. After the 1865 summer with Withers and Phillips, the only work he could get was playing comic Old Men for a season in a ragtag theatre company in Wilmington, North Carolina, and for a few managers who took him in out of pity for short engagements in minor roles. With no other work to be found, he withdrew from the stage and slipped irrevocably into poverty. His son, Felix, wounded in the war, died in

1869, but Spear's estranged wife got his army pension. By 1871 Spear was in dire straits, and benefits were staged for him in Boston that netted him enough to live on for five years, until he became only the second person to be admitted to the newly established Edwin Forrest Home for destitute and retired actors at the late star's country estate in Philadelphia. Confined to his bed for the final four years of his life, Spear passed away at age seventy-six on July 10, 1887, from "debility" and was buried in a Home plot in Cedar Hill Cemetery. Obituaries praised his jovial personality and comic timing.

Policeman-turned-actor **George Parkhurst** spent twenty years acting in small roles at Washington's National Theatre and Ford's Opera House, while also working as a government clerk. After losing his wife in 1881, he spent four years touring with Maggie Mitchell, finally making it to Broadway in 1888 in *Little Lord Fauntleroy*, where he played a small but important role. On July 2, 1890, he suffered a fatal stroke at home at age forty-nine, leaving a married son and young daughter. He was buried in Congressional Cemetery in Washington beside Kate, an infant whom they had lost in 1868, and a grandson.

James Lamb continued to paint scenery, routinely praised in reviews, for two more decades in Boston, Washington, and Baltimore, especially in theatres connected to the Fords. In 1890 he was still living, at age seventy-one, on Tenth Street in Southwest Washington.

Four more seasons of touring as Forrest's stage manager nearly exhausted **John Wright** (in six months in early 1872, shortly before Forrest's death, they traveled seven thousand miles to give 128 performances). Remarkably, the notoriously irascible star remained satisfied with Wright, which speaks well to Wright's competence and attention to detail. This was followed by several years working in New York for Augustin Daly's Grand Opera House and Charles Thorne's Niblo's Garden. In 1880 Wright retired, content to remain in Allston with Annie and their two remaining children. A diagnosis of cancer in 1889 led to declining, bedridden years and his death at age seventy-eight on August 9, 1893, with burial in Evergreen Cemetery in nearby Brighton. Although he never spoke publicly about the assassination, Annie granted several interviews after his death in which she narrated the horror of that night.

James Gifford continued to build, renovate, and maintain various Ford ventures in Washington and Baltimore. After a brief spell creating special mechanical effects for Broadway shows, he retired in 1879 to live with his wife and seven surviving children in the same house he had grown up in on East Fayette Street in Baltimore. In 1892 he contracted influenza but recovered, only to relapse the following year. His death on March 5, 1894, three days past his eightieth birthday, came just nine days before the death of his friend and patron, John Ford. Gifford's death certificate attributed his demise to "old age," and he was buried in Baltimore's Green Mount Cemetery.

Within a decade of the assassination, **John T. Ford** was being described as one of the wealthiest theatrical managers in America, with flourishing opera houses in three cities. By 1877, with 131 actors under contract, he was no longer just a manager, but a show business impresario, a term more respected in that era, implying visionary management of talent and bookings, beyond just that of buildings. Stunned by the suicide that year of his beloved first child, Annie, he plunged intensely into work, becoming one of the first managers in the United States to capitalize on the Gilbert and Sullivan comic opera craze that began with *H.M.S. Pinafore* in 1878. But he was slow to embrace the concept of combination companies and resistant to the demise of stock companies, which he only ceased hiring in 1881. He gradually lost his hold over formerly loyal stars like Owens, Mitchell, Jefferson, John Raymond, and Edwin Booth, who defected to other managers offering better terms and larger audiences. Worse, other managers were showcasing the newest rising stars, such as Sarah Bernhardt, Lillie Langtry, Henry Irving, and Ellen Terry. The 1884 financial panic rendered Ford nearly unable to meet his debts and cost him a sizable portion of his investments, yet he spent much of his remaining life engaged in widespread Baltimore philanthropy. In 1889 he was nearly killed by a runaway horse, and a few years later retired from management, leaving his sons in charge of his theatres. In January 1894 he contracted influenza and died on March 14, aged sixty-four. The tributes were extensive and eloquent as he was laid to rest in Baltimore's Loudon Park Cemetery, most citing his warmth of personality and universal respect. His epitaph fittingly quotes Hamlet: "He was a man, take him for all in all; we shall not look upon his like again."

Acting manager **H. B. Phillips** continued to perform "old man" roles. After his wife died in October 1866, he undertook two seasons of acting and managing Wall's Opera House in Washington with mixed results. For most of the 1870s and '80s, he acted steadily, touring with various combination companies and performing in Manhattan and in Brooklyn, to which he moved permanently in 1880. On the night of December 5, 1876, he barely escaped from one of the worst theatre fires in American history, at Conway's Brooklyn Theatre, which caused the death of 281 patrons and actors. In 1892 he closed out his fifty-five-year acting career and on September 25, 1896, died at seventy-seven at home in Brooklyn from a stroke. He was buried in the Actors' Fund plot in Evergreen Cemetery.

Costumer **Louis Carland**, doubtless disenchanted with Washington after his imprisonment, interrogation, and testimony, plied his trade for three more decades in Boston, Chicago, and New York, occasionally acting small roles. In his late fifties, he entered Bellevue Hospital in New York for repair of a hernia on November 11, 1900, but died in surgery. He was buried near Phillips in the Actors' Fund plot in Evergreen.

Ticket agent **Joe Sessford** readily found other employment in Washington, first at the National Theatre and then at Ford's new Opera House. Remaining in their Carroll Street home in Southeast Washington, he and

Sarah had two more sons. By the mid-1880s, he retired from theatrical work, signing on as a clerk with the federal government and later the Smithsonian Institution. He contracted influenza during an epidemic in early 1901, which, compounded by asthma and a weak heart, led to his death at home on March 8 at age sixty-seven, with burial in Washington's Congressional Cemetery.

Throughout the 1870s and '80s **John Mathews** continued to receive good reviews in supporting roles at over a dozen Broadway theatres. Like Phillips, he was trapped in the Brooklyn Theatre fire of 1876, escaping only by groping his way through a tunnel under the theatre. Except for his outreach work for the Actors' Fund, he preferred in his final years to remain in his room, devoted to his blind Irish setter until her death shortly before his own. For twenty-five years, he had never crossed anyone's threshold as a guest, he avowed, being particularly careful to avoid the company of women, toward whom he felt, asserted the *Mirror*, "a curious mixture of bitter antagonism, chivalrous esteem, and dread." Never married, he remained exceptionally close—romantically, she claimed—to his landlady, Martha Kimball, who found his body on the morning of January 11, 1905. Surrounded by theatrical souvenirs, he had died from a heart attack three weeks short of his seventieth birthday. Laid to rest in the Shriners' plot in Kensico Cemetery in Westchester County in a service attended by scores of fellow actors, this man of "odd peculiarities and idiosyncrasies" was eulogized as "an upright man of honor, without reproach" who "never recovered from the effects of the accusation" over Booth's letter, a controversy that continues to this day.[2]

Edwin Brink, who walked to the theatre with Booth that evening, soon grew frustrated in Richmond and left with Kittie to perform in upstate New York. After they divorced in the mid-1870s, he continued to play supporting and leading roles in well-known shows in smaller theatre companies in the Midwest and Canada. In 1901 he joined a vaudeville company touring Wisconsin and there, in Ashland, in June

1905, he contracted meningitis. Within five days, on June 29, he was dead at eighty-two, leaving a new wife but no children. He received a Grand Army of the Republic funeral with interment in the Civil War Veterans plot of Mount Hope Cemetery in Ashland.

Doorkeeper **John Buckingham** retired from the Navy Yard, but like Sessford had no trouble finding theatre work, first at the Washington Theatre and then at the National, where he proudly watched his favorite son, Harry, make his stage debut in 1874. At Albaugh's (formerly Ford's) Opera House, Buck became a lobby fixture for another twenty years, enjoying regular benefit nights, warmly greeting patrons, and swapping memories with visiting stars, including Harry Hawk, who came by on a tour in 1894. Buck was devastated in November of that year when his son Harry died in a Baltimore theatre fire; his grief was compounded by the death of his wife a short time later. In his mid-sixties, he retired for good, relishing the company of his many grandchildren and great-grand-children. Surprisingly, within a few years he remarried, to Katherine Cole of Maryland, who brought along eight sons and a daughter of her own. In the early years of the twentieth century, Buck's health began to fail and he moved in with his eldest son, John Jr., on Eighth Street in Northeast Washington, where he remained bedridden for nearly a year before his death at eighty-one on March 26, 1909. After a dignified Episcopal funeral, he was buried in Washington's Congressional Cemetery.

Property assistant **John Selecman** also remained in Washington, work-ing as a general carpenter and then cabinetmaker. In the mid-1870s, he married a New Jersey native, Louise, with whom he had two children, Marie and John Jr., the latter dying suddenly at age twenty-seven. By 1910 Selecman, sixty-one, still worked, living with Louise on Columbia Road, Northwest.

★ ★ ★

By the second decade of the new century, newspapers began speculating about the number and names of backstage survivors. Those who were contacted typically mentioned others with whom they were still in touch and provided updates on their own lives, in some cases pitching revised versions of the event, correcting small details or entire interpretations they insisted were erroneous. As might be expected, some spurious claimants appeared. As critic John Bouvé Clapp observed wryly in 1916, "It is estimated that enough players have been credited with acting at Ford's Theatre on April 14, 1865, to have filled the playhouse itself."[3]

In 1866 **May Hart** and new husband J. G. Saville headed for New York, snagging a few roles and an occasional laudatory review. In the 1870s she reached the peak of her career, first with E. L. Davenport, then as leading lady in Saville's new company at Washington's National Theatre, followed by leading roles in Philadelphia, New York, and Baltimore, earning good reviews. In 1878 she divorced Saville over his adultery and took her singing, dancing, and banjo-playing talents and her oft-mentioned good looks out West, performing in melodramas and flirtatious comedies opposite young James O'Neill (the father of playwright Eugene O'Neill). Returning east, she was wooed obsessively by wealthy Philadelphia lawyer/orator Charles W. Brooke, whom she married in her native Toronto in 1879. Settling into a luxurious home on Long Island, she began to appear regularly at high society Manhattan soirees. But by 1894, she and Brooke separated over his dalliance with their housekeeper, whom he married without divorcing Hart. (When he died in 1897, Hart was one of three widows who showed up to claim the rightful name and estate of Mrs. Charles Brooke, only to be rudely and publicly turned away penniless by Brooke's son, the estate's executor.) She turned to vaudeville, but her beauty had waned and tastes had changed, and she found few roles. Diagnosed with incurable cancer in 1911, with no immediate family, she admitted herself to Berkshire Hills Sanitarium in North Adams,

Massachusetts, where she died at sixty-six on March 25, 1913, and was buried in that town's Southview Cemetery.

Harry Ford, only twenty-one at the time of the assassination, spent the 1870s helping John manage his various theatres, southern tours, and Gilbert and Sullivan productions. In 1874, he married actress Blanche Chapman, twenty-three, and promptly began a family (four children by 1885) while maintaining a spacious home on Iowa (now Logan) Circle in Washington. After John's death, to accommodate Blanche's flourishing New York career, Harry retired from management and took the family first to Brooklyn and then in 1912 to Rutherford, New Jersey. On July 22, 1915, at age seventy-one, he died from surgical complications at St. Mary's Hospital in Passaic, New Jersey, and was buried in nearby Ridge-lawn Cemetery.

Harry Hawk, who spoke the last words Abraham Lincoln ever heard, never achieved real fame, but remained a competent gun for hire willing to act in any production, and so was almost constantly employed. Between tours he lived with his cousin in Bryn Mawr, Pennsylvania. After shaking off a spell of alcoholism that threatened his career in 1868 in California, he spent nearly fifty years touring the continent in dramas successful in their day but eminently forgettable today. Nearly twenty of those years were spent with Daly's Fifth Avenue Theatre Company, taking Hawk to almost every metropolis in America in dozens of major hits, including *Divorce*, *Article 47*, and *Camille*, and then with Palmer and Jarrett's mammoth revival of *Uncle Tom's Cabin*, which played London to mixed reviews. Usually, audiences loved him while critics deplored his improvised "gagging." Eventually, though, the Gilbert and Sullivan craze and the rise of vaudeville worked against him, not being a song and dance man. (He complained, "When you go into a dramatic agency now, but two questions are asked: 1. Can you sing? 2. Can you walk? If you can sing, they ship you off with a *Pinafore* company.") His greatest success came in the 1880s and '90s in support of stars Fanny Davenport and Fanny Janauschek and in long-running shows like *The Soudan, The English Rose,* and *Darkest Russia,* during which he earned a respectable hundred dollars a week. Playwright-producer McKee Rankin's company of *The Danites*—Hawk providing comic relief as a demeaningly stereo-typical wily Chinaman—took him back to England. Like Mathews he never married, but claimed to have fallen in love in England, returning there several times to see the woman, who remains unidentified. Despite a still-youthful appearance in his fifties, he began to feel his own mortal-ity, cheating death when trapped in a falling elevator car (his injuries requiring a lengthy recovery) in 1892, followed within months by having to clamber over rooftops to escape a fire in his athletic club. By the turn of the century, he stopped acting, choosing to raise chickens and dogs in Bryn Mawr and travel to the Channel Islands off the coast of Normandy for six months each year, which by 1911 became year-round. "I found in sunny Jersey," he said, "a place where I could live comfortably within my means." It is there that he is buried, after dying suddenly of a stroke at seventy-seven on May 28, 1916.[4]

After his divorce from Jeannie Gourlay, conductor **Billy Withers** never remarried, and began a rootless existence. He returned to Washington, to Saville's National Theatre, then signed on as "Premier Solo Violinist and Musical Director" for one of the first touring burlesque troupes, Lydia Thompson's "British Blondes." He reached the zenith of his career in 1877 as orchestra leader of New York's Park Theatre, but after one season headed west with a series of combination companies playing forgettable musicals in major cities. In the 1890s he returned to New York at Daly's Theatre, where he remained until retiring near the end of the century. In 1907 a stroke left him partially paralyzed and bedridden (but far from mute; interviews abounded) in a home he shared with his brother Reuben over their family store in the Bronx. Admitted to the

Bronx Home for the Incurables a few years later, he died from kidney failure at age eighty on December 5, 1916, and was buried in Greenwood Union Cemetery in Rye, New York.

Five weeks later business manager **James R. "Dick" Ford,** who ironically had been the frailest of the three brothers in 1865, yet lived the longest, passed away. He had married in 1866 and moved to Baltimore, where he and his wife, Hattie, raised two sons and a daughter. He assisted his brothers with their theatres there and their southern tours to a limited extent, but preferred to work at his Holliday Street tobacco shop and a bill-posting concern he founded. In the 1890s he became a Baltimore Police Department station-house clerk, affectionately known as "Uncle Dick," retiring in 1916, shortly after losing Hattie. He then moved in with his married daughter in Richmond Hills in Brooklyn, where he suffered a stroke and died on January 10, 1917, at age seventy-six. He was buried with his parents and brother John in Baltimore's Loudon Park Cemetery.

★ ★ ★

By the 1920s, a perverse sort of tontine developed for the honor of being the last survivor backstage at Ford's Theatre the night of the assassination. There were nine, but newspapers focused almost entirely on the actors. These nine saw a brave new world of automobiles, airmail, radios, and motion pictures, with two of them acting in that newest entertainment medium, one even playing the role of Abraham Lincoln.

Ned Emerson, who had played the foppish Lord Dundreary, soon realized not only that he would never achieve stardom, as he and John Ford had hoped, but that he could not sustain himself as an actor. After a few seasons trying his luck in Philadelphia and New York, receiving mediocre reviews in supporting roles, he retired from the stage in 1870, married, and moved to Lynchburg, Virginia, with his wife, Emma, and baby boy (the first of four children in rapid succession; a fifth died at birth). There he opened a book and newspaper depot on Main Street, remodeled and managed two theatres, and sidelined as a printer, bill poster, and paper hanger while Emma sold flowers. Four years after her death in 1893, he returned to Washington, married a considerably younger seamstress, and partnered with dry goods merchant Julius Lansburgh. Then, with his two oldest sons, he opened a prosperous stained-glass business on G Street, from which he retired in 1914. He died precisely on the fifty-seventh anniversary of the assassination, April 14, 1922, at his son's home in Alexandria, Virginia, from chronic nephritis at age eighty-two, and is buried next to Emma in Presbyterian Cemetery in Lynchburg.

Young **Helen Truman,** who revered President Lincoln for sparing her brother's life, moved to New York in 1866 and reclaimed her surname, acting for another sixteen years as Helen Coleman in insignificant supporting roles. While touring in 1873, she was badly burned in a fire which destroyed John Ford's Holliday Street Theatre. A year later she married actor Frank Wynkoop, and they formed a small touring company that achieved minor success, with Helen playing (in her thirties) leading "old woman" roles in folksy scripts in one- and two-night stands in small towns throughout the South, New England, and upstate New York. In 1883 she retired from the stage and moved to Los Angeles with Frank, who became a realtor, capitalizing on the early twentieth-century land boom in southern California. Her spine and hips were permanently injured in a 1913 train accident, and she withdrew from the public. She died of diabetes at age seventy-eight at her home on April 29, 1924, and is buried in Inglewood Manor, California.

Only twenty the night of the assassination, the best years of ingénue **Kate Evans**'s career came later. Following the early death of her husband, Johnny, she married prosperous Chicago merchant Henry Collins and moved there with her two children; they had three more together. Following his death in 1882, she returned to the stage using her middle name, as Kathryn (or Kate) Spencer, touring to hundreds of small towns across the country in lesser combination companies. The most successful of these, in the mid-1890s, was *Zeb, the Clodhopper*, a four-act comedy with singing and dancing about a hayseed Indiana family, that featured surprisingly elaborate stage machinery such as a moving sidewalk displaying more than three miles of scenery; Kate played "an old maid." In the early years of the twentieth century, she shifted honorably into "first old woman" roles for William Owen's Canadian Company and Lyman Twins and Company, also performing in vaudeville. By 1911 all five of her children had died, and by 1917, at age seventy-two, poverty and illness forced her after more than six decades of performing to give up the stage and enter the Episcopal Home for the Aged in Chicago. There she passed away at eighty-one from emphysema on June 14, 1926, and was laid to rest in Chicago's Rosehill Cemetery.[5]

Jake Rittersbach's foray into theatrical work lasted less than a month. He then plied his trade as a general carpenter for nearly thirty years in Washington, where by the early 1870s he and his new wife Louisa had bought a home. In 1901, following her death, he moved to Ohio, drawing an army pension as an invalid (due to partial deafness, chronic gastritis, and rheumatism). In 1913 he entered the Central Branch of the National Home for Disabled Volunteer Soldiers in Dayton, Ohio, where he died on June 28, 1926, at age eighty-six, making him the oldest assassination night survivor at death—but not the last to die. He was buried with military honors at Hampton National Cemetery in Hampton, Virginia.

Jeannie Gourlay Struthers, her husband Robert managing her career, performed in 1871 in London and the English provinces in an adaptation of *Fanchon* called *Fanchonette*. Reviewers praised her "spirit and vivacity," "great force and feeling," and versatility in playing light-hearted scenes like her "shadow dance"—in which, out of loneliness, her character frolics with her shadow, a scene made famous by Maggie Mitchell—

and in serious dramatic moments. For the next thirty years, except for a few interludes in New York, motherhood eclipsed acting; she bore seven children in thirteen years (1872–1884) and in 1888 forsook the stage permanently, settling in Milford, Pennsylvania. After Robert's death in 1907, she worked to preserve the scene of the assassination, corresponding with Lincolniana collector Osborne Oldroyd, who had converted the Petersen house into the first Lincoln Presidential Museum. In April 1910 she returned to Washington for the first time, visiting Ford's Theatre—where she was unable to bring herself to go inside, but instead walked around behind it to view the alley through which Booth had escaped—and Oldroyd's collection. In 1923 she unsuccessfully lobbied President Warren Harding to prevent the sale to auto maker Henry Ford of several assassination relics, including the chair in which the president had sat. A year later she drafted a lengthy eyewitness account of that night for the Reverend Patrick J. Cormican, S.J., archivist at Georgetown University. She died at age eighty-three at her daughter's home in Media, Pennsylvania, on March 5, 1928, survived by three daughters and a son; she was eulogized at the Edwin Forrest Actors' Home in Philadelphia and laid to rest next to Robert in Milford.[6]

Nearly the entirety of **Will Ferguson**'s career lay ahead of him in 1865, and he acted almost continuously for the next fifty-seven years in nearly every state in the Union and across Europe, including a remarkable thirty-eight original Broadway productions. As First Walking Gentleman at the New Memphis Theatre in 1867 he met Fannie Pierson, playing juvenile and "chambermaid" parts, and they married in New Orleans in 1873. His big break came the next year in New York, supporting Ford alumnus John T. Raymond in *The Gilded Age*, Mark Twain and Charles Dudley Warner's long-running, bitter satire on Washington corruption (Mathews was also in the cast). Another Broadway hit followed: *The Mighty Dollar* starring W. J. Florence, which ran nearly three years. After Fannie's death in 1878, Ferguson threw himself into performing in Philadelphia (joining May Hart) and New Orleans, ultimately returning to New York in 1883 and remarrying at age thirty-eight to seventeen-year-old Catherine Farrell. Their first child, Helen, was born two years later. For three more decades he played "character roles" to mixed reviews in long runs of popular shows such as *Hazel Kirke*; *Jim, the Penman*; *The Deep Purple*; *Charley's Aunt*; and *Beau Brummell*, frequently commenting on the state of American theatre. By 1908 he and Catherine had settled in Brooklyn and four years later doted on their first grandchild, named for her, whom they adopted as their own when Helen divorced. By age seventy, Ferguson had performed in six silent films, including the role of Lincoln in *Battle Cry of Peace* (1915). There would be ten more, six in 1922 alone. None were noteworthy and nearly all are considered "lost films" today. After 1920 he no longer acted on the stage, and two years later while filming in California fell in a hotel stairway, breaking his hip. Unable to work again, he died of pleurisy on May 4, 1930, a month short of his eighty-fifth birthday, while staying with his nephew in Pikesville, Maryland, and was buried in Baltimore's Western Cemetery. He never completed the full autobiography he had recently begun, but shortly before his death spelled out his three lifetime "claims to distinction": rolling and lighting a cigarette with manacled hands (required for a play), his performance in the original 1893 production of *Charley's Aunt*, and his presence backstage the night of the assassination. The *Washington Times* provided an apt assessment of his legacy: "He has shone brightly in more bad plays and has made good parts out of more poorly constructed dramatic works than any man on the stage."[7]

For years Ferguson had been regularly and erroneously identified as the last surviving actor from Ford's Theatre in 1865. But it was ironically—foes of the profession might say understandably—the performer who immediately quit the stage who lived the longest: **Charles F. Byrne**, who had played Captain De Boots. Moving to Philadelphia, he worked first for clothier Wanamaker and Brown and then for twenty-five years selling real estate and insurance. In the early 1870s, he married and fathered a son, Charles Thompson Byrne. Active in Philadelphia's reform movement in the early twentieth century, he ran unsuccessfully for state legislature in 1914. Widowed by 1910, he suffered a stroke in 1920 that left him paralyzed and unable to speak. His son's family cared for him until his death at eighty-six at their home on March 10, 1931, nearly sixty-six years after the assassination.

Two backstage survivors remained. Child bride **Kittie Brink** toured the United States and Canada in minor Shakespearean roles with small companies until 1878. After divorcing Edwin and losing her wardrobe in a theatre fire in Toronto, she quit the stage at age twenty-eight and returned to upstate New York to work as a household servant in Port Byron. There she fell in love with one of the home's occupants, Civil War Union Army veteran Nelson Armstrong, forty-two. In 1882, they moved to Huron, South Dakota, and married. For two decades, while raising two children, they struggled amid daunting frontier hardships to convert two shanties into a prosperous 480-acre hog and grain farm, where she continued to live after his death in 1903. On July 2, 1935, following a near-fatal bout of influenza and a week after falling and breaking her hip, Kittie passed away at eighty-five, the penultimate survivor of the Ford's Theatre crew the night of the assassination. She was buried next to Armstrong in Huron's Riverside Cemetery.

The final survivor was program boy **Joseph Hazelton**, who, that night, had been only eleven. Encouraged by both the assassin and his victim to pursue an acting career, Joe did just that after brief spells as a Senate page and a railway mail clerk. For six decades beginning in 1875, he acted in minor roles (some of them in blackface) in small companies, first in the West and then back in Washington. He tried forming his own company with a rural comedy called *Old Kentuck*, but was enjoined by the New York State Supreme Court from doing so, as he had not obtained the proper rights. In the closing years of the century, he tried writing romantic comedy-dramas set against the background of the Civil War, which were less than successful. For a decade he toured with combination companies in small, folksy character roles beloved by audiences, then in 1910 returned again to Washington, joining for two summer seasons the Columbia Players, one of the very few remaining stock companies in the United States. He also lectured on "Washington on the Motion Picture Screen." In 1912 he relocated to Los Angeles and performed in thirty-four silent films, nearly all forgettable "shorts," over eleven years. In 1927 he entered the Windsor Sanitarium in Glendale, California, and two years later was seriously injured in a 1929 automobile accident, ending his stage and film career. But he persisted in radio, delivering talks about the film industry, President Lincoln, the assassination, and life in Civil War Washington. The end came for Hazelton, the final backstage survivor of April 14, 1865, on October 9, 1936, more than seventy-one years after the event. He succumbed to pneumonia at age eighty-three at St. Vincent's Hospital and was buried in Hollywood Memorial Park Cemetery. He never married and had no known relatives. To his death, he maintained that John Wilkes Booth did not die in that burning barn but escaped to South America, returning years later to Enid, Oklahoma, under an assumed name, eventually confessing his crime and true identity just before ending his life with arsenic.

ACKNOWLEDGMENTS

THE MOST DAUNTING ASPECT of researching and writing this book has been knowing how much groundwork has already been laid, and how many words have been written, concerning this signal event in American history. Yet, I have been exceptionally fortunate to have available to me the prior work of outstanding, dedicated Lincoln assassination scholars, notably including James O. Hall, John Brennan, Mike Kauffman, Harold Holzer, Ed Steers, Roger Norton, Richard Sloan, Terry Alford, and Art Loux. The extraordinary generosity and guidance of these last two in particular as I began research were of immeasurable help and are tremendously appreciated.

The limitless dedication and shrewd insights to the assassination provided by members of the Surratt Society and through its publications and conferences, particularly the efforts of Laurie Verge, indefatigable director of the Surratt House Museum, with its superb research library, have guided much of my thinking and enriched my research and writing. Two online forums (lincoln-assassination.com and rogerjnorton.com/ LincolnDiscussionSymposium/index.php) have also been very helpful; it's possible to become lost in them for hours. Another invaluable resource was John Ford Sollers's doctoral dissertation on his grandfather, John T. Ford.

The staff of Ford's Theatre, especially former National Park Service Interpreter Gloria Swift, provided essential research assistance and motivation. The limitless knowledge, patience, and professionalism of the staff of the National Archives and the Library of Congress, especially its Newspapers and Periodicals Room and its Manuscripts Room, notably archivist Bruce Kirby, never cease to amaze me. The frequency of their mention in authors' Acknowledgments pages should underscore their enduring value; they represent public service at its finest. I am also indebted to the excellent staffs at the Maryland Historical Society, Historical Society of Washington, D.C., New York Historical Society, Pike County (PA) Historical Society, Folger Shakespeare Library, Billy Rose Performing Arts Division of the New York Public Library, Harvard Theatre Collection, Yale Sterling Library Manuscript Archives, and Georgetown University Library Special Collections. In Richmond, Mike Gorman of the National Park Service and Kelly Hancock of the Museum of the Confederacy were most helpful. In addition, Tom Tryniski's searchable website of historical New York newspapers (http:// fultonhistory.com) was a wonderfully rich resource.

I am grateful to the dedicated staff of the Hood College Library, particularly interlibrary loan officer Aimee Gil, for locating items that often did not want to be found. This gratitude extends as well to department chairs Ellen Koitz and Mark Sandona and Provost Kate Conway-Turner, for their support and friendship during my research.

Kate Powell, Terry Alford, and Paul Ganz provided helpful, insightful feedback on the manuscript as it evolved. James Bogar's proofreading was also helpful.

The keen insight, practical suggestions, and unwavering support of my agent, Joe Vallely, and dedicated editors Harry Crocker, Alex Novak, Tom Spence, and Lindsey Reinstrom, along with its outstanding art department, were invaluable and deserve the highest praise. Likewise, and paramount through the entire process, has been the steadfast, loving encouragement of my wife, Gail, who learned far more about the Lincoln assassination than she doubtless ever wanted to know.

NOTES

FSL = Folger Shakespeare Library

HSWDC = Historical Society of Washington, D.C.

HTC = Harvard Theatre Collection

JTF = John T. Ford

LOC = Library of Congress

MHS = Maryland Historical Society

NA = National Archives and Records Administration

OAC = *Our American Cousin*

CHAPTER 1

1.   *Washington Star*, February 9, 1913; Mathews testimony, July 1, 1867, Johnson Impeachment Investigation; *The Independent*,

April 4, 1895; *San Francisco Chronicle*, February 12, 1905; unidentified 1879 clipping in Laura Keene Files, Henneke Papers.

2.   It has often been stated in accounts of the assassination that Hawk
finished his line and the subsequent eruption of laughter covered
the sound of the shot, and that Booth knew the play well enough
to plan for just that eventuality. However, Hawk always insisted he
was interrupted by the shot and was opening his mouth to finish
the insult to Mrs. Mountchessington when Booth landed behind
him. See letter from Hawk to John B. Lober reprinted in *New York
Dramatic Mirror*, June 24, 1916.

3.   Diary of eyewitness Henry O. Nightingale, University of California
Merced Special Collections, 100; *New York Times*, July 9, 1883.
Booth's flat-topped, round-brimmed, black felt army-issue slouch
hat, seen by many earlier in the evening, was found later in the box.

4.   "Basket boys" or "bundle boys" at a theatre carried actors' costumes and personal hand props from their lodging to the theatre
before each performance and back again afterward in large wicker
champagne baskets and performed odds and ends of errands backstage.

5.   NARA RG 153, M599 (Hereinafter NA M599), 5/456-488; Kauffman, *American Brutus*, 8. Kauffman's account of the life of John
Wilkes Booth is exhaustively researched and a compelling read. See
also John T. Ford in *Washington Star*, April 18, 1888. Booth was
variously called John Booth and Wilkes Booth, depending on how
well one knew him, the former used primarily by close personal
friends; he was only theatrically billed as John Wilkes Booth.

6.   Mosby, 179; "Eyewitnesses to Lincoln's Assassination Live Here,"
Los Angeles Times, February 11, 1923, Section 3, 9.

7.   Rittersbach's version of Spangler's remark was vigorously rebutted
by John Ford in a Baltimore interview with a *New York World*
reporter on October 12, 1868, reprinted in the *Cincinnati Commercial*
on October 20, and by trial testimony of Louis Carland and James

Lamb. See "Testimony Concerning Edward Spangler" in Steers, *The Trial*, 97. The women were Mary Jane Anderson and Mary Ann Turner (M-599, 3/493 and 6/361), who gave strikingly similar testimony. See also Phillips in M-599 7/492. Rittersbach's name has been variously spelled Ritterspaugh, Rittersbaugh, Rittersback, Ritterspatch, Ritterspach, Ritterspick, and Riterspack, explainable in part by his illiteracy for much of his life. His military and death records, however, use Rittersbach (birth certificate is unavailable); the guttural German "-bach" could be interpreted as most of the above variants.

8.   NA M599 7/492; *Cincinnati Enquirer*, April 16, 1881; *Boston Sunday Herald*, April 11, 1897.

9.   According to the Pike County, Pennsylvania, Historical Society, Tom Gourlay took down the American flag that stood in the booth and handed it to Keene to use as a cushion for the president's head. That flag, with bloodstains still visible, is housed in the Society's showcase.

10. Munroe, 425.

CHAPTER 2

1.   For a thorough treatment of Ford's life and career, see Sollers (his grandson). Built in the late 1830s to replace the nearby Richmond Theatre that burned the day after Christmas in 1811 in one of the worst theatre fires in American history, the theatre was also known as the Marshall, for Richmond native Chief Justice John Marshall.

2.   It was from this era and these events that Maryland's state song, "Maryland, My Maryland," arose, its lyrics by James Ryder Randall today still proclaiming, "The despot's [Lincoln and the North] heel is on thy shore," along with the need to "Avenge the patriotic gore/That flecked the streets of Baltimore."

3.   James A. Herne, as told to his daughter, Julie A. Herne, in "James A. Herne: Actor and Dramatist." Unpublished Manuscript, no date,

University of California, Davis, 32; Scharf, *History of Baltimore City and County*, 130–31; Manakee, 23–38; Letters in Ford Papers, MHS.

4.   Kline, 353, 383; NA M599 2/845; *Richmond Enquirer*, October 9, 1861. An anonymous letter to the military tribunal conducting the trial of the assassination conspirators in May 1865 pointedly connected Ford and Kane, but was ignored.

5.   Bogar, *American Presidents*, 106, 108, 111; Forrest ALS to Ford, November 9, 1862 and August 8, 1864 in Ford Papers, LOC; Moody, 347.

6.   Oggel, 19; see also *Auburn* (NY) *Weekly News and Democrat*, December 23, 1886.

7.   J. Burdett Howe, *A Cosmopolitan Actor* (n.p.: Bedford, 1888) 126; Programs, Holliday Street Theatre, November 20 and December 23, 1860, March 9, 1861, cited in Sollers, 163; *Baltimore Sun*, December 22, 1860; Odell, 7:312; ALS to Hackett, June 26, 1863, in Ford Papers, FSL.

8.   "In parting from their encampment they cheered her gratefully for her kindness." Draft of petition, Ford to Stanton, c. May 11, 1865, cited in Sollers, 169; Maryland State Archives. http://aomol. net/000001/000367/html/am367-384.html.

9.   *Philadelphia Public Ledger*, July 8, 1907.

10. *Baltimore Sun*, February 21, 1862.

11. *Washington Post*, December 16, 1883.

12. Brooks, 294; *National Intelligencer*, March 6, 1865; *Washington Chronicle*, May 18, 1863.

13. Trollope, 14–15, 302.

14. *Washington Star*, November 12, 1863; Varhola, 110; Ellis, 385, 400–4, 458–61. Kauffman (122) places the number of brothels just above 100. Varhola places the number of prostitutes at 7,000.

15. Peskin, 149; Eytinge, 69.

16. "The Tragedy of the Nation," 1–2.

17. Vincent, 10; See also Riddle, 9.

18. NA M599, 2/845; *New York Clipper*, April 29, 1865. In general, however, Grover was a self-aggrandizing serial enhancer of the truth whose anecdotes about Lincoln and Ford cannot be accepted at face value.

19. *Washington Star*, January 3, 1862.

20. See Kauffman, 92. At some point after losing his own house, Gifford inherited the Baltimore house in which he had been born and in which he later died.

21. Burlingame, 322.

22. *Washington Chronicle*, August 23, 1863.

23. James A. Herne, 407; Julie A. Herne, 44–45; Perry, 8–13.

24. JTF Interview in *Baltimore American,* May 23, 1878; ALS JTF to John Wright, July 22, 1858, in JTF Papers, LOC. Ford did eventually yield to allowing bars in some of his theatres.

25. *Washington Post*, November 9, 1902, and March 28, 1909.

26. *Alexandria Gazette*, October 13, 1863.

27. *National Intelligencer*, February 26 and July 4, 1864. Persistent efforts to identify "Erasmus" have proven unsuccessful. It may have been editor John F. Coyle, who enjoyed the theatre, yet his friendship with the Fords would likely have precluded such harsh criticism. It may also have been Erasmus J. Middleton, whose father, James Middleton, knew Samuel Harrison Smith, the founder of the *National Intelligencer*.

28. ALS Ford to Wright, August 11, 1864, Wright Papers, HTC; Holliday Street pay schedule in JTF papers, MHS.

29. "Eyewitness Tells of Lincoln's Assassination," *New York Sun*, February 9, 1913.

30. ALS JTF to Wright, undated, in JTF Papers, NY Historical Society; *National Intelligencer*, December 15, 1864.

31. Letter, Wright to JTF, April 2, 1865, in JTF Papers, LOC.

32. Expenses quotation in *New York Clipper*, November 12, 1864. In a later interview, Ford said it was his practice to take the early train down to Washington on Mondays, Wednesdays, and Fridays, devoting those mornings to management of his theatre there, but others, including his two brothers, maintained that John's visits were irregular and less frequent.

33. According to his son, Harry's full name was Harry (not Henry) Clay Ford; Dick's was James Richard Ford.

34. *National Intelligencer*, November 28, 1864.

35. NA M599 3/683-4; 5/469-74.

CHAPTER 3

1. In testimony following the assassination, members of the cast and crew variously estimated that the rehearsal started between 10:00 a.m. and close to noon. The consensus is close to 11:00 a.m., however, and beginning rehearsal at that hour was the universal practice nationwide, in consideration of actors who had to stay up late the night before learning lines. The stage door, stage left, through which they entered was not the door Booth would use to flee after shooting the president; that one, in the far upstage right back wall, was so seldom used that even Wright was hardly aware of its existence.

2. *San Francisco Chronicle*, February 12, 1905.

3. Mary, born in 1825, was Phillips's second wife; his first wife, Catherine, whom he had married in the mid-1840s, died, likely in childbirth. In 1865 their three daughters, whom Mary was raising, were nineteen, seventeen, and fifteen.

4. Moody, 329.

5. George D. Ford, 302.

6. Bogar, *American Presidents*, 88; Sandburg, 3: 446.

7. *Washington Star*, November 2, 1863; *National Republican*, November 2, 1863; JTF to Owen Fawcett in *Detroit Free Press*, December 15, 1901; JTF in *Baltimore American*, June 8, 1893.

8. See Bogar, *American Presidents*, Chapter Nine.

9. Winter, *Vagrant Memories*, 46–47.

10. Jefferson, 206.

11. Mathews interview in Creahan, 138–39.

12. Jefferson, 193.

13. *New York Dramatic Mirror*, January 15, 1887; *Baltimore Sun*, November 8, 1873.

14. The curtain time of *Our American Cousin* is a continuing source of contention among assassination scholars; the advertisement closest to April 14, 1865, is that in the *Intelligencer* of November 14, 1864, which announces a 7:45 curtain, which was a common practice of the day, to ensure an actual commencement by 8:00, given typically dilatory audience arrivals. It also correlates with Ford's practice at his Baltimore Holliday Street theatre and with April 14 attendees' speaking of a long delay while the orchestra played patriotic airs.

15. Wright scrapbook, archives, Ford's Theatre National Historic Site, National Park Service; JTF Papers, LOC and FSL; Wright Papers, HTC and Boston Public Library; Clapp, 399–400, 468; Tompkins, 14–17, 35, 53–55.

16. Unidentified clippings, Wright Scrapbook, Ford's Theatre National Historic Site, National Park Service.

17. Clara Morris, 39–40.

18. Mitchell, 585; 598–99.

19. Ibid.

20. *National Republican*, September 29, 1864; *New York Clipper*, October 10, 15, and November 12, 1864.

21. Alford, 82; Bogar, *American Presidents*, 93.

22. Julie A. Herne, 26–27.

23. Ibid.

24. *The Story of Peggy the Actress* is Keene and Lutz's title, reflecting an adaptation of Charles Reade and Tom Taylor's original 1852 script, *Masks and Faces*, the name by which Keene performed it in most other cities. It tells the life story of actress Peg Woffington and provided one of Keene's more celebrated roles.

25. Rittersbach statement to Judge Advocate General Joseph Holt, Holt Papers, LOC, vol. 93, 253–54. Mrs. Scott's is listed in the 1865 Washington City Directory at 7th and H Streets, where it is also placed in testimony by the detectives who arrested Spangler and searched his room; yet in interrogation and trial testimony, Rittersbach and Spangler independently placed it at 7th and J and at 7th and G, respectively.

26. Spangler, 1–14; NA M599, 5/475–78, 87.

27. Gourlay interview in *Los Angeles Times*, April 11, 1914.

28. Although many sources, influenced by Pittman's trial transcript, have cited Maddox's assistant as John Sleichman, other sources, including reliable newspaper accounts, Superintendent Wood's records at Old Capitol Prison, and all census records, have him as John T. Selecman.

29. *Philadelphia Inquirer*, May 13, 1865; Kauffman, 418, fn. 32. Daniel D. Hartzler in *Marylanders in the Confederacy* (Silver Spring, MD: Family Line Publications, 1986) lists on page 153 a "James Gifford" as a private in the (Confederate) Maryland Guerrilla Zouaves and on page 408 identifies the source for this as "National Archives" and "Listing of members of Mansfield Lovell United Confederate Veterans Camp No. 843 of Rockville, Maryland." However, NARA's Maryland Guerrilla Zouaves rolls show no one by that name, and Louisiana State University libraries special

collections that house the national records of the United Confederate Veterans indicate that UCVA Camp 843 was that of Camp Jeff Davis in Augusta, Arkansas, and that Camp 518 (Camp Ridgley Brown) was located in Rockville, Maryland. Gifford appears on neither roster. No other UCVA camp in Maryland was named for Lovell.

CHAPTER 4

1. ALS Harry Hawk to George P. Morton, May 23, 1910, HTC.
2. Callboy (later Chicago theatre manager) Louis Sharpe in *Deseret Evening News*, December 24, 1886. The fear of Northern occupation of New Orleans was grounded in reality, especially after the Union capture of Ship Island off the coast of Mississippi in September 1861.
3. Harvey, 7; Kendall, 444–45; *New York Clipper,* July 22 and September 9, 1865. Hawk admits membership in the Guards in a 1912 letter to George Morton (Hawk Papers, HTC). See also Hawk interview in *Philadelphia Evening Telegraph*, July 8, 1907.
4. *Brooklyn Daily Eagle*, October 19, 1864.
5. *Philadelphia Evening Bulletin*, April 23, 1897.
6. Ferguson, *I Saw Booth Shoot Lincoln*, 15.
7. Ferguson, "I Saw Lincoln Shot!," 84.
8. George Ford quoting his father, Harry Clay Ford, in *Boston Daily Globe*, June 20, 1926. Information on the early life of John H. Evans is extremely scarce, and the commonality of his name thwarts search efforts.
9. Various ALS from Spear, primarily Fall 1858, to doctors and the Theatrical Fund, in Spear Papers, HTC; ALS Dr. Frank Whitman to F. C. Wemyss, n.d. (1856) in Spear Papers, HTC.
10. Spear ALS October 11, 1858, HTC; *Boston Herald*, July 12, 1887; *National Intelligencer*, November 4, 1864.

11. *National Intelligencer*, November 4, 1864; *American Civil War Research Database*, LOC; NA M378, Roll 7; playbills, Henneke Papers, Box 2, Folder 21.

12. Tom Taylor, *OAC*, Act I, Scene i, l. 273.

13. "How Wilkes Booth's Friend Described His Crime," 58.

14. *Alexandria Gazette*, August 27 and December 12, 1863; additional information provided by Henry Clay Emerson's great-great-grandson, David Hopkins.

15. "The Night that Lincoln was Shot," 180.

16. *OAC*, Act I, Scene i, ll. 206–59.

17. Charles Muzzy was a direct descendant of Isaac Muzzy, one of the first Minutemen to fall at Lexington Green in 1775.

18. "Eyewitnesses to Lincoln's Assassination Live Here."

19. *OAC*, Act I, Scene ii.

20. Ibid.

21. *New York Times*, May 11, 1886.

22. Mathews interview in *Boston Sunday Herald*, April 11, 1897.

23. *OAC*, Act I, Scene iii.

CHAPTER 5

1. "The Surratt Case," *Cincinnati Commercial*, October 20, 1868; Ford, "Behind the Curtain of a Conspiracy," 488.

2. Edward M. Alfriend, "Recollections of J. W. B.," Kimmel Collection; Ellsler, 123.

3. Alford, ix; Morris, 97–100.

4. Samples, 105–13. Brink was variously billed as Edwin/Edward Hunter/J. Brink; his headstone reads Edward H. Brink.

5. George Ford quoting his father in *Boston Daily Globe*, June 20, 1926; NA M599, 4/437-38, 7/490-92.

6. George Ford, 305.

7. NA M599, 5/456-88.

8. Ibid.

9. Ibid. See also JTF interview in *Washington Star*, April 18, 1885.

10. *New York Times*, February 14, 1926.

11. NA M599, 5/456-88.

12. *Washington Star*, April 18, 1885; "The Surratt Case," *Cincinnati Commercial*, October 20, 1868.

13. Thomas T. Eckert testimony, May 30, 1867, Johnson Impeachment Investigation.

14. "Actor Who Saw Lincoln Slain Recalls Memories of Tragic Night," *Philadelphia Public Ledger*, February 12, 1926. Byrne was billed erroneously as "C. Byrnes."

15. *OAC*, Act II, Scene i, ll. 384–87.

16. Gourlay's character is erroneously listed on the playbills of April 14 as Mary Trenchard; at play's end she is only promised to Asa Trenchard, not married. *Washington Star*, August 25, 1864.

17. *OAC*, Act II, Scene 2, ll. 67–68, 94.

18. Metropolitan Police Personnel File, 1863–65, NA. Parkhurst was allowed to resign as soon as the evidence against him was presented at a police board hearing. As part of the testimony in Parkhurst's dismissal hearing, "Roundsman Sheid" asked "Johnson" for the time. If this was actor L. Johnson, and a fellow patrolman, police files show no one by that name for those years. His name never reappears on any other playbill for a Ford theatre.

19. For elaboration on his brother William's role in the post-assassination search, see Kauffman 33. Hess seems to have been named after Presbyterian leader Cortlandt Van Rensselaer.

20. Brink interview in *Atlanta Constitution*, March 11, 1888. Brink's age at the time is open to debate. At his death in 1905 obituaries cited him as having lived to various ages, seventy-eight to eighty-three. His headstone reads "age 83," yielding a birth c. 1822. However, his notarized military enlistment papers give a birth year

of 1828, and his death certificate reads 1827. I have concluded that he followed the tendency of many actors and actresses of the day and shaved a few years off his age, which may also have helped him enlist and to marry Kittie.

21. *Atlanta Constitution*, March 11, 1888.
22. *OAC*, Act III, Scene i, ll. 11–94.
23. Jefferson, 196; *OAC*, Act III, Scene i, ll. 127–65.
24. *OAC*, Act III, Scene ii, ll. 44–81.
25. *OAC*, Act III, Scene ii, ll. 132–33.

CHAPTER 6

1. Various participants later provided conflicting times for the end of rehearsal, primarily due to confusion over the end of the play's rehearsal and the end of the singers'. The consensus regarding the former is close to 2:00.
2. *Boston Globe*, April 11, 1915.
3. Harry Ford statement April 20, 1865, to Colonel Olcott, NA M599, 5/487-88.
4. NA M599 5/392-93 and 5/475-78; Steers, *Trial*, 74. See Rittersbach's statement to Judge Holt, Holt Papers, LOC, Vol. 93.
5. Elwood, 22; NA M599, 5/473; Washington, D.C. City Directory 1865, LOC.
6. *Cincinnati Enquirer*, April 16, 1881.
7. Ferguson, *I Saw Booth Shoot Lincoln*, 17–18.
8. "Exemptions from the Draft," *Baltimore Sun*, December 30, 1863; NA M599 2/558, 3/488; 5/210; 5/477, 487-88; 5/500; 6/347-48. Under questioning on April 28, Maddox provided his address as "365 E Street between 10th and 11th," yet the 1865 Washington, D.C., City Directory lists him at First and G Streets.
9. NA M599 5/274-84.

10. Kimmel, *Mad Booths*, 208.

11. Carland testimony, June 12, 1865, Steers, *Trial*, 108.

12. NA M599, 5/397. Either Ferguson erroneously recalled DeBonay as "Tribonia" or the transcriber of his testimony (who placed a space before the final accented "á" and a question mark after the name and recorded it a second time as "Triboni à") misheard.

13. Ferguson, "I Saw Lincoln Shot!," 15; "Lincoln's Death," 37.

14. Mathews testimony, Johnson Impeachment Investigation, July 1, 1867.

15. Ibid.

16. Ibid.; see also Mathews letter to *National Intelligencer*, July 17, 1867.

17. NA M599 5/384, 5/479, and 7/489.

18. "This Man Saw Lincoln Shot," 20–21.

19. Ibid., 112, 115.

20. Ibid., 116.

21. *New York World*, February 12, 1911; *Baltimore American*, July 15, 1905.

CHAPTER 7

1. Hawk letter to father quoted in *New York Clipper*, April 29, 1865; Hart interview in *San Francisco Chronicle*, February 12, 1905.

2. H. C. Ford interview in *Washington Evening Critic*, April 15, 1885.

3. H. C. Ford interview in *New York Evening Post*, July 8, 1884; *Good Housekeeping*, 116.

4. Annie Wright interview in *Boston Globe*, April 11, 1915; Bogar, *Presidents*, 115.

5. Kittie Brink interview in Huron, South Dakota, *Huronite*, February 12, 1929.

6. OAC, Act III, Scene 2, ll. 19–22.

CHAPTER 8

1. James R. Ford interview in *Atlanta Constitution*, December 11, 1885.

2. Bryan, 189; Truman interview, *Oakland Tribune*, February 11, 1923.

3. *Impeachment Investigation*, 783. Within days fellow actor Sam Chester did testify to Mathews's connection to the Baltimore trunk.

4. *National Intelligencer*, July 18, 1867; *Impeachment Investigation* 286; *Chicago Tribune*, December 4, 1881. The controversy continues to this day over whether or not Mathews was truly able to memorize the letter; I have chosen to believe his assertion that his actor training allowed him to do so.

5. "Easter Recalls Lincoln," *Brooklyn Daily Eagle*, April 12, 1914. In an April 11, 1915, interview in the *New York Herald*, a man identified only as "F. Petersen of Washington, D.C., the son of William Petersen at 516 Tenth Street [which had been 452 before the numbering was changed in the 1870s]" asserts that he crept into the room where Lincoln lay dying early in the morning of April 15 and was present at the moment of death. He makes no mention of Ferguson, however.

6. Byrne Interviews, *Philadelphia Public Ledger*, February 12, 1926, and *Philadelphia Evening Bulletin*, February 12, 1929.

7. Richards telegram in Butler Papers, LOC.

8. Kathryn M. Evans interview, *Dayton* (OH) *Daily Journal*, August 26, 1893, and letter, *New York Dramatic Mirror*, February 4, 1905.

9. NA M599, 6/468-71. By mid-May the *Pittsburgh Commercial*, reprinted in the *Clipper* of May 20, asserted that Booth had an accomplice at the ready to shut off the gas, a story that may have been planted by Withers.

10. NA M599, 7/485-86; interview with Tanner, unidentified clipping with dateline Washington D.C. April 15, 1905, in bound collection,

"Newspaper Clippings on Lincoln Assassination," Hay Library, Brown University. Keene's statement in *New York Clipper*, March 2, 1867. The *Richmond Dispatch*, October 28, 1885, though, asserts that George F. Adams, a proprietor of the *Washington Star*, informed by Keene, was the first correspondent to telegraph Booth's identity to the Confederate capital.

11. NA M599, 7/490-92.

12. Jeannie Gourlay Struthers ALS written c. January 1924 in Cormican papers, and interview, *Los Angeles Times*, April 11, 1914.

13. Steers, *Trial*, 108.

14. *Dorchester* (MA) *Beacon*, April 11, 1896; *Boston Globe*, April 11, 1915.

15. Brooks, 260–61.

16. Ibid.

17. Creahan, 25.

18. Eyewitness recollections of newspaperman Will Kent, *St. Louis Globe Democrat*, December 5, 1891.

19. NA M599, 4/135-137 and 6/201-4; JTF Papers, MHS, File 371.

20. James R. Ford interview, *Atlanta Constitution*, October 11, 1885; NA M599, 6/508-9; telegram request slip in Butler Papers, LOC.

21. See the telegram on April 19 from Middle Department Command-ing General Lew Wallace to Major General Ord in Richmond: "Not a single pass has been given by my [Baltimore] Provost Marshal to any one to go to Richmond. If any one has such a pass it is a forgery. The orders of the War Department are carried out to the letter." Telegraph to War Department in Wallace Papers.

22. ALS from C. G. Thompson to JTF April 9, 1865 in JTF Papers, LOC. More than eight hundred buildings had burned in the tumul-tuous abandonment of the Confederate capital as the Union Army entered it.

23. ALS JTF to Getz, April 16, 1865, cited in Sollers, 199.

24. Interview in *Washington Star*, December 7, 1881.

25. *Trial of John H. Surratt*, 826; Nightingale Diary, 117.

26. NA RG153, Files MM3961, MM4050, OO940; Roy Morris, 117; *New York Clipper*, May 6, 1865.

27. *New York Clipper*, April 29, 1865; Clara Morris, *Life*, 104–7.

28. NA archival ALS Police Superintendent A. C. Richards to Colonel Timothy Ingraham (provost marshal general, defenses north of the Potomac, Washington, D.C.), April 15, 1865.

CHAPTER 9

1. Hart interview in *San Francisco Chronicle*, February 12, 1905.

2. Anderson stuck to her erroneous identification throughout the trial of the conspirators, saying she had "looked right wishfully" at Booth/Emerson.

3. Emerson claimed that Hart was forced to dress in the presence of the arresting officers, who had burst forcefully into her hotel room, but Hart, in telling the story of the arrest in the *San Francisco Chronicle*, February 12, 1905, omits anything of the sort.

4. Hart interview in *San Francisco Chronicle*, February 12, 1905.

5. Interrogative addendum to Spangler's December 3, 1867, notarized statement to William Gleason in Butler Papers, Box 195.

6. Phineas D. Gurley, *The Voice of the Rod* (Washington, D.C.: W. Ballantyne, 1865), 14–15; Robert M. Hatfield, *The Theater: Its Character and Influence* (Chicago: Methodist Book Depository, 1866), 19–38; Ruggles, 185–86; Eytinge, 84.

7. Steers, *Trial*, 108; JTF Papers, MHS, File 371.

8. *Harrisburg Daily Telegraph*, April 17–19, 1865.

9. NA M599, 2/52-54; *Baltimore Sun*, April 19, 1865; *Harrisburg Daily Telegraph*, April 17–19, 1865; Telegrams in Butler Papers.

10. *Philadelphia Evening Telegraph*, July 8, 1907. Hawk in 1897 recalled their being held in Harrisburg for four days; he may have

been thinking of the date of their opening in Cincinnati, or it just felt like four. He never revealed the assumed name.

11. NA M599, 5/392-95.

12. NA M599, 4/127-132.

13. Davis, 208; Doster, 105.

14. The three Southern governors were Joseph E. Brown of Georgia, Zebulon B. Vance of North Carolina, and John Letcher of Virginia.

15. Wood in *Washington Sunday Gazette*, September 14, 1884.

16. NA M599, 5/490-91.

17. Record Book of Old Capitol Prison in NA M598, reel 110; NA M599 2/917, 3/337 and M345.

18. O'Bryon telegraph request slip in Butler Papers.

19. Letters Received by the Office of the Adjutant General 1861-1870 ("Lincoln Assassination Reward Files") in RG 94, Records of the Adjutant General's Office, 1780s–1917, NA M619, 456/544-558.

20. "Confession of Samuel B. Arnold" in "Lincoln Assassination Reward Files," NA RG 94.

21. *Baltimore Sun* and *Baltimore American and Commercial Advertiser*, April 19, 1865.

22. Ibid.

23. JTF Papers, MHS, File 371.

24. NA M598, reel 110, Record Book of OCP; NA M599, 6/510-12.

25. NA M599, 6/510-12.

26. "John T. Ford's Record of His Imprisonment," JTF Papers, MHS, File 371.

27. Ibid.

28. NA M599, 5/395-99.

29. NA M599, 6/348-49.

30. Miles was erroneously recorded as "John Morris."

31. NA M599, 5/250-61 and 6/166-69.

32. NA M599, 6/447-49.

33. NA M599, 5/448.
34. NA M598, 110; NA M599, 6/48-49; Williamson, 29, 67; Boyd, 225; See also Davis, 219–21.

CHAPTER 10

1. *National Republican*, April 22, 1865.
2. *New York Clipper*, April 22 and 29, 1865.
3. *New York Evening Post*, July 8, 1884.
4. Ibid.
5. All Harry Ford quotes from this interrogation session are NA M599, 5/456-488.
6. Record Book of Old Capitol Prison, NA M598, reel 110; NA M599, 2/917, 3/337; NA M345; *New York Evening Post*, July 28, 1884.
7. NA M599, 5/304-6.
8. NA M599, 5/307-9.
9. NA M599, 5/309-11.
10. NA M599, 5/310-14.
11. NA M599, 2/63-64. Prison records do not list Mathews among its inmates, and John Ford, who monitored and recorded everything he could while incarcerated, maintained that Mathews was never a prisoner there, merely held briefly for questioning. When Wood testified during the Johnson impeachment hearings in 1867 that Mathews was *in* Old Capitol, he was perhaps recalling this session.
12. JTF Papers, MHS, File 371; NA M599, 2/917, 4/196, 6/348-49.
13. NA M599, 3/873-877; Jeannie Gourlay Struthers interview, *New York Sun*, February 6, 1916.
14. JTF Papers, MHS, File 371.
15. NA M599, 4/64-66.
16. NA M599, 4/66-70.

17. The Record Book of Old Capitol Prison, NARA M598, lists Harry Ford as arrested in Baltimore, but Records of the Superintendent, OCP, NA RG 393, have him arrested in Washington "on order of Gen. C. C. Augur," which in its specificity would seem to trump the former.

18. In her April 25 statement, Hart said she lived in Baltimore but that her address would soon be Richmond, Indiana; nothing, however, indicates that she had family there or ever actually relocated there.

19. JTF Papers, MHS, File 371.

20. ALS JTF to Hall, April 19, 1865, in JTF Papers, LOC.

21. ALS Hall to JTF and ALS W. E. Bartlett to Mrs. Ford, in JTF Papers, LOC.

22. *Atlanta Constitution*, March 11, 1888. One of Brink's obituaries has him remanded back to Old Capitol after this identification for three months, but his name does not appear on prison rolls.

23. *Washington Post*, November 9, 1902.

24. NA M599 5/477, 487-88.

25. NA M599 5/274-77, 500.

26. NA M599 5/277-82.

27. NA M599 5/282-84.

28. NA M599 5/500.

29. NA M599 6/347-48. Carpenter Clark was also arrested, on April 30, but no record remains of his questioning and, not being a stage-hand needed for shifting scenery, he may not have been present backstage the night of April 14.

30. NA M599, 2/553-56 and 2/743-46.

31. NA M599, 5/441-43.

32. NA M599, 5/444-47.

33. NA M599, 5/448-54.

34. Unidentified Baltimore newspaper clipping, April 19, 1865, in Wallace Papers.

35. NA M599, 5/497.

36. NA M599, 5/498.

37. "Carroll Prison Memo," rough notes, JTF Papers, LOC; "John T. Ford's Record of his Imprisonment" in JTF Papers, MHS.

38. ALS JTF to Stanton, undated but likely May 10, 1865, in JTF Papers, LOC.

39. JTF Papers, MHS; "Memoranda of Arrest and Imprisonment," JTF Papers, LOC.

40. NA M599, 4/170; Baker, 555.

41. NA M599, 4/202-205.

42. Ibid.

CHAPTER 11

1. NA M599, 5/345-47.

2. NA M599, 1/40 and 2/861-64.

3. Selecman was misidentified in his warrant as "Slackman."

4. JTF in *Cincinnati Commercial*, October 20, 1868.

5. Ibid.; "John T. Ford's Statement" and "Record of his Imprisonment" in JTF Papers, MHS; NA M599, 906-13; *New York Times*, July 17, 1867.

6. List in Joseph Holt Papers, LOC, Vol. 93, 241.

7. Account as told by Spangler to Ford in JTF Papers, MHS, File 371. The hoods had been ordered by Stanton, ostensibly because another accused conspirator, Lewis Powell, had tried to kill himself by slamming his head against the bulkhead of the *Saugus*.

8. Account as told by Spangler to Ford in JTF Papers, MHS, File 371.

9. Letter in James O. Hall research library, Surratt Society, Clinton, MD.

10. Unidentified clipping, Lincoln Obsequies scrapbook, LOC rare book room, 181; Brooks, 270; *Washington Star*, May 12–19, 1865; *Washington Globe Democrat* December 3, 1891; *New York Times*,

May 15, 1865; *New York World*, May 19, 1865; *Philadelphia Inquirer*, May 13, 1865; "The Tragedy of the Nation" in Porter Papers; Wallace Papers, Series 11, OVA Graphics; "Signs of Character," 19.

11. "Gath" (George Alfred Townsend) in *San Francisco Chronicle*, July 30, 1882; *New York World*, May 19, 1865; Brooks, 271; *New York Times*, May 15, 1865.

12. ALS Ewing to Sherman, May 1, 1865, in Ewing Papers, LOC.

13. Steers, *Trial*, 73. No one ever pointed out during the trial that C. V. Hess, who had been too ill to perform but had approached Gifford and Carland at "ten minutes after ten," wore a mustache and before changing into performance attire might have been considered "ruffianly."

14. Steers, *Trial*, 78–79.

15. Ibid., 80–81.

16. Ibid., 73–74. This near-definitive version of trial testimony, based on the official Pittman transcript, omits occasional details reported by newspapers, such as the *Washington Star*'s including on May 16 Selecman's admission in his testimony that he accepted Maddox's offer to join them all for a drink.

17. Steers, *Trial*, 73–74.

18. NA M599, 1/41; Steers, *Trial*, 77–78.

19. Records of the Superintendent, Old Capitol Prison, NA RG 393.

20. Steers, *Trial*, 76.

21. Ibid., 97.

22. Ibid., 98.

23. Ibid.

24. Ibid.; NA M599, 1/45. An exhaustive search of all extant records of Baker's activities, communications, and payments to spies, including the Baker-Turner papers in NA, failed to establish a direct link between Baker and Rittersbach, however.

25. ALS to JTF from J. M. Varnum, May 31, 1865, in JTF Papers, LOC. A May 29 letter from the members of the Holliday Street orchestra also supported Ford.

26. *New York Clipper*, June 10, 1865.

CHAPTER 12

1. JTF Oct. 6, 1884, letter to *Washington Evening Star* in JTF Papers, LOC.

2. NA M599, 3/873-877.

3. *New York Clipper*, April 29, 1865.

4. Untitled rough notes written prior to trial testimony in JTF Papers, MHS.

5. Ibid.

6. Ibid.

7. May 27, 1865, letter from William Spangler to Gifford in JTF Papers, LOC.

8. Untitled rough notes written prior to trial testimony in JTF Papers, MHS.

9. *Washington Star*, May 30, 1865.

10. Steers, *Trial*, 109.

11. Ibid., 102.

12. Ibid., 103.

13. Ibid., 103–4.

14. NA M599, 6/111-14.

15. *San Francisco Chronicle*, July 30, 1882; ALS McCullough to JTF, June 2, 1865, JTF Papers, LOC.

16. Steers, *Trial*, 105.

17. Ibid., 107–8.

18. NA M599, 1/40 and 2/861-64.

19. Steers, *Trial*, 109–10.

20. NA M221, 281/003-10.

21. Steers, *Trial*, 104.

22. NA M599, 3/710; James R. Ford recollections in JTF Papers, MHS.

23. Steers, *Trial*, 108.

24. Mary Porter, 19–20.

25. Steers and Holzer, *The Lincoln Assassination Conspirators*, 115, 125–26; Gray, 626–36.

26. Steers, *Trial*, 276–88. Herold's account of Booth's sympathy for Spangler is cited in Kauffman, 174, from NA M599, 4/463.

27. JTF letter in *New York World*, July 2, 1865.

28. Ibid.; *Washington Star*, June 21, 1865.

29. Robert Summers, "Conviction," Dr. Samuel A. Mudd Research Site, http://www.samuelmudd.com/ conviction.html; Lew Wallace to Susan Wallace, undated, but likely June 26, 1865, in Wallace Papers.

30. ALS Ewing to JTF July 8, 1865, in JTF Papers, LOC; Gray, 633.

31. Gray, 633; *Baltimore American*, January 18, 1869.

32. Hartranft Papers. Dodd was breveted on Hartranft's recommendation on July 8.

33. Guard Captain William Dutton, interview in *Washington Chronicle*, August 9, 1865; *New York World*, August 4, 1865; *Washington Star*, August 3, 1865.

34. William Frederick Keeler, *Aboard the U.S.S. Florida: 1863–65*, http://www.samuelmudd.com/7271865-paymaster-keelers-1st-letter.html.

35. *Washington Chronicle*, August 9, 1865.

36. Mary Porter, 36–37; unidentified clipping, Lincoln Obsequies scrapbook, 111.

37. Mary Porter, 37.

38. *New York Times*, June 26, 1892; ALS Calvin Shedd to his wife, June 9, 1863, Shedd Letters.

39. Prison Records of Dry Tortugas, Florida, 1864–1865, NA RG 94; Muster Rolls of General Prisoners documenting the period 1863–1865, NA RG 249; "The Tragedy of the Nation," 22.

40. *Washington Chronicle*, August 9, 1865; Arnold, 63–125.

41. *New York Herald*, August 2, 1865; Captain W. R. Prentice, "On the Dry Tortugas," *McClure's* (April 1902), 569.

42. *New York Herald*, August 2, 1865; Spangler interview, *Philadelphia Evening Telegraph*, June 24, 1869; Holder, 561.

43. *New York Daily News*, October 12, 1865, reprinted from *Baltimore Commercial*.

44. "Attempted Escape," Dr. Samuel A. Mudd Research Site, http://www.samuelmudd.com/attempted-escape.html.

CHAPTER 13

1. *Washington Chronicle*, May 7, 1865; *Washington Daily National Intelligencer*, April 28, 1865.

2. *Washington Weekly Chronicle*, May 13, 1865; *Washington Daily Constitution*, April 26, 1865.

3. Power, 210; *Washington Chronicle* quoted in *Washington Post*, April 11, 1965.

4. Boyle also testified briefly in defense of Mary Surratt, his parishioner, on May 25.

5. *New York Clipper*, April 29, 1865.

6. *New York Clipper*, June 24, August 5, and October 6, 1865.

7. *New York Clipper*, June 10, October 6, and November 25, 1865; *Titusville Herald*, January 3, 1866.

8. *Titusville Herald*, January 3, 1866.

9. Darrah, 10, 32, 83, 140; "Tappan's Mushroom City"; "A Peak [sic] at Pithole's Past."

10. Memorandum of arrests and closing time of theatre, July 1865, in JTF Papers, LOC; Sollers, 192.

11. *New York Times*, June 28, 1865; NA M-221, 281/15-18, 21 and 85–86.

12. *New York Clipper*, July 15, 1865.

13. ALS JTF to Wright, July 2, 1865, in Wright Papers, HTC.

14. John T. Ford, "Behind the Curtain of a Conspiracy," 484–93; "Notes made by J. T. Ford" prior to writing the "Conspiracy" article, in JTF Papers, MHS.

15. John T. Ford, "Behind the Curtain of a Conspiracy," 485.

16. ALS Ewing to JTF July 8, 1865 in JTF Papers, LOC.

17. *Washington Star*, July 12, 1865; Letter from Emerson to H. D. Bowen, Paris, Texas, April 21, 1920, in Barbee Papers, Box 4, File 231.

18. Gideon Welles, *Diary of Gideon Welles* (Boston: Houghton Mifflin, 1925), II, 331.

19. ALS JTF to Thomas Ewing Jr., July 13, 1865, in JTF Papers, LOC.

20. *Washington Chronicle*, July 14, 1865.

21. Ibid. Ford also alluded to a chain of presidential theatregoing since George Washington; it remains unbroken to this day. Ford made his case even more eloquently for the edifying nature of theatre as "a very ancient, honored and indispensable institution" in 1871 in an essay entitled "The Pulpit and the Stage," which he printed in his theatre programs.

22. *New York World*, July 15, 1865; *New York Observer*, July 27, 1865; *New York Herald*, July 12, 1865.

23. ALS Davis and Schley to Stanton, July 18, 1865, in JTF Papers, LOC. Draft of the agreement in Davis's handwriting in JTF Papers, New York Historical Society; "Gath" (George Townsend), "The Experience of a Veteran," *New York Daily Graphic*, April 7, 1879; *Washington Star*, August 15, 1865.

24. ALS JTF to Forrest, October 1, 1865, in Forrest Papers, University of Pennsylvania; Henry Winter Davis to J. A. J. Creswell, December

15, 1865, cited in Sollers 227; ALS JTF to Ewing, August 8, 1865, November 20, 1865, and January 17, 1866, and Ewing to JTF, January 12, 1866, in JTF Papers, LOC. For a thorough assessment of Ford's financial outcome, see Sollers, 228–30.

25. *Syracuse (NY) Daily Courier*, March 23, 1865.

26. *Memphis Public Ledger*, February 13, 1866; Faulkner, 77; ALS Withers to Wright June 30, 1866, HTC.

27. *New York Times*, June 30, 1878; T. Allston Brown letter of May 15, 1905, in Mathews file, HTC; *New York Clipper*, December 2, 1865.

28. *New York Herald*, October 2, 1865; *New York Clipper*, October 13, 1865.

29. *New York Times*, October 8, 1865.

30. ALS Keene to W. D. Booth, December 25, 1865, HTC; *Chicago Tribune*, January 13, 1866.

31. *Milwaukee Daily Sentinel*, February 2 and 10, 1866.

32. *New York World*, January 4, 1866.

33. *New York Clipper*, February 17, 1866; *Chicago Daily Tribune*, September 18, 1876.

CHAPTER 14

1. ALS JTF to John Wright, April 17, 1866, in HTC; ALS JTF to Forrest, October 1, 1865, in Forrest Papers, University of Pennsylvania; ALS Thomas Ewing to JTF, January 12, 1866, and ALS JTF to Ewing, January 17, 1866, in JTF Papers, LOC. The deed for the sale of Ford's Theatre was not recorded, however, until November 18, 1873.

2. ALS JTF to Wright, November 22, 1866, New York Historical Society; ALS JTF to Wright, April 17, 1866, HTC.

3. Nettie Mudd, 165, 276; ALS JTF to Ewing, January 17, 1866, and ALS Spangler to JTF, June 30, 1867, in JTF Papers, LOC.

4. ALS JTF to Johnson, April 4, 1866, in JTF Papers, LOC; ALS Ewing to Thomas Ewing Sr., July 7, 1865, in Ewing Papers, LOC. Although Ford was convinced Spangler was "wholly innocent," he must have entertained some doubts, for he also asked Wright for "your ideas about Spangler's complicity or innocence." (ALS JTF to Wright, November 1866, New York Historical Society.)

5. JTF to Ewing, January 13, 1867, in Foreman M. Lebold Collection of the Lincoln College Museum, reprinted in *The Lincoln Newsletter* 19, no. 1 (Spring 2000): 1.

6. *Impeachment Investigation*, 490–92. Wood, however, misidentified him as "Thomas Mathews."

7. Ibid., 533–35.

8. Butler Papers, LOC. A copy of this December 3, 1867, notarized statement, part of Gleason's report to Butler, was found by Mudd in Spangler's tool chest after his death.

9. All he had seen, said Gifford, was the president's carriage with its livery man, Carland, Hess, and an actor he misidentified as "George Harry," which could have been Johnny (John Harry) Evans or Edwin Brink.

10. *Trial of John H. Surratt*, 557–63.

11. Ibid., 583, 594.

12. Ibid., 814–18.

13. Ibid., 819–20.

14. Ibid., 821–28.

15. John D. Lawson, ed., "John H. Surratt" in *American State Trials* 9 (St. Louis: F. H. Thomas Law Book Co., 1918), 93; *New York Clipper*, September 29, 1866.

16. *Titusville Herald*, December 9, 1865.

17. Jeannie Gourlay later claimed to have performed with Edwin Booth on the night of his triumphant return to the stage (January 3, 1866), but she was still performing in Memphis then. Maggie's son, William Gourlay Shiels, lived only until June 18, 1872.

18. *Baltimore Sun*, February 20, 1868.

19. ALS Edwin Booth to JTF, July 15, 1867, in JTF Papers, LOC.

20. H. H. Kohlsaat, "Booth's Letter to Grant," *Saturday Evening Post*, February 9, 1924.

21. Telegram, JTF to Edwin Booth, February 15, 1869, in Booth Papers.

22. Bryan, 310–11. A 1911 newspaper account of the gathering also names as being present James Mattox [sic], which is not possible given Maddox's death the year before. The reporter's source was "one of the men who identified Booth's body." Mitchell in 1882 named "Anna Booth" as providing the lock of hair, but no one by that name was present, unless Ford's sister Anna or daughter Annie (more likely) was also present.

23. Mudd's notes on Yellow Fever epidemic, October 27, 1867, Summers, Dr. Samuel A. Mudd Research Site, http://www.samuelmudd.com/yellow-fever.html.

24. *National Intelligencer*, April 8, 1869, and *New York Times*, April 10, 1869, quoting *Baltimore Sun*, April 7, 1869.

25. *New York Herald*, February 21, 1875; Roger J. Norton, *Abraham Lincoln's Assassination*, http://rogerjnorton.com/Lincoln24.html. See also Higdon, 206; Kauffman, 390; Steers, *Blood on the Moon*, 328.

26. Reignolds interview, Creahan, 68.

27. *New York Clipper*, January 12 and March 2, 1867.

28. Hutton's manuscript diary, Henneke, 256.

29. *Utica Daily Observer*, November 19, 1873. Keene's two daughters would also die within a decade at ages twenty-seven and thirty-five, respectively.

30. *New Hampshire Sentinel*, July 23, 1874. Although the 1870 census lists Otis Reed in New Hampshire as having a wife, Alice, and two children, none of his obituaries mention them.

31. Ireland, 2:428.

32. *New Orleans Commercial Bulletin*, January 26, 1868; ALS Dyott to unknown "Madame," April 7, 1874, in Dyott Papers, HTC; *New York Times*, December 10, 1871.

33. ALS Dyott to Joseph Ireland, July 28, 1869, in Brander Matthews Papers. Others claimed to hold the slain president's program as well.

34. *New York Clipper*, December 2, 1876.

CHAPTER 15

1. *Atlanta Constitution*, March 11, 1888. While Brink's enlistment records in the National Archives prove his Navy service, there is no record of his service in "Baker's Rangers," also known as the 1st D.C. Cavalry.

2. Ferguson, "Lincoln's Death."

3. *New York Herald*, June 25, 1878; *Washington Star*, December 7, 1881.

4. *Brooklyn Daily Times*, March 12, 1928.

5. Letter from Hawk to J. B. Clapp, New York, January n.d., 1894, opposite page 62 in Lincoln Assassination scrapbook titled "April Fourteenth, 1865" in McClellan Collection, Hay Library, Brown University.

6. Frank Ford letter to George Olszewski, April 13, 1962, Olszewski, 124.

7. Letters Received by the Office of the Adjutant General 1861–1870 ("Lincoln Assassination Reward Files"), NA RG 94 Records of the Adjutant General's Office, 1780s–1917, M 619, 456/544-558.

8. Sinn in *New York Independent*, April 4, 1895.

9. *New York Tribune*, January 10, 1870; *New York Dramatic Mirror*, December 23, 1896.

10. Ruggles, 253.

11. *Macon (GA) Weekly Telegraph*, February 26, 1910.

12. *San Francisco Bulletin*, February 4, 1890; *Biloxi (MS) Herald*, November 26, 1892; *Toledo Blade*, March 28, 1896; *New York Tribune*, February 10, 1909; *New York World*, February 12, 1911; unidentified clipping dated July 14, 1905, in Lincoln Assassination file, Brown University Hay Library. See also a lengthy account of the assassination that Withers wrote for Osborne Oldroyd and various letters to Oldroyd, all 1908, in Oldroyd Papers.

13. *New York Dramatic Mirror*, December 28, 1895; *Independent*, April 4, 1895; "Easter Recalls Lincoln," *Washington Post*, February 12, 1899; Ferguson, "I Saw Lincoln Shot!," 82; *Brooklyn Eagle*, March 25, 1913.

14. *New York Dramatic Mirror*, February 26, 1913; Weik, 561–62; "Find Actor's Story of Lincoln's Death," *New York Times*, February 14, 1926. The use of the shutter is further corroborated by eyewitness J. F. Troutner, Sioux City, IA, *Journal*, June 10, 1915.

15. ALS Jeannie Gourlay Struthers to A. I. Mudd, May 16, 1916, in Mudd Papers. The details of Struthers's account, consistently specific and in many cases corroborated by those of others, have been integrated throughout this work.

16. Given the remarkable similarity of Truman's words and biography among these interviews, they were likely generated by the press department of the Rockett Film Company, whose Lincoln film was being released, and which had invited her to its premiere.

EPILOGUE

1. *Baltimore Sun*, May 12, 1883; *New York Mirror*, May 7, 1885; *New York Sun*, April 11, 1915. Actor William H. Crane in 1890 wrote that the translation of a play in which he was performing had been translated by Angela Sefton, "who afterward married John DeBonay, an actor of whom I have not heard in a number of years." There is no mention of John in Angela Sefton's own obituary.

2. *New York Times*, June 22, 1878, July 13, 1887, and January 12, 1905; *New York Tribune*, January 19, 1905; *Washington Post*, January 12, 1905; *New York Dramatic Mirror*, January 21, 1905.

3. *Boston Evening Transcript*, June 9, 1916.

4. *Detroit Free Press*, March 29, 1879; ALS Hawk to George P. Morton, August 6, 1913, in Hawk Papers, HTC.

5. Kate may have divorced Collins, as she identified herself on the 1920 Census as being both widowed and divorced; no record of such a divorce is extant.

6. *The Era* (London), September 24 and October 8, 1871.

7. Unidentified obituary in Crawford Theatre Collection, Box 323; *Washington Times*, March 13, 1915.

BIBLIOGRAPHY

BOOKS

Aldrich, Thomas. *Crowding Memories*. Boston: Houghton Mifflin, 1920.

American College Theatre Festival. *The American Theatre: A Sum of Its Parts*. NY: Samuel French, 1971.

Arnold, Samuel Bland. *Defence and Prison Experiences of a Lincoln Conspirator*. Hattiesburg, MS: The Book Farm, 1943.

Baker, Lafayette C. *History of the United States Secret Service*. Philadelphia: L. C. Baker, 1867.

Barber, James G. *Alexandria in the Civil War*. Lynchburg, VA: H. E. Howard, 1988.

Barrett, Lawrence. *Edwin Forrest*. Boston: J.R. Osgood, 1881.

Berg, Albert Ellery. *The Drama, Painting, Poetry and Song, Embracing the Complete History of the Stage*. New York: P. F. Collier, 1884.

Bogar, Thomas A. *American Presidents Attend the Theatre*. Jefferson, NC: McFarland, 2006.

———. *John E. Owens: Nineteenth Century American Actor and Manager*. Jefferson, NC: McFarland, 2002.

Boyd, Belle. *Belle Boyd in Camp and Prison*. South Brunswick, NJ: Yoseloff, 1865, rpt. 1968.

Brennan, Walter C. *The Ford Theatre Lincoln Assassination Play-bills*. Philadelphia: Priv. print, 1937.

Brinkerhoff, Roeliff. *Recollections of a Lifetime*. Cincinnati: Robert Clarke, 1900.

Brooks, Noah. *Washington, D.C. in Lincoln's Time*. 1895, rpt. Herbert Mitgang, ed. Athens, GA: University of Georgia Press, 1989.

Brown, T. Allston. *History of the American Stage Containing Biographical Sketches of Nearly Every Member of the Profession That Has Appeared on the American Stage, from 1733 to 1870*. New York: Benjamin Blom, 1870, rpt. 1969.

———. *A History of the New York Stage*. 3 vols. 1903, rpt. New York: Benjamin Blom, 1964.

Bryan, George S. *The Great American Myth*. 1940, rpt. Chicago: American House, 1990.

Buckingham, John E. *Reminiscences and Souvenirs of the Assassination of Abraham Lincoln*. 1894, rpt. Port Tobacco, MD: J. Barbour, 1980.

Burge, James C. *Lines of Business: Casting Practice and Policy in the American Theatre, 1752–1899*. New York: Peter Lang Publishing, 1986.

Burlingame, Michael, ed. *Lincoln's Journalist: John Hay's Anonymous Writings for the Press, 1860–1864*. Carbondale, IL: Southern Illinois University Press, 1998.

Carson, William. *The Theatre on the Frontier: The Early Years of the St. Louis Stage*. New York: B. Blom, 1965.

Chamlee, Roy Z., Jr. *Lincoln's Assassins: Complete Account of Their Capture, Trial, and Punishment*. Jefferson, NC: McFarland, 1990.

Clapp, William Warland, Jr. *A Record of the Boston Stage*. Boston: J. Munroe, 1853.

Clark, Champ, ed. *The Assassination: Death of the President*. Alexandria, VA: Time-Life Books, 1987.

Clarke, Asia Booth. *John Wilkes Booth: A Sister's Memoir*. Edited by Terry Alford. Jackson, MS: University Press of Mississippi, 1996.

———. *The Unlocked Book: A Memoir of John Wilkes Booth*. 1938, rpt. New York: Arno Press, 1977.

Creahan, John. *The Life of Laura Keene*. Philadelphia: Rodgers, 1897.

Cropsey, Eugene. *Crosby's Opera House: Symbol of Chicago's Cultural Awakening*. Madison, NJ: Fairleigh Dickinson University Press, 1999.

Darrah, William Culp. *Pithole, the Vanished City*. Gettysburg: William Culp Darrah, 1972.

Detzer, David. *Dissonance: The Turbulent Days between Fort Sumter and Bull Run*. Orlando, FL: Harcourt, 2006.

Dormon, James H., Jr. *Theater in the Antebellum South, 1815–1861*. Chapel Hill, NC: University of North Carolina Press, 1967.

Doster, William E. *Lincoln and Episodes of the Civil War*. New York: G. P. Putnam's Sons, 1915.

Duvergier de Hauranne, Ernest. *A Frenchman in Lincoln's America*. 2 vols. Translated and edited by Ralph H. Bowen. Chicago: Lakeside Press, 1974–1975.

Ellis, John B. *The Sights and Secrets of the National Capital*. New York: United States Publishing, 1869.

Ellsler, John A. *The Stage Memories of John A. Ellsler*. Edited by Effie Ellsler Weston. Cleveland: Rowfant Club, 1950.

Elwood, George M. "Some Earlier Public Amusements of Rochester." *Rochester Historical Society Publication Fund Series*. Monograph in Rochester and Monroe Co. NY Library. Rochester, NY: Rochester Historical Society, 1922.

Evitts, William J. *A Matter of Allegiances: Maryland from 1850 to 1861*. Baltimore: Johns Hopkins University Press, 1974.

Eytinge, Rose. *The Memories of Rose Eytinge*. New York: F. A. Stokes, 1905.

Ferguson, W. J. *I Saw Booth Shoot Lincoln*. Boston: Houghton Mifflin, 1930.

Fishel, Edwin C. *The Secret War for the Union: The Untold Story of Military Intelligence in the Civil War*. Boston: Houghton Mifflin, 1996.

Ford, George D. *These Were Actors: A Story of the Chapmans and the Drakes*. New York: Library Publishers, 1955.

Ford, Thomas. *A Peep behind the Curtain: By a Supernumerary*. Boston: Redding, 1850.

Furgurson, Ernest B. *Ashes of Glory: Richmond at War*. New York: Alfred A. Knopf, 1996.

Furtwangler, Albert. *Assassin on Stage: Brutus, Hamlet, and the Death of Lincoln*. Urbana, IL: University of Illinois Press, 1991.

Gilbert, Anne (Hartley). *The Stage Reminiscences of Mrs. Gilbert*. Edited by Charlotte M. Martin. New York: Charles Scribner's Sons, 1901.

Goldberg, Isaac. *The Story of Gilbert and Sullivan*. New York: Crown, 1935.

Good, Timothy S. *We Saw Lincoln Shot*. Jackson, MS: University Press of Mississippi, 1995.

Gough, Monica. *Fanny Kemble: Journal of a Young Actress*. New York: Columbia University Press, 1990.

Graham, Franklin. *Histrionic Montreal: Annals of the Montreal Stage with Biographical and Critical Notices of the Plays and Players of a Century*. New York: B. Blom, 1969.

Green, Constance McLaughlin. *Washington: Village and Capital, 1800–1878*. Princeton, NJ: Princeton University Press, 1962.

Grieve, Victoria. *Ford's Theatre and the Lincoln Assassination*. Alexandria, VA: Parks and History Association, 2001.

Harvey, E. T. *Recollections of a Scene Painter*. E. T. Harvey, 1916, rpt. General Books, 2009.

Henneke, Ben Graf. *Laura Keene: A Biography*. Tulsa, OK: Council Oaks Books, 1990.

Hewitt, John Hill. *Shadows on the Wall; or, Glimpses of the Past*. Baltimore: Turnbull Brothers, 1877.

Higdon, Hal. *The Union vs. Dr. Mudd*. Gainesville, FL: University Press of Florida, 2008.

Holzer, Harold, Craig L. Symonds, and Frank J. Williams. *The Lincoln Assassination*. New York: Fordham University Press, 2010.

Hoole, William Stanley. *The Ante-Bellum Charleston Theatre*. University, AL: University of Alabama Press, 1946.

Horton, Judge William Ellis. *Driftwood of the Stage*. Detroit: Winn & Hammond, 1904.

Howe, J. Burdett. *A Cosmopolitan Actor*. Bedford: n.p., 1888.

Impeachment Investigation: Testimony taken before the Judiciary committee of the House of Representatives in the investigation of the charges against Andrew Johnson. Second session, Thirty-ninth Congress, and first session, Fortieth Congress. Washington: Government Printing Office, 1867.

Ireland, Joseph. *Records of the New York Stage*. 2 vols. New York: T. H. Morrell, 1866–67.

Jampoler, Andrew C. A. *The Last Lincoln Conspirator*. Annapolis: Naval Institute Press, 2008.

Jefferson, Joseph, III. *The Autobiography of Joseph Jefferson*. New York: Century, 1889.

Kauffman, Michael W. *American Brutus: John Wilkes Booth and the Lincoln Conspiracies*. New York: Random House, 2004.

Kendall, John S. *The Golden Age of the New Orleans Theater*. New York: Greenwood Press, 1968.

Kimmel, Stanley. *The Mad Booths of Maryland*. New York: Dover Publications, 1969.

Kline, Michael J. *The Baltimore Plot*. Yardley, PA: Westholme, 2008.

Kunhardt, Dorothy Meserve, and Philip B. Kunhardt, Jr. *Twenty Days*. New York: Harper and Row, 1965.

Laas, Virginia, ed. *Wartime Washington: The Civil War Letters of Elizabeth Blair Lee*. Urbana, IL: University of Illinois Press, 1991.

Lankford, Nelson. *Richmond Burning*. New York: Viking, 2002.

Lawson, John D., ed. "John H. Surratt" in *American State Trials*. St. Louis: F. H. Thomas Law Book, 1918. IX: 93.

Leale, Charles A. *Lincoln's Last Hours*. New York: Charles A. Leale, 1909.

Leech, Margaret. *Reveille in Washington*. New York: Harper and Brothers, 1841.

Leman, Walter. *Memories of an Old Actor*. 1886, rpt. New York: B. Blom, 1969.

Lindsley, Maggie. *Maggie!* Southbury, CT: M. D. Mackenzie, 1977.

Mammen, Edward William. *The Old Stock Company School of Acting*. Boston, MA: Trustees of The Public Library, 1945.

Manakee, Harold R. *Maryland in the Civil War*. Baltimore: Maryland Historical Society, 1961.

Moody, Richard. *Edwin Forrest: First Star of the American Stage*. New York: Knopf, 1960.

Morris, Clara. *Life on the Stage*. New York: McClure, Phillips and Co., 1901.

Morris, Roy, Jr. *Ambrose Bierce: Alone in Bad Company*. New York: Crown Publishers, 1995.

Mudd, Nettie, ed. *The Life of Dr. Samuel A. Mudd*. New York: Neal, 1906.

Odell, George C. D. *Annals of the New York Stage*. 1927–49, rpt. New York: AMS Press, 1970.

Oggel, L. Terry, ed. *The Letters and Notebooks of Mary Devlin Booth*. New York: Greenwood Press, 1987.

Olszewski, George J. *Restoration of Ford's Theatre*. Washington, D.C.: U.S. Government Printing Office, 1963.

Perry, John. *James A. Herne: The American Ibsen*. Chicago: Nelson-Hall, 1978.

Peskin, Allan. *Garfield: A Biography*. Kent, OH: Kent State University Press, 1999.

Phelps, Henry P. *Players of a Century; A Record of The Albany Stage*. 1880, rpt. New York: B. Blom, 1972.

Porter, Mary. *The Surgeon in Charge*. Concord, MA: Rumford Press, 1949.

Power, Tyrone. *Impressions of America During the Years 1833, 1834, and 1835*. 2 vols. in 1. 1836, rpt. New York: B. Blom, 1971.

Reck, W. Emerson. *A. Lincoln: His Last 24 Hours*. Jefferson, NC: McFarland, 1987.

Rees, Terence A. L. *Theatre Lighting in the Age of Gas*. London: Society for Theatre Research, 1978.

Reid, Thomas. *America's Fortress*. Gainesville, FL: University Press of Florida, 2006.

Rhodehamel, John, and Louise Taper. *"Right or Wrong, God Judge Me": The Writings of John Wilkes Booth*. Urbana, IL: University of Illinois Press, 1997.

Riddle, Albert Gallatin. *Recollections of War Times*. New York: G. P. Putnam's Sons, 1895.

Rinear, David L. *Stage, Page, Scandals, and Vandals: William E. Burton and Nineteenth-Century American Theatre*. Carbondale: Southern Illinois University Press, 2004.

Roscoe, Theodore. *Web of Conspiracy: The Complete Story of the Men Who Murdered Abraham Lincoln*. Englewood Cliffs, NJ: Prentice-Hall, 1959.

Ruggles, Eleanor. *Prince of Players: Edwin Booth*. New York: W. W. Norton, 1953.

Samples, Gordon. *Lust for Fame: The Stage Career of John Wilkes Booth*. Jefferson, NC: McFarland, 1982.

Sandburg, Carl. *Abraham Lincoln*. New York: Scribner's, 1926–1940.

Scharf, J. Thomas. *Chronicles of Baltimore*. Port Washington, NY: Kennikat Press, 1874.

———. *History of Baltimore City and County*. Philadelphia: Louis J. Everts, 1881.

Sherman, Robert L. *Chicago Stage, its Records and Achievements*. Chicago: n.p., 1947.

Smith, Gene. *American Gothic*. New York: Simon & Schuster, 1992.

Spangler, Edward W. *The Annals of the Families of Caspar, Henry, Baltzer and George Spengler, Who Settled in York County, Respectively, in 1729, 1732, 1732 and 1751*. York, PA: York Daily Publishing, 1896.

Steers, Edward, Jr. *Blood on the Moon*. Lexington, KY: University Press of Kentucky, 2005.

———. *The Lincoln Assassination Encyclopedia*. New York: Harper Perennial, 2010.

———. *The Trial: The Assassination of President Lincoln and the Trial of the Conspirators*. Lexington, KY: University Press of Kentucky, 2003.

Steers, Edward, Jr., and Harold Holzer, eds. *The Lincoln Assassination Conspirators: Their Confinement and Execution, as Recorded in the*

Letterbook of John Frederick Hartranft. Baton Rouge: Louisiana State University Press, 2009.

Stoddart, James H. *Recollections of a Player*. New York: The Century, 1902.

Swanson, James L. *Manhunt: The 12-Day Chase for Lincoln's Killer*. New York: William Morrow, 2006.

Taylor, Tom. *Our American Cousin*. New York: n.p., 1869.

Tidwell, William A., with James O. Hall and David Winfred Gaddy. *Come Retribution: The Confederate Secret Service and the Assassination of Lincoln*. Jackson, MS: University Press of Mississippi, 1988.

Titone, Nora. *My Thoughts Be Bloody*. New York: Free Press, 2010.

Tompkins, Eugene. *History of the Boston Theatre, 1854–1901*. New York: B. Blom, 1969.

Toomey, Daniel Carroll. *The Civil War in Maryland*. Baltimore: Toomey Press, 1983.

Townsend, George Alfred. *Katy of Catoctin; Or, The Chain-Breakers*. New York: D. Appleton, 1887.

Trial of John H. Surratt. 2 vols. Washington, D.C.: U.S. Government Printing Office, 1867.

Trollope, Anthony. *North America*. New York: Harper & Brothers, 1863.

Union League of Philadelphia. *While Lincoln Lay Dying*. Philadelphia: The Union League of Philadelphia, 1968.

Varhola, Michael J. *Everyday Life during the Civil War*. Cincinnati: Writer's Digest Books, 1999.

Vincent, Elizabeth Kipp. *Girlhood Recollections and Personal Reminiscences of Life in Washington during the Civil War*. Gardena, CA: Spanish-American Institute Press, 1924.

Wallack, Lester. *Memories of Fifty Years*. New York: Charles Scribner's Sons, 1889.

Weisert, John Jacob. *The Curtain Rose: A Checklist of Performances at Samuel Drake's City Theatre and Other Theatres at Louisville from the Beginning to 1843*. Louisville, KY: n.p., 1958.

———. *A Large and Fashionable Audience: A Checklist of Performances at the Louisville Theatre, 1846–1866*. Louisville, KY: n.p., 1955.

Welles, Gideon. *Diary of Gideon Welles*. Boston: Houghton Mifflin, 1925.

Williamson, James Joseph. *Prison Life in the Old Capitol and Reminiscences of the Civil War*. West Orange, NJ: n.p., 1911.

Wilmeth, Don. B, and Christopher Bigsby, eds. *The Cambridge History of American Theatre: Volume I Beginnings to 1870*. New York: Cambridge University Press, 1998.

Wilson, Arthur Herman. *A History of the Philadelphia Theatre, 1835 to 1855*. New York: Greenwood Press, 1968.

Wilson, Francis. *John Wilkes Booth: Fact and Fiction of Lincoln's Assassination*. 1929, rpt. New York: B. Blom, 1972.

Wilson, Garff B. *A History of American Acting*. Bloomington: Indiana University Press, 1966.

———. *Three Hundred Years of American Drama and Theatre*. Englewood Cliffs, NJ: Prentice-Hall, 1973.

Wingate, Charles E. L. *Shakespeare's Heroines on the Stage*. New York: T. Y. Crowell, 1895.

Winik, Jay. *April 1865*. New York: Harper Perennial, 2001.

Winslow, Catherine Mary Reignolds. *Yesterday with Actors*. 1887, rpt. Freeport, NY: Books for Libraries Press, 1972.

Winter, William. *Life and Art of Joseph Jefferson*. New York and London: Macmillan, 1894.

———. *Vagrant Memories, Being Further Recollections of Other Days*. 1915, rpt. Freeport, NY: Books for Libraries Press, 1970.

NEWSPAPERS AND PERIODICALS

"Actor Who Saw Lincoln Slain Recalls Memories of Tragic Night." *Philadelphia Public Ledger*, February 12, 1926.

Cate, Wirt Armistead. "Ford, the Booths, and Lincoln's Assassination." *Emory University Quarterly* V (1949): 11–19.

Davis, Curtis Carroll. "The 'Old Capitol' and Its Keeper: How William P. Wood Ran a Civil War Prison." *Records of the Columbia Historical Society* 52 (1989): 206–34.

"The Decent Drama Discussed by Manager Ford." *Pittsburgh Dispatch*, September 25, 1887.

"Easter Recalls Lincoln." *Brooklyn Daily*, April 12, 1914.

Emerson, E. A. "How John Wilkes Booth's Friend Described His Crime." *Literary Digest* 88 (March 6, 1926).

"Eyewitnesses to Lincoln's Assassination Live Here." *Los Angeles Times*, February 11, 1923, III, 9.

"Eyewitness Tells of Lincoln's Assassination." *New York Sun*, February 9, 1913.

Ferguson, William J. "I Saw Lincoln Shot!" *The American Magazine* (August 1920): 84.

———. "Lincoln's Death." *Saturday Evening Post*, February 12, 1927.

Ford, John T. "Behind the Curtain of a Conspiracy." *North American Review* 148 (April 1889): 488.

———. "The Dramatic Season." *Baltimore American*, May 23, 1878.

Gray, John A. "The Fate of the Lincoln Conspirators: The Account of the Hanging, Given by Lieutenant-Colonel Christian Rath, the Executioner." *McClure's Magazine* XXXVII (1911): 633–35.

Harris, Gayle T. "John Thompson Ford: A Chronicle from Letters." *Library of Congress Performing Arts Annual* (1988): 132–49.

Hazelton, Joseph H. "The Assassination of President Lincoln." Broadside distributed by Hazelton, Hollywood, CA, c. 1929.

Herne, James A. "Old Stock Days in the Theatre." *Arena* 6 (September 1892): 407.

Holder, Emily. "At the Dry Tortugas during the War: A Lady's Journal." *Californian Illustrated Magazine* 2, no. 4 (September 1892): 561.

Hotchkiss, L. D. "Ford Theater Actress Tells of Emancipator; Los Angeles Woman Whose Brother Won Pardon and Prison Release Witness at Assassination." *Los Angeles Times*, February 10, 1924, B19, 23.

"How Wilkes Booth's Friend Described His Crime." *Literary Digest*, March 6, 1926, 58.

Kohlsaat, H. H. "Booth's Letter to Grant." *Saturday Evening Post*, February 9, 1924.

"Last Living Witness Tells of Shooting of Abraham Lincoln." *New York Herald*, February 6, 1916.

"Lincoln's Death." *Saturday Evening Post*, February 12, 1927, 37.

"Lincoln's Last Hours," in *Twenty-fifth Annual Report of the American Scenic and Historic Preservation Society, 1920, to the Legislature of New York*. Albany: J. B. Lyon, 1920, 330–34.

Mitchell, Maggie. "Success on the Stage." *North American Review* 135 (December 1882): 598–99.

Mosby, John S., Jr. "The Night That Lincoln Was Shot." *Theatre Magazine* 17 (June 1913): 179–80.

Mudd, A. I. "Members of Cast in Play on Night of Lincoln Tragedy." *Washington Post*, January 22, 1917, 8.

Munroe, Seaton. "Recollections of Lincoln's Assassination." *North American Review* CLXII (April 1896): 425.

Murray, J., ed. "New Sadler's Wells." *The Academy, a Weekly Review of Literature, Science, and Art* XVII (May 29, 1880): 394.

"The Night that Lincoln was Shot." *Theatre Magazine* 17 (June 1913): 180.

"A Peak [sic] at Pithole's Past." *Pittsburgh Post-Gazette*, August 12, 1996.

Prentice, W. R. "On the Dry Tortugas," *McClure's* (April 1902).

Robertson, James I. Jr. "Old Capitol: Eminence to Infamy." *Maryland Historical Magazine* LXV, no. 4 (December 1970): 394–99.

"'Signs of Character': Physiognomy. The Conspirators. A personal description of the assassins on Trial at Washington. Mrs. Surratt, Harold [sic]. Payne. Atzerott. O'Laughlin [sic]. Spangler. Dr. Mudd. Arnold. 1865." *American Phrenological Journal (1838-1869)* 42(1): 19.

"The Silent Drama." *Life*, September 21, 1922.

"A Southern Manager." *Houston Post*, November 8, 1885.

Sturm, Jean. "Ford's Theatre on Stage." *American History Illustrated* XX (February 1986): 10, 20–23.

Summers, Robert. Dr. Samuel A. Mudd Research Site. http://www. samuelmudd.com.

"The Surratt Case." *Cincinnati Commercial*, October 20, 1868.

"Tappan's Mushroom City." *New York Times*, September 8, 1884.

"This Man Saw Lincoln Shot." *Good Housekeeping*, February 1927, 20–21.

Townsend, George "Gath." "The Experience of a Veteran." *New York Daily Graphic*, April 7, 1879.

Weik, Jessie W. "A New Story of Lincoln's Assassination," *Century Magazine* (February 1913): 561–62.

West, E. J. "Revolution in the American Theatre: Glimpses of Acting Conditions on the American Stage 1855–1870." *Theatre Survey* I (1960): 43–64.

Alexandria (VA) Gazette

Atlanta Constitution

Auburn (NY) Weekly News and Democrat

Baltimore American and Commercial Advertiser

Baltimore Gazette

Baltimore Sun

Biloxi (MS) Herald

Boston Daily Globe

Boston Evening Transcript

Boston Herald

Brooklyn Daily Eagle

Brooklyn Daily Times

Chicago Tribune

Cincinnati Commercial

Cincinnati Enquirer

The Critic

Daily Arkansas Gazette

Dayton (OH) Daily Journal

Deseret Evening News

Detroit Free Press

Dorchester (MA) Beacon

The Era (London)

Georgia Weekly Telegraph

Harrisburg (PA) Daily Telegraph

Idaho Daily Statesman

The Independent

Lincoln Log [editor: Richard Sloan, Seaford, NY]

London Morning Post

Los Angeles Times

Macon (GA) Weekly Telegraph

Memphis Public Ledger National Intelligencer

Milwaukee Daily Sentinel

National Police Gazette

(Washington) National Republican

New Hampshire Sentinel

New Orleans Commercial Bulletin

New Orleans Daily Picayune

New York Clipper

New York Daily Graphic

New York Daily Tribune

New York Dramatic Mirror

New York Evening Post

New York Herald

New York Independent

New York Mirror

New York Observer

New York Spirit of the Times

New York Sun

New York Times

New York Tribune

New York World

Oakland (CA) Tribune

Philadelphia Evening Bulletin

Philadelphia Evening Telegraph

Philadelphia Inquirer

Philadelphia Public Ledger

Pithole (PA) Daily Record

Pittsburgh Commercial Gazette

Richmond Dispatch

Richmond Enquirer

San Francisco Chronicle

San Francisco Daily Dramatic Chronicle

San Francisco Daily Evening Bulletin

St. Louis Globe Democrat

Surratt Courier

Syracuse (NY) Daily Courier

Titusville (PA) Herald

Toledo Blade

Utica Daily Observer

Washington Chronicle

Washington Daily Capitol

Washington Daily Constitution

Washington Evening Critic

Washington Gazette

Washington Globe Democrat

Washington Post

Washington Star

Washington Times

THESES AND DISSERTATIONS

Cooley, Edna Hammer. "Women in American Theatre, 1850–1870: A Study in Professional Equity." Ph.D., University of Maryland, 1986.

Faulkner, Seldon. "The New Memphis Theater of Memphis, Tennessee, from 1859 to 1880." Ph.D., State University of Iowa, 1957.

Fletcher, Edward Garland. "Records and History of Theatrical Activities in Pittsburgh, Pennsylvania, from Their Beginning to 1861." Ph.D., Harvard University, 1931.

Fuller, Charles Franklin, Jr. "Kunkel and Company at the Marshall Theatre, Richmond, Virginia, 1856–1861." M.A., Ohio University, 1968.

Herbstruth, Grant. "Benedict DeBar and the Grand Opera House in St. Louis, Missouri, from 1855 to 1879." Ph.D., University of Iowa, 1954.

Jones, Cecil Derwent, Jr. "The Policies and Practices of Wallack's Theatre, 1852-1888." Ph.D., University of Illinois, 1959.

Kile, Sara A. "John B. Wright's Staging at the National Theatre, Boston, 1836 to 1853." M.A., Ohio State University, 1959.

McNeill, Sarah Brown. "The Theatre of Owen Fawcett: Half a Century as a Supporting Player, 1853–1903." Ph.D., University of Tennessee, Knoxville, 1973.

Melebeck, Claude, Jr. "A History of the First and Second Varieties Theatres of New Orleans, Louisiana, from 1849 to 1870." Ph.D., Louisiana State University, 1973.

Neel, Charles David. "The Stars' 'Golden Era': A Study of the Craft of Acting in America, 1850–1870." Ph.D., Cornell University, 1966.

Schaal, David George. "Rehearsal Direction Practices and Actor-Director Relationships in the American Theatre from the Hallams to Actors' Equity." Ph.D., University of Illinois, Urbana-Champaign, 1956.

Sollers, John Ford. "The Theatrical Career of John T. Ford." Ph.D., Stanford University, 1962

Swinney, Donald Henry. "Production in the Wallack Theatres, 1852–1888." Ph.D., Indiana University, 1962.

Taylor, Dorothy Jean. "Laura Keene in America, 1852–1873." Ph.D., Tulane University, 1966.

Withers, Nan Wyatt. "The Acting Style and Career of John Wilkes Booth." Ph.D., University of Wisconsin–Madison, 1979.

NATIONAL ARCHIVES

RG 94 Records of the Adjutant General's Office, 1780s–1917

M-619 Letters Received by the Office of the Adjutant General 1861–1870

M-797 Case Files of Investigations by Levi C. Turner and Lafayette C. Baker, 1861–1866

RG 109 War Department Collection of Confederate Records

M-378 Index to Compiled Service Records of Confederate Soldiers who Served in Organizations from the State of Louisiana

M-598 Selected Records of the War Department Relating to Confederate Prisoners of War, 1861–1865

RG 111 Records of the Office of the Chief Signal Officer

T-252 The Mathew B. Brady Collection of Civil War Photographs

RG 153 Records of the Office of the Judge Advocate General

M-599 Investigation and Trial Papers Relating to the Assassination of President Lincoln

RG 351 Records of the Government of the District of Columbia

Metropolitan Police Detective Department Blotter 1862–1867

Metropolitan Police Personnel Files 1863–65

RG 393 Records of the U.S. Army Continental Commands, 1821–1920

Records of the Superintendent, Old Capitol Prison

Records Relating to Prisoners 1865–1870

MANUSCRIPT COLLECTIONS

Boston Public Library
John B. Wright Papers

Brown University Hay Library
Special Collections

Columbia University Library
Brander Matthews Papers

Dartmouth College
"The Tragedy of the Nation" in George Loring Porter Papers

Folger Shakespeare Library
Edwin Forrest Papers
John B. Wright Papers
John Mathews Papers
John T. Ford Papers
Laura Keene Papers

Ford's Theatre National Historic Site, National Park Service
John B. Wright scrapbook

Georgetown University Library Special Collections
David Rankin Barbee papers
Rev. Fr. Patrick J. Cormican, SJ papers

Gettysburg College Musselman Library
John Frederick Hartranft Papers

Harvard University, Houghton Library, Harvard Theatre Collection
Lincoln Assassination records and scrapbooks
Actors' Files and Photographs

Historical Society of Washington, D.C.
Washington Theatre Files

Indiana Historical Society
Papers of Lew and Susan Wallace

Indiana University, Lilly Library
Osborne Oldroyd Papers

Library of Congress
American Theatre Playbills and Programs

Benjamin F. Butler Papers
John T. Ford Papers
Laura Keene Papers
Lincoln Obsequies scrapbook
Thomas Ewing Family Papers

Lincoln College Museum
Foreman M. Lebold Collection

Lincoln Museum, Fort Wayne, IN

Maryland Historical Society
John T. Ford Papers

Maryland State Archives

New York Historical Society
John T. Ford Papers

New York Public Library, Billy Rose Performing Arts Division, Lincoln
    Center
A. I. Mudd papers

Pike County (PA) Historical Society, Special Collections
Gourlay Family Papers

The Players Club, New York
Edwin Booth Papers

Princeton University
William Seymour Collection

Surratt House Museum, Clinton, MD
James O. Hall Research Library

University of California, Davis, Special Collections
Herne, Julie A. "James A. Herne: Actor and Dramatist." Unpublished
    manuscript, n.d.

University of California, Merced, Special Collections
Henry O. Nightingale Diary

University of Miami Library
Calvin Shedd Civil War Letters

University of Pennsylvania, Rare Books and Special Collections
Edwin Forrest Papers

University of Tampa
Stanley Kimmel Collection

University of Tulsa
Ben Graf Henneke Papers

Yale University Sterling Library
Crawford Theatre Collection
Theatre Manuscripts Collection

INDEX